What Almost Did Not Happen

What Almost Did Not Happen

A Self-Portrait

JAMES WILLIS

iUniverse, Inc.
Bloomington

What Almost Did Not Happen
A Self-Portrait

Copyright © 2011 by James Willis.

All rights reserved. No part of this book may be used or reproduced by any means, graphic, electronic, or mechanical, including photocopying, recording, taping or by any information storage retrieval system without the written permission of the publisher except in the case of brief quotations embodied in critical articles and reviews.

iUniverse books may be ordered through booksellers or by contacting:

iUniverse
1663 Liberty Drive
Bloomington, IN 47403
www.iuniverse.com
1-800-Authors (1-800-288-4677)

Because of the dynamic nature of the Internet, any web addresses or links contained in this book may have changed since publication and may no longer be valid. The views expressed in this work are solely those of the author and do not necessarily reflect the views of the publisher, and the publisher hereby disclaims any responsibility for them.

Any people depicted in stock imagery provided by Thinkstock are models, and such images are being used for illustrative purposes only.
Certain stock imagery © Thinkstock.

ISBN: 978-1-4620-4045-2 (sc)
ISBN: 978-1-4620-4046-9 (hc)
ISBN: 978-1-4620-4549-5 (ebk)

Printed in the United States of America

iUniverse rev. date: 10/14/2011

DEDICATION

Writing a self-portrait shows you are not who you thought you were.
—Michel de Montaigne

###

My chronicle is written for Jaeger Orrin Willis Hepp, born July 31, 2009, the great-great-great-great-great-great-great-grandson of James Willis, the great-great-great-great-great-great-grandson of Redding Willis, the great-great-great-great-great-grandson of William Jessie Willis, the great-great-great-great-grandson of William Alphus Willis, the great-great-great-grandson of John Milton Willis, the great-great-grandson of William Earl Willis, the great-grandson of James William Willis, the grandson of James Wesley Willis, and the son of Bethany Willis Hepp; and for my children, step-children, grandchildren, cousins, friends, acquaintances, ex-wives and the curious.

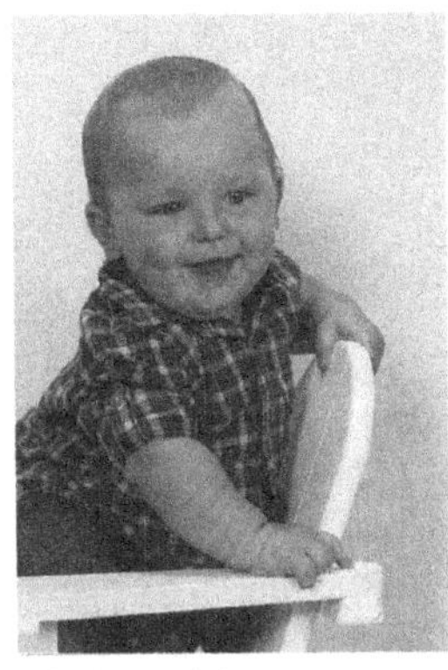

Jaeger at one year

Author at one year

THANX—CJ

INTRODUCTION

There are things which a man is afraid to tell even to himself, and every decent man has a number of such things stored away in his mind.
—Fyodor Dostoyevsky

* * *

There is nothing dishonorable about talking about your life. People like it.
—Pam Hulbert, character on *The Office*

##

In his reminiscences *Some Jottings Down* Dad encouraged me to write an account of my life. That thought appealed to me not at all.

Writing my memoirs is attractive to me now because I will soon pass into inevitable oblivion. My name will be spoken less and less until it passes from thought and then from memory; the world will close around the hole where I used to be. Not the least nor faintest track will remain in the dust to show I was here, that I passed this way.

The only unique thing a person owns that cannot be lost, stolen or diminished, the only thing one can leave behind for others, is one's personal story. Another like it has never been and never will be.

My oldest grandchildren Bethany and Jonathon have frequently, strongly urged me to write my story. Since my old age has found me, I am slipping into death; no longer am I emerging into life. I have begun to realize I would treasure chronicles written by my ancestors, family and friends.

I would agree with those who believe trying to understand a man by reading the most complete narrative of his life is no more helpful than observing the shadow of his statue. About the American Civil War, Walter Whitman wrote, “No prepared picture, no elaborate poem, no after narrative could be what the thing itself was.”

I have no ambition for my story to be who I *myself* am. Nor is my ambition for it to ensure when my ashes are gone, a faint track in the dust shall remain to show I was here, I passed this way.

My ambition for my self-portrait is for the shadow of my statue to remain.

To amuse myself in my declining years, assuage curiosity of grandchildren and promote the shadow of my statute, I present the James William Willis story.

CHILDHOOD
1938-1956

I always thought that if she had a dog she'd name him Spot—without irony.
If I had a dog I would name him Spot, with irony.
But for all practical purposes nobody would know the difference.
—Flannery O'Connor

* * *

This is who I am because this is how I began.
—John Kotre

##

Shakespeare said, "Every man's life is a history." The problem writing a history is where does one begin, where does one end and what does one omit?

I was somebody before I was born. I will begin there.

A night in December 1937, in the bed I now sleep, in an instantaneous, haphazard moment of natural selection, my father's twenty-three specific pairs of chromosomes and my mother's twenty-three specific pairs of chromosomes joined to form the extremely small, single cell that developed into my cesarean birth in Monticello, Arkansas September 10, 1938, as the only child of William Earl and Lela Adalade (McKinstry) Willis.

These forty-six chromosome pairs were individual and precise. If a tiniest part of one of them had been the least teensy, tiny bit different, I would be different, as surely as siblings born of the same parents, raised within the same family are different, including identical twins.

The nature-versus-nurture conundrum poses the question: which is more important in influencing our development, genetic inheritance or upbringing? Hundreds of millennia of genetic lines since the origin of modern man, chromosomes combining and sharing genetic codes, became my parents and were imprinted into me to create a human who was never before, nor ever will be again.

In accordance with my genetic recipe that I inherited and the environment into which I was born, my genes were turned into proteins and cells, my brain formed so that I learned to think and desire and talk and adept my self to the culture soup in which I was swimming. Each culture takes itself as its standard.

These chromosomes that created the eventual human me at that exact, precise moment were single and particular. It almost did not happen. If I had inherited any but these, I would have become a different person. My life after that instant moment of conception would have unfolded differently.

My father was 6'3" and weighed 185 well-proportioned, muscular pounds. When he and Mother married, she was 4'10" and weighed 90 pounds. She told Dad she was 4'11" and weighed 100 pounds. They were a couple whom people considered "cute" and "darling"—words used to describe them as a couple but not as individuals. As individuals they were two extraordinarily strong, intelligent, willful and independent persons, with decidedly separate personalities.

My birth was cesarean. Cutting too deeply into Mother's womb, the surgeon, John Price, M.D, sliced into my back. His error complicated the birth process, and I almost did not survive. The scar on my back has grown as I have, in proportion to my size. The complications from my birth kept Mother from having additional children.

Author's mother about the age she met author's father.

Author's mother, her first year teaching; class is grades 3-4-5. She is third row, center. One of the boys was nineteen, older than the author's mother.

Author's Dad about the age he met author's Mother.

If the surgeon had cut half a smidgen deeper, the rest of my life would have unfolded differently, if it had unfolded at all.

Before I was born, an elderly man in Monticello, told people he could remember when he was born. If anyone seemed about to express doubt, before they could, he quickly offered as proof, "I remember I could not hardly get my breath."

I do not recall my birth. I was affected by it, because it was often discussed in the family with me present, even when I was old enough to understand. I was sometimes asked to remove my shirt to show the scar to visiting strangers. I do not recall the details of anyone else's birth in the family being discussed.

* When I was born, Dad said I was the ugliest baby he ever saw. One of Mother's several guiding principles was a person should say nothing about another, unless it is something good; she said I had the prettiest head of any baby she ever saw.

Author's father, with slight smile, holding the ugliest baby he ever saw, fall, 1938.

When I was an infant, I was allergic to raw milk. Mother heated it during the day. For the night feeding, Dad woke up, heated the milk, and put it in a baby bottle. After several weeks, he realized he could heat the milk before he went to bed and put it in a thermos, which allowed him to sleep a half hour longer.

In his later years, Dad said each time he thought he might be becoming smart enough to know when to come in and to go out, he was humbled by his recalling how long it had taken him to realize how easily he could have gained a half hour of sleep each night.

* For the first twenty-two years of Dad's life, he lived on a farm that had not changed since the 1850s. Tools were manipulated by hand, and all power for them was muscle of mule and man. His life was one of brutal labor and little comfort. His home had

no utilities, no running water, no insulation and its seven rooms were heated by two fireplaces—one in the living room, one in his parents' bedroom.

He was the fourth of five children and the second of three sons. He had almost nothing of his own. He had one pair of pants to wear to high school, located on today's University of Arkansas at Monticello campus. To attend, he walked two and a half miles one way on a pig trail path through the woods that had been first trod by his two older sisters. He took with him a corn pone that he himself had prepared to eat for lunch, and returned home to a cold supper of leftovers.

My Dad's childhood experience is important in my story because it impacted my childhood, as I shall explain.

My mother's family was considerably more affluent than Dad's, albeit after she and Dad married in Star City, Arkansas, the day after Christmas 1936, they continued living the less affluent life Dad had lived, with a major exception: he was no longer farming. He was teaching at Drew Central High School, a school in Drew County, after he had taught for two years at Wilmar, also in Drew, where he met Mother.

During my first year, we lived in the *Babb House*, so called because a man named Babb built it. Today the site is a vacant lot, forty feet south of the intersection of Highway 425 and Highway 172. At this intersection is also White Hall Grocery, established in 1927. Today this building is an antique (junk) store. Its exterior remains unchanged.

During my second year, we lived in the White Hall store. Mother ran it in the day, while Dad was at Drew Central. One day she was not present, and my Uncle Hugh, Dad's youngest brother, was watching the store and me. He made for me a sandwich of tuna salad Mother had prepared. (Mother made great tuna salad with apples and eggs.) For whatever reason, which I suspect I did not know at the time, I threw the sandwich across the room.

Author's parents with their new born baby.

John Willis Family, Christmas, 1938. Author is front center held by his grandma. His grandpa is top left. His parents are top right. Others in the picture are: two women top are Grace and Mary; man in back with hat is Wesley; women to his left is Clara; to her left is Hugh; standing; behind author's grandma is Warren; boy left front is John; girl in front right with face turned from camera in Betty Jane

Uncle Hugh smacked my bottom and gave me the sandwich back. I silently held it until Mother got home and threw it again. Uncle Hugh explained the situation to Mother; she spanked me harder than my uncle and gave me the sandwich and told me to eat it. I sat on the couch and held it until the moment Dad walked through the door; I threw it the third time.

Uncle Hugh and Mother told him what was happening. He spanked me much harder than my uncle and Mother put together and told me to eat the sandwich. I sat on the couch and held it until I fell asleep.

I have long thought I remembered in real time sitting on the couch, waiting for Dad to walk through the door, and all events that preceded it; however, as I was not yet eighteen months old, family adults persuaded me I recalled this scene from hearing it repeated several times by my parents and Uncle Hugh, with what I thought was a tone of reluctant pride in their voices.

However, the July 2010 issue of *Scientific American* features an article stating latest research shows that humans retain memory from age six months and "know far more than ever expected." After reading this piece, I am more certain I remember in real time my out break of sandwich-throwing.

February 1940: My parents moved into a house on the Drew Central campus that had become vacant after the agriculture and shop teacher had moved away. The house was given to Dad by his mentor, Superintendent Walter Massy, who had taught Dad's mother at the one-room Jones School in White Hall in the 1890s. This was the same school Dad had attended through grade eight before he began his pig trail trek through the woods to high school.

The campus house had electricity, gas heat, a six-party-line telephone (the entire number was 529-J2.), indoor plumbing, including hot water, and a state newspaper delivered every day. Dad wrote in *Some Jottings Down*, when we moved there, he thought he had "died and gone to heaven."

Author with his first dog Pedro, named by his Uncle Hugh

* The most confusing and distressing experience during my childhood began in fall 1942. My mother had reentered Arkansas A&M College (today University of Arkansas at Monticello) to obtain her secondary teaching certificate. A decade previously, she had obtained her License to Instruct, which was suitable for teaching only grades one through eight.

My parents concluded Dad's job, Mother's school and a four year-old child were too much to handle. Their solution was to place me beyond their bother. They sent me to live with my Grandpa and Grandma Willis.

I don't recall my parents discussing with me why they were sending me away.

Author with Cousin Betty Jane, who has her face turned away from camera in the John Willis Family picture.

Dad and Mother did not select a day care option for my absence. They did not take me there in the morning and pick me up in the afternoon, though I was two and a half miles away on a good road and they had a car each could drive. Their plan was a weekly room-and-board option that continued for two years, except summers, until I began first grade in September 1944.

The separation from my parents was exacerbated by my grandparents' not having a phone, which insured no communication with my parents.

The usual procedure was I went home with Grandpa and Grandma after church in White Hall and Dad picked me up on Friday after school. When he and Mother had something to do on Friday night, Dad picked me up Saturday morning. On some weekends, I did not go home at all.

Neither of my parents was demonstrative. Neither exhibited sadness when I left them nor happiness when I returned. No affectionate hugs and kisses; no special treats; no favorite food for my supper. My absence was routine, no big deal.

I adopted the attitude they modeled toward our separation. Parents were grandparents; grandparents were parents. Both were the same. No change; no problem; especially no emotion.

My grandparents were hard-working people who had emerged from a depression decade struggling in rural poverty. Also, at their house were two of my cousins, Warren and John McCullers, twelve and ten years older than I, respectfully. Their single mother, my dad's sister, Grace, was teaching at Snyder in Ashley County, where circumstances required her to room and board.

My cousins caught a school bus to Drew Central High School each morning and returned on it each afternoon. At that time in Arkansas, school year was eight, not nine, months. It began after Labor Day and ended before Memorial Day

Also living there was Dad's other sister Clara, who worked as assistant registrar (later registrar) at Arkansas A&M. She was six feet tall and usually displayed a focused, somber expression of consentration. Her size and countenance projected an imposing presence that belied her kindness, forgiving character, and friendly personality.

I slept with her in her bed. To facilitate my going to sleep, she told me the story of the Bremen Town Musicians, a fairy tale about a donkey, a dog, a cat and a rooster.

The four animals worked on four farms where they had grown too old to work. Each owner told them they could not afford to feed them if they did not work and turned them out. They met along the road. After talking among themselves about what to do for a livelihood, they decided to go the Bremen town fair to make music. They ran into trouble along the way; therein is the story.

It was a wonderful story, and Aunt Clara was a marvelous storyteller. She had different voices and expressions for each character.

My relationship to Aunt Clara was not unlike that of a feral cat that had found a person who feeds it and would not leave; she had created a monster. Every night afterward, I could not, or persuaded her to believe I could not, go to sleep until she told me about the Bremen Town Musicians. For a change up, she sometimes told me about Br'er Rabbit and the Tar Baby. She also sang to me *Shortnin' Bread*.

As an adult, I have had occasions with children to tell these fairy tales. A friend, a woman from Kentucky, vacationed in Europe. In Bremen, Germany; she bought for me a brass statuette of the donkey, on whose back sat the dog, on whose back sat the cat, on whose back sat the rooster, as depicted in the story with which Aunt Clara put me to sleep each night. My friend's gift is among my stuff in my library.

* After Clara, Warren, and John went to work and school each morning, I was alone with my grandparents, who had plenty to do without me getting in their way. I do not recall wanting to be involved in their day-to-day activities; in any case, I was not.

At my grandparents', when I was alone, I was much alone. No other human being was present; none was in sight. No outside mental stimulation was available: no radio; no television; no telephone; no newspapers; no magazines; no books, except a Bible; no crayons; no coloring books; no pin; no paper; no dogs; no cats—nothing, except chickens.

I was fascinated with the preacher in the pulpit at the small church all the Willis family attended. I was impressed with how adults listened to him and respected him. He used his voice and presence to be the center of everyone's attention.

Author's Aunt Clara several years older than when she put him to sleep telling him the story of *The BremenTownFair Musicians*

Sometime, while living with my grandparents, I stood on top of a stump in their backyard and gave a sermon to the chickens. I modulated my voice, used gestures and expressed a presence, continuing for several minutes. My first audience?

I did not know Grandma was watching me. She told everyone.

As did everyone who lived with my grandparents, I drank water from a dipper in a bucket, drawn from a cistern filled by runoff water from the roof of the house. I peed on the ground and defecated in an outhouse during the day and in a chamber pot at night. I washed my hands before each meal with home made lye soap in a wash pan of cold water; before going to bed, I washed my feet in the same pan with cold water.

My feet were dirty because I was often barefoot. I washed them because the dirt came off onto the sheets, a result of which I vividly remember Grandma did not approve. I do not recall anyone mentioning to me about brushing my teeth, much less how to brush them; I do not recall brushing them.

I bathed on Saturdays only. When I was staying with my grandparents on the weekend, baths were taken in the kitchen in a number-three washtub, in which were two or three inches of water at the most. When hot water was desired, all of it came from one iron kettle heated on the wood-burning cook stove, often by Aunt Clara. In the winter, the kitchen could be very cold. That kettle is in my living room.

When at my parents' on Saturday, I took a bath in a tub in a bathroom. Hot water was drawn from a ten-gallon tank, and the room had a gas stove for heat in the winter. Ten gallons is not much water by today's standards, but more than a teakettle.

Food at my grandparents' was simple, ample, scrumptious; seasoned with lard, butter, salt, and pepper. Grandma's cooking remains among my favorite dishes.

Many afternoons, Grandma retired to her and Grandpa's bedroom to regenerate. She often invited me into her bedroom, where she taught me to count to one hundred, say my ABCs and whistle. She also piece-quilted in there; I was fascinated watching her. She would talk to me about each piece as she selected it for her quilt. For her, quilting was a labor of love.

I was too young to assist Grandpa on the farm. In the house, I fetched whatever Grandma called for and helped her get the table ready for dinner, the main meal of the day, eaten at noon. When she was ironing, I brought the hot irons to her from the fireplace. She called out the number that designated the iron's weight, size and distance from the fire. Two of these irons are in my living room today.

I also went into the chicken pen, where chicken poop mashed up between my toes; caught a squawking bird; and handed it to grandma, who wrung its neck. It walked about a while as a chicken does with its head off, until it could no longer stand, and flopped around in the dust.

When it stopped moving, grandma placed it in a black iron wash pot of boiling water, where it stank terribly. This procedure loosened the feathers so that she could pluck it. She cut off its legs, removed the innards, and cut it into proper pieces for frying; never baking. It was a nauseating sight and a disgusting smell for a five-year-old. I was well grown before I could enjoyably eat chicken.

* The single, most lasting effect on me of living with Dad's parents was I met and closely associated with Grandpa Willis. (His children and his other grandchildren called him Papa.) I grew to love him dearly; at that time in my life, I loved him not more than anyone else but more than everyone else.

The first minutes of my first day there, I vividly recall, when Dad left, Grandpa was at the door, I was lying on my back on the couch in the living room against the east wall. Grandpa came back to me and sat on the couch's edge next to me. With an easy smile, he put his hand on my stomach under my shirt and talked quietly and kindly with me. No one had ever touched me so intimately, so lovingly.

As a grown man with my own family, when I was leaving my parents' home after visiting them, I would hug Mother and say, "I love you, Mother." It was many years before Mother told me she loved me.

Dad took several more years to say the word *love*. When I was leaving after visiting them, I would, as I did Mother, hug Dad and say, "I love you, Dad." Visibly uneasy, Dad would answer, "I understand."

After several years of this exchange, I told him I did not want him to understand. I wanted him to say he loved me. After he retired and moved to Monticello, he still could not say he loved me, until Mother laughed at his reluctance. On the next visit, when I told him I loved him, with difficulty, he said, "I love you, Son."

Author's Grandma Willis at about age she met his Grandpa

Author's Grandpa Willis, 1900

Author's Grand parents, seated 1954; Children standing L-R and by age are Grace, Wesley, Clara, Earl and Hugh.

Like getting the first olive out of the bottle, it became easier for him to say he loved me. Every time we spoke afterwards even on the phone we ended our conversation saying to each other, "I love you."

Loving my grandpa was as natural for me as a duckling bonding to a mother substitute when its real mother is unavailable.

Grandpa's goodness flowed like an artesian well from deep within the kindness and sweetness of his character. John Willis was always on his oath, whether with children or adults. He absolutely never, ever raised his voice or hand to anyone nor indulged in vulgar speech, nor was he negative; he never whined or complained. He never spoke unkindly or even carelessly of others. He never forgot a promise.

Though he laughed easily, he never laughed loudly. I never heard him tell a joke or a humorous story. To have done so would have put him at the center of attention, which he avoided, because he believed nothing was ever about him, or at least ought never to be. His education consisted of a one room, three month school that he attended for three years but never on the first or last day. The school was miles away across today's Hy 425 east of Mildred McGinnis' childhood home.

I do not recall him ever beginning a sentence with the words "I don't like" or "Why did you" or "You can't" or "I can't." He had within him many beautiful places. John Willis was proud that his wife never worked in the fields. She rarely, if ever, worked in the garden. Grandpa planted it, picked it and brought into the kitchen; Grandma canned it and cooked it.

In the Sermon on the Mount, Jesus says, "Blessed are the meek . . ." The Greek word *praotes*, translated here as "meek," can also be translated as "gentle." Ergo, "Blessed are the gentle, for they shall inherit the earth." John Willis was not meek; he was gentle, having a mild and kind nature and manner.

When he died decades later, Mr. Stephenson the funeral director told Dad that Grandpa's funeral was the largest one he had ever seen.

My Great Grandfather William Alphus Willis married Rody Jane Jordan, thus combining in kinship their Willis and Jordon descendents. Jack Jordon married Maud and they had nine children. One consequence of this union was almost all, if not all, people living in White Hall were Willis or Jordon or married to a Willis or a Jordon. Bobby, Alvin and Shelby Jean were the Jordon cousins nearer to my age; We enjoyed our childhood time together. Shelby Jean was in my class at school for twelve years. Alvin was best man at my first wedding.

Left to right: Alvin, Shelby Jean and Bobby Jordon,
Author and Betty Jane Willis.

* Hanging on the wall to the west of the front door in the living room of my grandparents' house was the only picture in the house, I recall, that was not of family members. It was the picture of a lone wolf in moon light, in the snow on a hill overlooking a cozy scene of a village below. I imagined how the wolf was feeling and what he was thinking.

Author's Grandpa Willis with his cows, 1940s.

Author's Grandma Willis with her chickens, 1940s.

I decided the lone wolf did not feel lonely. He would be appalled if he thought someone felt sorry for him. He was what the picture was about—the center of attention of all who looked at it. He had an audience; how could he be lonely?

On my frequent visits returning to my grandparents' house after I began to live with my parents, I continued to study that picture. I decided, if the lone wolf had a philosophy, it would be *If the whole world passed away and I had one rock to stand on, I would be okay*. To ensure I not be lonely when I was alone, I assumed the lone wolf's philosophy as I imagined it was.

When Aunt Clara moved to Galbert Street in Monticello in the early 1950s, Grandpa and Grandma moved with her and brought the lone wolf picture. It hung in Aunt Clara's bedroom. She had noticed my attention to the picture and said I could have it when she died; she told me where it would be.

When she passed, Dad went with me to pick up my picture. He uneasily followed me, suspiciously I think, from room to room. It was not where she told me it would be. I asked each cousin about it. No one knew anything.

This same picture was in Archie Bunker's living room, in the television show, which can be seen on reruns. This set was displayed at the Smithsonian Museum of American History, during some of the times I visited DC.

I saw some lone wolf pictures in antique stores but not the exact same picture until 1999. I found the exact same picture in the exact same frame, in an antique store in Tennessee. It hangs in my living room now, above my television set. The man wanted twenty dollars. I did not haggle.

* When I was a child, I was often ill. I had pneumonia in both lungs when I was two. When I was eight, all of my teeth were so rotten they poisoned my immune system. All were removed by a surgeon, while I breathed ether through gauze.

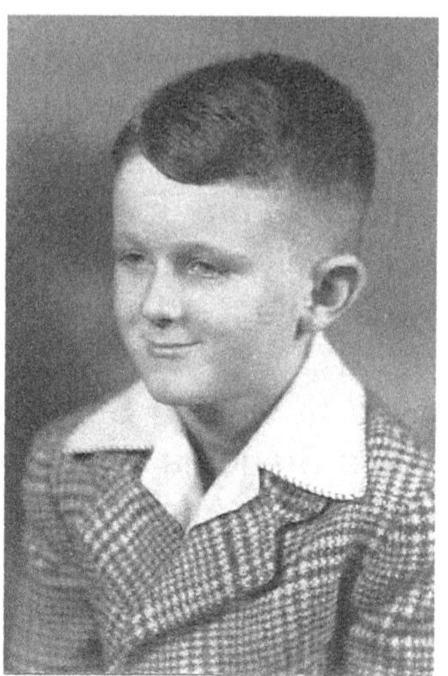

Author dressed up by his mother, age 6.

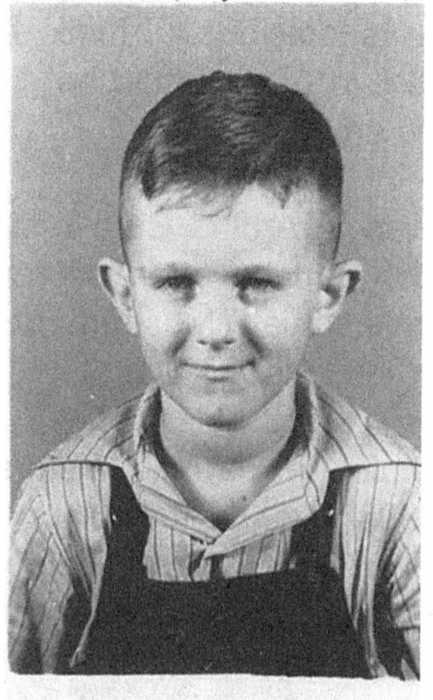

Author in grade two

My most crippling, challenging childhood illness was serious asthma. I was allergic to many common things besides raw milk, including chicken and chocolate. Outdoors, I was allergic to hay and various grasses, flowers, and weeds. But what I was especially allergic to was indoors: house dust.

In spring 1945, when I was six, I came close to death one night because of my allergy to house dust. At least my parents and I were convinced I was because my wheezing became louder and my breathing more labored and I grew weaker.

At three o'clock that morning, Dad called one of the Hyatt brother physicians in Monticello. Dr. Hyatt drove that night to our home three miles south of Monticello and gave me an adrenalin shot. My breathing improved immediately and continued to improve until it became normal. I still recall that frightful night.

After this episode, my parents took me to an allergist in Little Rock. He found fifty-two substances to which I was allergic, and prepared an anti-allergy serum. I took the serum by hypodermic injection weekly for a year followed by one every two weeks for another year. I took them at the office of John Price, M.D., the same physician who had surgically removed my teeth, and had sliced me when I was in my mother's the womb.

His office was where the *Hope for Women* office is today, on the west side of South Main Street where it crosses the railroad. Mother unfailingly drove me there.

The area of my arm that was injected quickly swelled to the size of tennis ball; shrank within hours. After two years of injections, I was retested and found to be allergic to absolutely nothing. The allergist discontinued my shot therapy. I have not had an asthma attack since I began taking the shots.

Since completing the anti-allergy serum regimen, I have been free of all allergies, even hay fever. Being free of allergies during my life has contributed much to my ease of mind, well-being, and ability to function as an adult.

Often as a child, and sometime still, I sit or lie quietly under a tree and listen to my breath going in and out, always in. The pleasant sound provides security and confidence. Nothing is more frightening to me than being unable to take a breath.

Author as a child in standard professional photographer pose at that time.

Free of allergies, I continued to encounter usual childhood illnesses: colds, ear aches, a small bout with measles and a large one with intestinal flu. Before being free of allergies, I cried often, felt bad and was not fun to be around. I believe I never reached anything approaching *infant terrible*, but I was not a loveable child.

* My parents and I visited Little Rock during Christmas 1945, staying overnight at a downtown hotel. No malls were in Little Rock then; important shopping was done among a few shops, called department stores, along Main Street. *Crowded* hardly begins to describe the throng of people on Little Rock's Main Street the first Christmas after the war.

Mother and I were in a store on Main Street when she told me where we were going next. I thought I knew where that next place was, and when we walked out the store onto the sidewalk,

I turned to right, the direction I thought we were going to go, and Mother turned left. We separated in a pressing crowd; neither found the other.

When I realized I was lost, I began searching for a policeman. After what seemed a long time, I found two on the sidewalk next to their car and approached them in tears and said I had lost my mother. They asked me my name and in what hotel we were staying.

I had no idea; I had only learned what a hotel was the day before. They asked me to describe it. I told them it had a lobby—I had never seen or heard such thing and assumed it was unique to my hotel—and I told them the doors never shut but went round and round (I found out later these were called revolving doors), which I also had never seen before and thought were unique to my hotel.

In the meantime, Mother had returned to the hotel crying, and told Dad I was lost. He called the Little Rock Police Department headquarters.

The policemen called their headquarters and were told my parents were in the Lafayette Hotel. They then called them to say they had found their lost son, drove me to the hotel in their super, cool police car, turned on the siren when I asked them and took me in an elevator to my parents' room. Everyone was glad to see each other.

Days later, Mother asked me, "How did you know to find a policeman?"

"I don't know. It just made sense," I answered.

If I had not found the two policemen, which almost did not happen, the rest of my life could have unfolded differently, perhaps tragically.

Author's father, 1940

Author's mother, 1940

* The sudden leap in Dad's good fortune when we moved to the Drew Central campus caused him to believe that, as a child, I would become spoiled if I had too much come too easily to me. He intended to assure I did not have a carefree childhood.

Consequently, in my formative years, he deliberately set about being sure I never developed an assumption of privilege or permission. When I asked for something, he frequently said no without an explanation, nor did he give me one when I asked. More importantly in ensuring my childhood not be carefree, he found work for me.

My regular jobs were to keep the grass cut, the yard clean, my room clean, wash and dry the dishes after supper and assist Mother cleaning house on Saturdays. I had several jobs outside the home as a boy because my father rarely let a chance pass him by to direct me toward one.

I cleaned mortar off several thousand old bricks at a dollar per thousand. Beginning in the summer after grade eight, I worked on Drew Central's construction crews, always for less than anyone else was making. I washed the school's busses and removed from under them the greasy, messy, near-solid mass known as gunk.

Once, Dad had me rake the entire grounds in front of the old red-brick high school, an area of several acres full of oak and maple trees, today filled with Drew Central's buildings.

Dad thought, when I finished raking, the ground must be void of *every* leaf. I was not just to make the school's campus appear cleaner with *almost* all leaves gone. I never heard dad mention any philosophers, albeit he seemed to follow the existentialist philosopher Nietzsche's "What does not kill us makes us stronger."

* My parents were members of the White Hall church called Shady Grove Baptist Church, which had a total attendance of about thirty persons, including children. It was heated by a woodstove; it had no electricity or plumbing. We had Sunday school every Sunday; our preacher came two Sundays a month. We had a revival every August. The revival preacher was a visitor.

They worked hard at "saving souls." In the1950 revival, the preacher began each evening by saying, "You all are one day closer to judgment and to hell if you have not accepted the Lord Jesus Christ into your heart as your personal savior." He spent the rest of the sermon preaching the wonders of heaven, the torments of hell and death everlasting. I was *saved* and baptized in Aunt Grace's pond, which is still where it was in 1950.

The congregation sometimes discussed whether the church was a Missionary, Southern, or hard-shell Baptist. It seemed one of the differences was the belief that someone saved could *backslide*, which means the saved person did not behave as a Christian. Some believed if one is saved, one is always saved. I do not remember what we called ourselves in 1950. I probably did not know then.

Every Sunday, my parents and I went about doing whatever we each did to get ready to go to church. It was never discussed. Our church had a strong Sunday school program with proper and attractive literature.

Author with his mother

* Dad and Mother continued to leave me home on occasions as they went through their week-to-week affairs. They had hired a woman who lived on Midway Road near Scroughout, to help Mother with the washing, ironing, and general house work. Her name was Julia; she was a large, congenial black woman who helped Grandma Willis with her washing. She was well known to everyone in the Willis family; all liked her and held her in high esteem, as did I.

When my parents needed me kept, they hired Julia to take care of me at home. She also prepared lunch and supper for herself and me.

I do not recall trying to disobey her or even considering it. Albeit, her method to keep me in her control was to show me the scariest picture she could find in one of my parents' magazines, tell me what was going on in that picture, and say the same was going to happen to me if I did not do as she said.

If she could not find a picture, she made up a scary story to tell me. I believed her as surely as I would my parents telling me these things.

I was unaware adults could lie or make up stories out of whole cloth. Magic is reality to a child, serious reality, something I could neither defeat nor escape.

Her approach to child care had an unintended consequence: it created within me a fear of the dark that veiled my sight until the known became the unknown. This fear continued until high school. I was never afraid of a person or *something alive* waiting, lurking in the darkness. I was afraid of something neither human nor animal: nameless, supernatural, evil spirits that roam the earth in the darkness.

Man does not need the mortar of truth to seal the
prison of his fear.
—Michel de Montaigne

My fear was irrational and consequently boundless. When it began, it took me over, until all I could think about was to flee or hide. It literally crippled me. This was not a mild trembling fear. When I was in its grip, I was held by sheer terror until paralyzed into helplessness. My pores opened and fear rushed in.

A message I received from this experience while overcoming my fear was if one gives credence to anything one can not touch, smell, taste, see or hear, he can step off into a hole with no bottom.

Superstition is a great enemy of man . . .
—Swami Vivekananda

Without working up a drop of perspiration, Julia scared the stem-winding green snot out of me.

I never mentioned this to my parents. I did not understand for sure what was happening to me at the time it occurred. Also, I did not think they would believe me. Looking back on it, I can understand why molested children or abused spouses keep that portion of their lives from everyone. It was a helpless feeling.

In 1950, a spate of information began in the radio, newspapers, and magazines—and television, perhaps, though I had not yet heard of one—marking the end of the first half of the twentieth century, emphasizing it as a milestone in human progress.

That year was my twelfth one, and I became caught up in the concept of measuring progress. I was convinced a boy's twelfth year is his last one of childhood, or if not, it should be. If I was no longer a child; I had to stop being afraid of things that go bump in the night—something unreal, things I had never seen nor, I eventually realized, had anyone else.

Years would pass before I heard of Lao Tzu (Sixth Century B.C. Chinese philosopher and founder of Tao), who was to become my favorite philosopher. He wrote, "Man's enemies are not demons, but human beings like himself." I was pleased I had figured that out without anyone's help.

To overcome my fear, I began going alone into the woods with my dog and closest companion Spot. By the next summer, Spot and I began camping overnight. On my army surplus utility belt, I carried an army surplus hatchet, a marine KA-BAR knife, field shovel and canteen. In my army surplus backpack, I had an iron skillet (the same one I make cornbread with today), bacon, potatoes, an onion, several slices of light bread and matches

In the iron skillet, I fried the bacon; I cut potatoes and onions into small chunks and fried them in bacon grease. Today, this is still among my favorite things to eat, especially if some of the potatoes and onions are nearly burned. Mother called them American fried potatoes.

As Spot and I spent nights alone with a fire, I began to figure out Julia, her stories and what caused me to be afraid. I eventually viscerally understood of what I was afraid did not exist and I began to get well. I named my fear, brought it out of the darkness and with difficulty it became controllable.

If I had not overcome this irrational fear, which almost did not happen, my life would have unfolded differently.

* Decorating the house for Christmas was a big deal with Mother. I helped her. The main thing I did to help was cut the tree and drag it home. Mother preferred a cedar, but a well-bushed pine was satisfactory. Dad squared the bottom and steadied it upright, until I became old enough to do it.

Once, while dragging a tree from about a quarter of a mile east of today's Highway 425 to our house on the Drew Central campus, my fingers on my right hand became frostbitten. I learned it is not the freezing weather that causes pain and distress; it is inadequetately dressing for it.

Mother, whose understanding of the healing arts always surprised me, plunged my hand into a pan of cold water with ice cubes. When enough feeling returned to my fingers to feel the water, she *slowly* added warmer water, until it was at room temperature. Thawing safely required about one and a half hours.

If I remember correctly, I did not have gloves that day. I kept my left hand warm in my coat pocket and dragged the tree with my right. I had an army surplus hatchet and a canteen on my army surplus utility belt.

For some years afterward, these frostbitten fingers got colder before those on my left hand. When I was grown, I noticed no difference.

Mother decorated the cedar growing in front of our house with only large blue outdoor lights. The combination was stunningly beautiful; several of her friends commented on it.

At that time in school, I was taught matching colors from a commercially prepared color chart. The chart, therefore, the teacher said that blue and green absolutely did not match.

I told Mother about the color coordination chart and what my teacher said about blue and green. She smiled and said, "Blue sky, green grass." She was ahead of her time in several ways about what combinations look good and taste good together that were contrary to conventional thinking.

Christmas presents I remember were a bicycle—actually two of them, the first one I never learned to ride because I was afraid I would fall—Lincoln Logs, and Erector Sets. I added to these over succeeding Christmases. When I was ten, I received my Daisy Red Rider BB Gun. With it I learned the fine art of shooting, and I began my lifelong love of guns and shooting.

Erector sets provided a wonderful side benefit. Two pretty girls in Bowser, Anna Ray and June Webb, slightly younger than I would come with their mother to my house to visit. We would go to my room and build stuff with my erector sets. They had never seen an erector set and made a fine audience for me. We have recalled those time as years have passed.

In tenth grade, June was my girl friend for a couple of weeks. She may have not known she was, as I never mentioned it to anyone.

By age thirteen, I began to ask for clothes rather than toys for Christmas. I often returned clothes my parents gave me, as they did not suit me. They soon figured this out and began to give me money for Christmas, and I bought my own. A couple of Christmases, I worked at the Model, a department store on the square, owned by David Anderson. I took most of my salary in clothes.

When I joined the married world, I was astonished by the number of couples I came to know whose wife selected the husband's clothes and laid out each morning what he was to wear that day.

Such behavior was outside my experience growing up among the Willis and McKinstry families. My dad's paramount vanity was clothes. From as early as I can remember, he selected and purchased for himself every thread he wore. It probably never occurred to anyone who knew him that he required help. Or if they thought he did need help, they were surely certain he did not want any.

* Dad and Mother each had four siblings; their offspring amounted to fourteen first cousins: seven McKinstry and seven Willis. Among us fourteen cousins, I was the only one without a sibling.

The first cousin nearest my age, a week younger, was Ralph Lynn McKinstry. Everyone, including his parents, called him Bubba. In 1954, Bubba had moved to Bastrop, Louisiana; that summer, he and I spent several days with Grandma McKinstry at her large grand old home on Highway 278 (old Highway 4), on Main Street in Wilmar.

Grandma McKinstry cooked and served a big breakfast—eggs, meat, biscuits and gravy, and potatoes—each morning at six thirty, to which everyone had to be on time. To summon everyone, she rang an old school bell that had been in her family before anyone could remember. This rule was her only one; otherwise we did pretty much as we pleased. The bell I have on a shelf in my library.

What pretty much pleased us that summer was to steal watermelons, which we gave to a skinny, friendly good old girl who ran a tiny café in Wilmar on Highway 4 on the west end of town. We called her *Skinny Minnie Fishtail*, which were words that were part of a popular song then. She liked our calling her that and for lunch served us cold watermelon at no charge with her delicious cheeseburgers.

Today, the exterior of the building in which was her tiny café is unchanged, except for a fading hand-painted sign on raw plywood identifying it as *Bait Shop*.

Our usual method of stealing melons was Hardy McKinstry, one of Mother's first cousins and three years older than Bubba and I, would drive slowly, after dark, in his truck with his lights off by a large watermelon field beside Highway 4, about half a mile west of Wilmar, the first field past the railroad on the right.

Bubba, two or three other Wilmar boys, and I would jump out of the truck bed, climb over the fence and go into the field to get the melons.

Oldest McKinstry cousins on Grandpa Mckinstry's horse. L-R are: Larry Mckinstry, Author, Bubba Mckinstry and Wayne Groce. Not yet born are: Wayne's brother Dennis; Larry's and Bubba's sister Mary Kay; Aunt Artie's two children Tommy and Sissy Robinson

Hardy would drive, lights off, down the road, turn around and come back, stop, and wait for us to return with the stolen goods that we loaded into his truck. We sometimes went back for more. When we stole watermelons, we did it at the same time of night and from the same field, a consistency that came back to haunt us.

One night, just as we got well out into the field as we always did, we were expected. Someone from the edge of the woods bordering the field on the south fired a large-caliber shotgun. We hit the dirt. As we lay there, we could see Hardy driving by slowly back and forth. After a while, we began to crawl toward the highway, not on our hands and knees but on our bellies, a low crawl, hugging the dirt. We stopped at the field's edge.

After hearing nothing more from the woods for several minutes, we saw Hardy coming, climbed over the fence, jumped into the back of his truck, and sped away.

Hardy is a bright, likeable and humorous man. I have heard him tell this stealing-watermelons story with more humor than I felt that night. I would probably have thought it funny too if I had been in the truck watching Hardy crawling in the dirt. He eats breakfast at Lena's Café almost every morning.

The next night, Bubba and I lay in bed and clawed our chigger bitten legs. Grandma provided us with some baking soda and vinegar; things improved. None among us thieves mentioned going back to the watermelon patch.

While in Wilmar, I spent some time with Glynis Reap, who lived across the road and a little east from Grandma. I did not have access to a car, which meant spending of our time together was sitting on her front steps. Glynis had the three most important qualities I admired in a girl: she was smart, pretty, funny and liked me, not necessarily in this order.

I imagine the only reason she would see me was her parents would not let her go with boys in cars. I did not care why she would see me.

We were sitting on her front steps one night. The moon had set; gathering clouds had entombed the stars. We did not notice how dark the night had become and did not turn on the porch light.

It was three o'clock when suddenly the light came on. Mr. Reap burst through the door with a big iron on his hip and a double-barrel twelve gage in his arm. The sudden light and noise startled Glynis and me. We quickly stood.

He saw me and exclaimed, “Are you still here!” Without slowing, he started toward me. In my anxiety to get out of his way, I fell backward into the yard.

Without a glance in my direction, Mr. Reap strode into the night.

Glynis explained her father was town Marshall and had probably received a call about trouble and was heading out to take care of it. I understood this information was pertinent at some level but was of no help to me at that moment. At that moment, I could think only of being sure I was not late for Grandma’s breakfast.

Today, the Reap house is still intact, front steps included, on the south side of Main Street, near Eighth Street in the middle of town.

Glynis resembled Jennifer Jones, the beautiful, sultry actress in *Duel in the Sun*, with Gregory Peck and Joseph Cotten. Jones died at age 90 in December 2009.

* That summer, Hardy’s girlfriend was Carol Wiley, Glynis’s friend. The Methodist church welcomed a new pastor who had a seventeen-year-old son. He asked Carol to go with him to a movie in Warren, and her mother (according to Carol) made her go. Hardy had an idea.

Hardy, Bubba, a couple of other Wilmar boys, and I, the same bunch who stole watermelons, went to Warren and found the young man’s car on the movies’ parking lot. We picked up the back end off the pavement and slipped a block under the rear drive axle, so the back wheel was about a half an inch of the ground. Back in the day, if one rear wheel did not get traction, the vehicle could not move. In the darkness one could not see the wheel was off the pavement.

Glynis in her yard with her cat. Building in background is Wilmar's Baptist church, long ago razed and replaced with a larger, brick one.

Among the parked cars in the darkness, we hid and watched. Carol and her date came out and got into the car; he started it and put it in reverse. It did not move. He opened the hood and saw nothing wrong. We came out of the darkness. Carol saw us, screamed, "Hardy!" and ran to him.

Hardy told Carol's date to get back in the car while he would look under the hood. While he was looking under the hood, the rest of us stealthily removed the block, and the car was ready to move. Hardy told him, "Try it now." He drove back to Wilmar very slowly, with us following at Carol's insistence.

I saw Hardy at Lena's Café several months ago and asked him if he ever told Carol what we had done. He grinned with the memory and shook his head.

* In 1955, I spent Halloween with Bubba in Bastrop. Halloween that year was on a Monday, a school day. Because Sunday was Sunday, Bastrop celebrated that holiday on Saturday night.

A friend of Bubba had a pickup or at least access to one. Among the first things we did was remove from a Gulf gas station a large standing orange sign reading, *Clean Bathrooms Inside*, and placed it in the immaculately manicured yard of a large, beautiful house in Bastrop's nicest neighborhood that was the home of the ex-girlfriend of one of Bubba's friends who was with us.

By the time we got around to the night's main event, it was one o'clock; we drove into the country to steal sugarcane. We went in the truck to a farmer's field but had to park about a hundred yards away from the cane field that was on the other side of a creek that we crossed on a railroad trestle. The farmer's family house was dark, one hundred feet from the trestle.

We walked over the trestle in a single line, carefully stepping on the crossties as not to fall between them. The sky was clear; the moon, two days from full, was nearly set.

After we gathered the cane and started back over the trestle, the moon had set. In the dimmed light, we moved over the trestle more gingerly than we had come.

I was bringing up the rear when a large dog began to bark at the farmer's house. The front stoop light came on, and the farmer stepped out into the light with a large-caliber rifle, not a shot gun.

He raised it and aimed; I was the only target he had. The others had gone into the darkness of the woods toward the truck. I was on the trestle, alone in the pale starlight of the cloudless, moonless sky. I stood silently, stone-cold still.

I thought surely the man would fire in the air, if he would fire at all; instead, he fired at me. I heard the zing of the bullet as it passed. I ignored the old adage, *Look before you leap*, and jumped into the darkness twelve feet off the trestle. I had no idea how deep the water was; I grasped my arms full of cane as would a drowning man so many pieces of straw.

I waded out of the three-foot-deep creek, made it to the pickup, heaved the cane into the bed on top of the rest of our booty, and jumped on top of all of it. The driver already had the truck started; we roared off into the Louisiana night.

Bubba died from a heart attack in Texas about 1994. I had not seen him since all the cousins were together at our Grandma McKinstry's funeral on January 6, 1977. He left three children and a beautiful wife.

If I had been shot off that railroad trestle instead of jumping that Halloween night in that Louisiana sugarcane field, the rest of my life would have unfolded differently, if I had a rest of my life.

* Except for Bubba, I was closer to my Willis than my McKinstry cousins. This was not a deliberate choice but a natural one. While I was growing up, Dad's siblings lived within a short driving distance from the old Willis home and gathered there frequently, usually for no special reason.

When it was summer, we often ate homemade ice cream on the east side of my grandparents' house. My mother always brought it, as the family agreed hers was the best. I have her recipe and make it when I remember how good it was long enough to do something about it.

According to Mother's friends, her recipe was original with her. It is too delicious to be lost. As it may not be found elsewhere, It is presented here:

Lela Willis's Vanilla Ice Cream

> Beat 6 eggs until light yellow. Add 2 cups of sugar and heat in double boiler until a consistent mix. Add juice of 1 lemon and enough whole milk to make a workable amount in a double boiler. Cook on low heat until mixture coats to spoon. Set aside and add 2 teaspoons of real vanilla and 1 can of Eagle Brand milk, 1 pint of half-and-half, or ½ pint of whipping cream. Add enough whole milk to bring the amount to within 1 to 2 inches of top of freezer can. (Any substitutions will influence taste.)
>
> Mix everything thoroughly before pouring into freezer can. Add layers of ice cream salt and ice. Turn it until you can not.

In my second book, Professor Miller says of Bill Butler's Ma's apple pie, "It is good enough to prove the existence of God or at least establish the purpose of man." The professor could have said the same of my Mother's ice cream.

My friends at school rode a bus each day and were not around weekends, evenings, or during the summer. Most of them, if not all, did not have telephones until they were in junior high or later. Being an only child and growing up largely isolated from children, first with my grandparents and then at school, I learned to relate easier to adults than to persons my age.

Child psychologists of the next generation observing me may have noticed, in their lingo, "He does not play well with others."

* I am sure my parents had conversations when I was not present, albeit they never asked me to leave their presence when they were conversing, literally never.

They discussed important subjects of the day, activities among friends and our extended families, and the events at Drew Central, where my dad was superintendent and Mother taught English. If they said it, I heard it. I learned early discretion is the better part of valor.

One evening, at the dinner table with guests present, I made an accurate but indiscreet observation about someone not present. Mother reproved me on the spot. "James William, you do not have to say everything you are thinking." This helpful advice I have sometimes ignored to my regret.

When my parents decided I was old enough to know how to behave among a group of adult strangers, they rarely left home without me. I went with them to Arkansas A&M faculty parties, often the only child there; or if another was there, I was usually the only one who wanted to be there.

Mother liked to entertain friends with a formal sit-down dinner. Grilling out was not her thing. I looked forward to these adult affairs because of the interesting conversation and the menus Mother prepared and served.

Back in the day, adult social entertainment was card playing, and conversation for which the dinner table provided an excellent setting. My father was a skillful raconteur and was at ease in this environment.

My favorite menu was Mother's roasted standing pikes peak beef with gravy from the drippings caught in the drip pan, served with twice-baked potatoes, other vegetables, green salad, pickles, olives, and hot yeast rolls with butter. Her favorite desert was light fluffy cheesecake. It was the best food I ate in my youth. No other home I visited offered such a meal.

When I left home and began cooking, I was amazed that she prepared and served these meals with one small, unsophisticated, regular kitchen stove and oven, without warmer, microwave, or pre-prepared dishes, and without assistance, except mine, which was limited to setting the table.

Mother owned a set of nice china, linen napkins and sterling silver tableware. She instructed me *exactly* where and how each item was to be placed and why.

Perhaps, one may think Mother's feat was not so amazing when one considers my Grandmother Willis, by herself, cooked daily for several people a variety of delicious dishes on a wood-burning cook stove. Her grandmother cooked everything in an open, wood-burning fireplace.

As no one in McKinstry's or Willis's family fished or hunted for food, we ate pork and chicken. Pork was made into ham, bacon, or sausage and cured by smoking. Chickens remained alive until killed and eaten fresh.

I vividly recall the first beef I ate; I was nine. Mother prepared chunks of it with natural gravy, served it with stiff-mashed potatoes, prepared with whole milk and butter. I excitedly asked Mother what this wonderful stuff on the potatoes was. "Beef," she said. She asked me to go with her into the backroom of the house.

Stacked in the corner on the floor were dozens of shinny tin cans. "All of these cans are full of beef," Mother said. I would have suffered from an embarrassment of riches if I had known what that meant.

These cans of beef were from the cow Dad and a neighbor raised, staked out in Weevil Lake, the only place grass could grow during that driest of summers. They took it to the local butcher shop, where it was prepared and canned. At that time, almost no homes, if any, had freezers; meat was fresh, such as chicken, and smoked, such as pork. Beef was dried or canned.

* When I was seven, after second grade, Mike and Pat McGinnis moved in across the street, where dormitory, Bankston Hall, is today. Mike was two years older than I; Pat was a year younger. Billy Webb, Mike's age, lived in Bowser, a rural community south of Arkansas A&M. Things picked up a little, but I never learned to relate comfortably to people my age in casual situations.

Mike and Pat's parents and mine became close friends; they played bridge most Saturday nights at either's house. Mike and Pat's father John McGinnis, an A&M chemistry professor, was the neighbor who raised the cow with Dad.

In spring 1947, immediately after school was out after third grade, I began to feel bad and thought I had a fever. I did not tell anyone because Mrs. McGinnis and Mother were taking Mike, Pat, and me to see *Snow White and the Seven Dwarfs* at the theater in Monticello. I intended to see that movie no matter what. I was not disappointed.

The next morning, Mother noticed I was in bad shape; I did not dispute her. She put me under covers to sweat, another example of her medical acumen, and fed me hot, hot lemonade. I soon broke out all over, as she had anticipated, with German measles.

* A couple of days later, I was still in my bed recovering. Aunt Artie, Mother's middle sister, was staying with me. I was asleep but suddenly awoke with a wonderful dog licking my face and walking about on me and my bed! He had come to our front door; Artie let him in.

He went immediately to my room, according to Artie, jumped on the chair next to my bed and then on my bed. She fed him, and he spent the day with me. Artie loved dogs; she believed my parents would want a dog in my bed; or if they did not, they ought to.

Author's life long friend Mike McGinnis high school senior picture

When Dad got home, he told me we had to find out to whom the pup belonged, which turned out to be a student in married housing on Arkansas A&M campus, two hundred yards from our house. The man came and got him. Next day, he was back; that afternoon Dad returned him. Next day, he was back; that afternoon, Dad returned him again. The man realized the dog had adopted me and asked Dad if I could keep him.

He was twenty-two inches high and stocky in body. He was white with three black spots; one was on his right eye, another on his tail, and a large, prominent one on the middle of his back. After unsuccessful attempts at creativity, I could not ignore the obvious and named him Spot. His previous owner told Dad Spot was eight months old.

He developed the habit of going to the campus slaughter house and dragging home for a half a mile the biggest bone he could find. The bone was longer than he was, and it was a struggle for him. He put his treasure down by our front door and gnawed it.

If my parents noticed a large gnawed bovine femur on our front stoop, they never said anything, nor did any visitors of whom I heard.

When people acted as if they desired the bone, Spot put his mouth around it and growled with harmless fury. One who enjoyed Spot's bone game was Ira Lafayette "Doc" Jones, high school principal; he began playing the faux femur game with Spot when he visited our house.

Soon afterward, Spot saw Doc walking from the old red brick building, the original Drew Central High School, to the mailbox across the road, which he did almost every day. Spot grabbed his bone and ran and put it down in front of Doc for him to put his foot on. This became a daily routine for them, one that Doc told everyone about and of which neither tired.

One occasion, Spot saw Doc walking but could not find his bone. He panicked momentarily, but recovered in time to drag the largest limb he could find over to Doc and put it down in his path. Doc put his foot on it and Spot, with the limb in his mouth, growled menacingly.

Spot chased birds he saw on the ground until they flew away; then he jumped in vain attempts to catch them. One day he caught one just as it got into the air. Suddenly, to his total amazement, he had a mouthful of fluttering, screaming bird.

He had the most surprised look on his face I have ever seen on man or beast. He was negotiating with himself what to do with what he had caught in his mouth; freeing his captive was never on the table.

Wesley and Monteene McCoy moved in next door, and though ten years younger than Dad and Mother, they became closest of friends with my parents. Monteene said recently the four were like siblings.

Monteene would sometimes put food in a bowl for Spot. He would pick up the bowl at Monteene's house, bring it to our house without spilling any of the food, eat it, and return the bowl where he found it.

In the hot days of summer, Spot would amble along to Weevil Lake for a refreshing swim and saunter back.

When I took off on my bike or walking, Spot followed and walked or ran beside me, except to school. Mostly, Spot was just with me. He was always glad to see me. We chased each other and fell on the ground to wrestle.

Often when playing, he would scratch my arms, hands, or face with his claws, but I never cared. Once he jumped and caught the soft tissue between my nostrils with his teeth, which hurt like all get out.

Spot followed me when I rode my bike to Grandpa's house. He would lag behind as much as an eighth of a mile but always remained in sight. When I stopped for him to catch up, instead of catching up, he stopped where he was and lay down. When I continued, he continued. I was careful to never get out of his sight.

I do not know and have never known what love is. My quandary is persons who think they are in love feel and act exactly as people who really are in love. Regardless of my problem with understanding love, I knew at that time I could count on the fingers of one hand, without a thumb, people for whom I felt authentic affection as much as I did for Spot.

An obvious emotion a dog feels is unadulterated jealousy. Everyone has witnessed a dog caught up in this emotion. Jealousy is one of humans' most debilitating emotions. Knowing dogs feel jealousy, one must wonder what other human emotions dogs feel, such as heartbreak, loneliness and angst.

Unlike every human I know, Spot was always glad to see me, never judged me, and never cared what clothes I wore, what grades I made or how much money I had. He believed I could do no wrong, a belief from which he never wavered, no matter if I mistreated him or how foolishly I sometimes acted.

Unlike humans, Spot was never mad at me; he never complained, whined or offered excuses. He was never negative; he never pouted; he never withheld his love, seeking emotional revenge for some slight of mine, real or imaged.

Spot never lied. I cannot imagine the origin of the simile *He lies like a dog*. It is impossible for a dog's guileless heart to deceive.

In my life's sojourn, I have met many people of both sexes, all ages, most ethnic groups and many faiths. Some persons were very good; some not so good; some very bad. I have never met a bad dog, except those humans had made so.

Spot was by far and away the most important dog in my life, my closest childhood friend, and one of my life's more important influences. There is not much an intelligent person cannot learn from a good dog. A not so intelligent person could too, if he had enough sense to get out of his own way.

I told Dad how I felt about Spot. He said he understood why I felt that way, but I probably ought not to tell anyone. I also knew if dogs cannot go to heaven, I did not want to go. This thought I kept to myself without being prompted. Subsequent association with dogs and humans has not changed my view. I still miss him.

Hercule Poirot, the Belgium criminal investigator and connoisseur of human nature observed to a young lady, "Mademoiselle, so many people are disgusting about so many things"—*Three Act Tragedy*; Masterpiece Theater, 2011.

I was in the army in Europe when Spot died. His passing was a traumatic experience for Dad who was with him. More than forty years later, Dad wrote in *Some Jottings Down*, "I still become physically sick every time I think about Spot dying." Dad loved Spot. He probably never told him.

Dad buried Spot under the large white oak on the west side of our house, on a limb on which was my bag swing that Dad had prepared for me. He also built a thirteen-foot ladder off the top of which I could jump onto the swing. I whiled away many afternoons on that swing, alone, in the shade, with Spot watching.

Limb from which my swing hanged is gone; the remainder of the tree appears relatively prosperous. The house was razed years ago. The site is a fenced play area for children of Drew Central Primary School.

Spot

* When I was home on weekends from Dad's parents, Dad and I began a Saturday routine: he and I would attend the Saturday afternoon western movie at the Drew Theater in Monticello. When I returned to live with my parents, we continued going to the Saturday movies, which were always Westerns.

Author and Spot.

The theater was located where the Commercial Bank parking lot on its west side is today. It burned in 1953. Dad drove me there to watch it burn. He commented to a friend of his standing with us, "This is going to be hard on James William; it's his second home."

When I was eleven, on Saturdays, I began to hitchhike alone three miles from my house at Drew Central campus to the movie theater in Monticello, something I looked forward to the whole week, especially if it was a Roy Rogers movie.

I caught a ride in front of my house to town and at the Methodist church curve on South Main to return home. Sometimes Mike or Pat or both went with me.

Without talking to me, as far as I know they may not have talked to each other, my parents allowed me to go anywhere within a one-day round-trip walking distance from our house. I usually walked there along the railroad. Sometimes I walked on Midway Road. I walked south to my grandparents, sometimes on the pig trail path my father and aunts had walked to school.

Basically, I walked everywhere I went, usually alone. As incredulous as it seems today, back in the day, nothing seemed strange about a boy walking alone for miles in the woods and on the roads and byways, including Monticello's streets.

It never occurred to me to leave a note saying where I was going; usually I did not know when I left. I don't recall my parents ever asking me where I had been when I returned.

* My parents belonged to the Book of the Month Club; seriously, quietly reading was a daily, evening activity for them. They also read the daily *Arkansas Gazette* and weekly magazines. I adopted their habits and began reading *Time*, *Look*, *Life*, *Collier's Weekly*, the *Saturday Evening Post*, and the jokes in *Reader's Digest*. I do not recall reading one of their many books. My lack of interest seems strange to me today, and I am at loss for a reason.

I recall the cover and title of *The Iron Mistress* struck my thirteen-year-old fancy. Dad told me it was the story of Jim Bowie. I did not read it then but recently ordered a copy from Amazon and read it.

In the evenings, I lay in bed and listened to the radio; the programs were frequently drama and comedy, with some news. This comedy was mostly borrowed from vaudeville, which still may be the origin of the best comedy in America.

Entertaining myself, rather than participating in an activity with others, was, and remains, a major form of my entertainment.

I often took a deck of cards to bed with me. Playing various card games is pretty much the extent of my social entertainment; that and a pleasant dinner conversation. Reading and watching television I enjoy alone.

I told my fourth wife, Dawn, that if the world passed away and I had a rock to stand on, I would be fine. With a friendly smile, she replied, "You'd have to have a TV."

In college, both of my parents majored in English. Dad's minor was history. If Mother had a minor, I do not know what it was. Dad had few hours in math and less in science because he did not like science. As superintendent, he taught algebra at Drew Central because he could not find certified math teachers.

My parents put a great emphasis on speaking grammatically. Without hesitation, they corrected my grammar and often got into grammar debates between themselves. I remember one continuing over several evenings about how to correctly diagram the sentence: *Over the fence is out.*

They also debated the antecedent of the pronoun *it* as in *It is raining*.

My parents would have wholeheartedly agreed with Jason Chamberlain, president of the University of Vermont, who said in his inaugural address 1811, "Morals and manners will rise or decline with our attention to grammar."

Dad fired at least two teachers because they spoke with improper grammar, including incorrect subject and predicate agreement. I remember he said, "If a person had any pride, he would at least speak with noun and verb agreement."

Today, I will sometimes make a grammar slip and think, "Sorry, Momma."

* Dad began smoking in 1933, at age eighteen, while he spent that summer helping his oldest brother Wesley on his farm. When he became superintendent of Drew Central, he began to smoke more than two packs a day. I never heard him or Mother talk about it. Back in the day, no one noticed or cared where, when, what, how often or if a man smoked.

In summer 1950, Dad, Mom, and I, together with Mom's siblings and my McKinstry cousins, were visiting Mother's family in Wilmar. We boys and men were standing around outside the house on the east, between the big east porch and a very large oak, which still stands in good health. Today, nothing about the house site shows any evidence of past human presence.

On that day, without antecedent or a word to anyone, Dad dropped on the ground the cigarette he was smoking and stomped it out. Quietly, with a wane smile, he said only to me, "That's my last one." He had smoked cigarettes for at least seventeen years. Suddenly, he reduced his cigarette consumption to zero.

He never smoked another one, ever. As I grew older, I became impressed with what he had done. He went cold-turkey from more than two packs a day to none. As was his nature, he never mentioned it or made a fuss about it to anyone. Years later, if others brought up the subject of quitting smoking and asked him about it, I heard him tell them without elucidation it was the most difficult thing he had ever done. I never heard him and Mother speak of it.

During the first few months after he quit, he would often go home from his office during the day, undress, and go to bed. In Civil War soldier vernacular, he went "plumb to bed," but did not go to bed to sleep or nap or even rest. He went to bed solely not to smoke; in bed and in church were the only places he never smoked.

Whatever it took; he was determined not to smoke again. He never wore a nicotine patch or chewed nicotine gum, if such things were even available. He smoked a pipe for a while but soon quit, perhaps because I sometimes smoked his pipe when he and Mother were out for the evening. Neither ever said anything to me. I assumed they knew and I quit before they decided to approach me about it.

We never talked about it, but I believe Dad quit smoking so he could have moral authority to demand I not smoke. Moral authority was important to him.

He never, I mean never, cursed for the same reason.

When I was a small child, Dad's expression when frustrated was *I'll swear*, which means, if one thinks about it, he is declaring he intends to swear. I have never heard anyone else say that the way he did. Before I understood what it meant, I said *I'll swear* in some personal, perturbing situation or another, thinking that was what a man was supposed to say in these circumstances.

Dad sternly said, "No, you won't!"

I innocently asked what it was he did not want me to do. With my question, Dad realized what he had been saying. He never said it again. Sometimes he would tell a joke or story in which he would quote someone who swore, usually *damn*.

My many iniquities are not visited on me by my father; they are all my own.

* The first time I saw my parents cry was when they learned FDR had died. Dad came home from school and told Mother he had heard it, but did not know whether it was true; neither wanted to believe it and wondered how they could know. We did not have a radio in April, 1945.

We three went outside and looked west toward the college. The United States flag, which was on a pole immediately east of today's administration building and the first thing one saw while approaching the campus, was being lowered to half-mast by the sailors in the cadet program at Arkansas A&M, while taps was played.

In April 1945, I was six and in the first grade. I did not know what a president was, much less who he was, and was distressed to see my parents in such state and wondered what it meant for me. They explained to me their angst. The only president they had known since they were teenagers and had led the nation during the depression and World War II had suddenly died.

This event caused me to begin to pay attention to political talk among adults, and to politics and government in general. I have been a political news junkie since. I clearly remember listening to the 1948 Democratic Convention with Dad and exchanging views about it.

On Tuesday, August 14, 1945, my family was at the home of my mother's parents in Wilmar. Some other family members were there. That afternoon, I was napping in one of the upstairs bedrooms. Dad entered the room, woke me, and as exuberant as I ever saw him, exclaimed, "The war is over! The war is over! Japan has surrendered!"

He and Uncle Olen, Mother's brother, got in Grandpa's pickup, with Bubba and me in the back, and took off for Monticello. Olen blew the horn at every vehicle we met. On the square in Monticello were a throng of people on the sidewalks screaming and waving and a swarm of vehicles, including the four of us in the truck, driving around the square all yelling and waving back. Olen drove around the square a few times, and we returned to Grandma McKinstery's, still honking and yelling.

My Uncle Hugh, who had been in the Philippines, was on a troop ship moving toward Japan for the anticipated invasion.

May 1, 2011, sixty-six years to the day after Hitler killed himself in his bunker in Berlin, U.S. Special Forces shot dead Osama bin Laden and dumped his remains into the Arabian Sea. That evening, after President Obama's told the nation, spontaneous, ecstatic crowds in the thousands gathered in Times Square, Lafayette Square and other towns and universities across the nation. I recalled that Tuesday afternoon in 1945.

First Lieutenant Hugh Willis in Philippines, 1945.

* When in my early teens, Artie Harris, two years younger than I, moved into a college faculty house across from Weevil Stadium on the west. His parents were the entire music department faculty at the college. He attended Drew Central. I enjoyed his company and went to his house often. While there, I witnessed two interesting phenomena I vividly recall.

One of them was when a sudden rain began, with a strong wind that drove Artie and me to his house. We stood on the front porch and watched it. The rain stopped as quickly as it began. In his front yard, we saw small fish flopping in the wet grass!

They were not there before it rained. They were probably two inches long and shaped like small gold fish. We gathered some and put them into jars with water.

I have since read about raining fish. Reports have been made worldwide for hundreds of years. Such a thing happens somewhere in the world about ten times a year, according to Google.

The other event occurred when Artie and I were outside in his east yard with our bows and arrows. We were shooting the arrows straight up and watching them fall. Artie went into his house for some reason. While he was gone, I shot an arrow straight up.

As I was watching the arrow, a shiny, silver, round object suddenly appeared above me from the east. It remained above me not moving for at least a full minute. I never took my eyes off it. The sky was bright and clear of clouds; consequently, I could not get a fix on how high it was or how big it was. I heard no sound.

During the minute I watched it, I could add nothing to its description that I have not said; it was shiny, silver, and round, whether round as a penny or a ball or a saucer, I could not discern.

While keeping my eyes on the object, I began to yell for Artie. He hurried out, allowing the front screen door to slam behind him. Just as I heard the noise of the slamming door, the flying object I could not identify, after hovering, took off west; moving faster than anything I have ever seen. Artie never saw it.

* Sometime in my youth, I ran across writings of Bertrand Russell, British author, mathematician, and philosopher (1872-1970). He writes, "One should respect public opinion in so far as it is necessary to avoid starvation and to keep out of prison, but anything that goes beyond this is voluntary submission to an unnecessary tyranny."

His attitude toward public opinion helped put my own about it into focus, and I took comfort that I was not alone and no weirder than Lord Russell. My hero is Howard Roark, the architect in Ayn Rand's *The Fountainhead*. My hero is fiction; in reality, I never wanted to be anyone but myself.

When I returned to live in Monticello in 2005, a woman who had gone to school with me for twelve years, since we were in first grade, and had not seen me in forty-nine years, said about me to a Monticello friend, “He’s weird, you know.”

My mother would have been proud. She would have been disappointed If I had spent my life searching for the proper manila envelope to be filed under *conventional*. She supported authenticity.

Einstein said, “Innovation is not the product of logical thought.”

Not for nothing in high school did girls called me *Freak* in a friendly manner. They and I considered Freak a compliment in a weird way.

Boys called me *Peg*, shortened from *Peg Leg*, a name given to me in grade five, after I broke some small bones and tore ligaments in an ankle playing Fox and Hounds. I tore it up pretty good and had to walk with a crutch.

This nickname of mine was begun by my friend Skippy Cates, whom many teachers believed would end up in jail before he got out of school. I liked Skippy’s easy, unassuming manner. He lived near today’s Highway 425 and walked to school. Sometimes, he would walk home with me and we would watch the Weevil football team practice, my daily habit during the season.

Skippy added to my life in a significant way neither of us imagined. I had some sort of pocket knife that he took a shine to and wanted to buy. I do not recall any particulars about it. I have carried a pocket knife since I was a young boy. I would not sell my knife or swap for it.

He showed up the next day with a beautiful silver coin, the size of a United States dollar. It was an 1874 Bavarian funf (five)-mark coin. The bust of Bavaria’s (Mad) King Ludwig II was on one side. On the obverse was the Bavarian’s imperial eagle. I had never imagined such a delightful thing and gladly exchanged my knife for his coin.

A few days later, he approached me with a big smile and said the knife had fallen apart while he was trying to sharpen it. I apologized and tried to return the coin to him. He said it was not my fault and refused to take it. He thought the whole affair was funny, a great joke on him.

This large silver coin opened up a world to me I did not know existed. Uncle Hugh had served in the Philippines in World War II, where he had obtained coins from a fifty cent to one cent that he gave me. I suddenly had a foreign coin collection that I spent many years adding to and much enjoyed.

A coin dealer in Monterey, California, told me the Bavarian five-mark coin's silver content of 99.99 percent is among the highest of all the world's silver coins.

I have not been an active collector for three decades, but I still have the collection of hundreds of coins. Today, the world has 203 countries, a number that fluctuates. If I remember correctly, the last time I paid attention, I had coins from 157 different coin-producing entities, some of which no longer exist.

I also collected foreign paper currency. Among the most beautiful are prerevolutionary Mexican (the Mexican Revolution began in1910) and prerevolutionary Russian (before 1917).

The Bavarian five-mark coin with King Ludwig II was struck from 1874 to 1876. I have wondered how Skippy, a lad in Drew County, Arkansas, came to obtain such an exquisite object. Many who knew Skippy had a story about which they wondered.

Skippy did not return to school after fifth grade. I have never known anyone who knew where he went. It was rumored his beautiful mother was a war widow. She lived alone with only Skippy. I could not find him in Google Search.

* When I was thirteen, Mother told me to choose wallpaper for my room. I selected forest green with black shapeless random accents. I hung on my wall Roy Rogers comic book covers, and pennants I collected from trips my parents and I had taken.

I also selected my bed covers and curtains. My bed was the iron one Dad and Mother slept in on their wedding night. I painted it battleship gray and stuck an Arkansas A&M emblem on it. I sleep in it today.

Mother showed me how to clean my room; how to sweep, mop, and dust; and how to make my bed. She said if I made my bed every day and cleaned my room once a week, she would never come into my room unless invited. To my knowledge, she never did.

She taught me how to separate laundry, wash, and hang clothes on a line to dry. When I was fourteen, I wanted my blue jeans starched and ironed with a crease. She refused to do that but showed me how to. Clothes were starched in a dish pan, into which were put Argosy starch powder and warm water. Spray starch was years away.

To be ironed, they had to be sprinkled as were starched shirts. She taught me to iron my shirts, and I often got compliments on them. Some people did not believe I ironed them. Most of these people were girls my age.

Mother said she was teaching me to live alone. She said many men could not live without a woman because men did not know how to take care of themselves.

* My Grandmother McKinstry did not teach any of her four daughters to cook. Her notion was that cooking is difficult enough without having people around trying to help who did not know what they were doing. When Mother married, she literally could cook almost nothing; but she quickly learned and became

an excellent cook. Speaking from her experience, Mother said, “Anyone can learn to cook who is not lazy and can read.”

She had a great knack for understanding how different flavors go together and taught me some of what little I know about cooking today.

Dad was a meat-and-potatoes man. He always ate purple hull peas and butter beans, but never a salad. With a smile, he once observed, “I don’t know why Lela says I don’t eat vegetables; I eat ’em both, peas *and* beans.”

When he went to Nashville for three summers to go to school at Peabody College in the late forties, Mother took advantage of his absence and encouraged me to eat a variety of foods.

Her instruction began the first day of his absence at lunch, when she placed my plate on the table with food on it I had never seen. I told her, “I do not like this stuff, and I’m not going to eat it.” She calmly suggested that, since I had no idea what it was or tasted like, I should try it, which made absolutely no sense to me at all, and I told her so.

I had Mother where I wanted her; she desperately wanted me to do something I did not want to, and she could do nothing about it. When I came to supper without eating all afternoon, a plate with the exact, same food was before me.

The only thing that had changed was I was hungry. Letting me get hungry is how she taught me to enjoy a variety of foods.

Dad came home from Nashville and saw me eating what he called rabbit food and eventually began to eat it himself. He never learned to eat asparagus or okra. The first, he said with good humor, was grass; the other was a weed. He did not even like fried okra, which is wrong on many levels.

Today, with many kinds of food available in small-town cafés and groceries that were unheard of in rural Drew County sixty years ago, times have passed by my mother's efforts to teach me to eat different foods but have done nothing to lessen the most important takeaway from her efforts to get me to eat different foods.

Namely: I should never think I don't like something because it is different, if I have not tried it. In other words, my not understanding something does not mean it is stupid.

* I was anxious to get my driver's license; Dad began to teach me, and I drove many times with him in the car. I learned to apply my breaks before I got into the curve; my lights were for me to be seen, not just for me to see; and I learned to straighten the car when getting into a skid, to driver slower when it rains, and what to do with a front-tire blowout.

I went to the courthouse to take the written test. I had scanned the driver's manual. I assumed the test was to see if people knew how to drive before the state gave them a license; I could already do that.

The test's specificity was unexpected by me.

I failed the test by one question. The state policeman, who was in Monticello only one day a week, was not going to allow me to drive. In the office that day was Mr. Clyde Ross, superintendent of Monticello schools. He told the officer I really did know how to drive and asked him if he would let me show him. Mr. Ross was sure if the officer would see me drive, he would award me a license. The officer agreed. I got my driver's license. Whew!

I did not learn the lesson I was supposed to learn from this incident.

* Singing in public and playing baseball were *the* two most important pastimes of my dad's life until well after he was grown.

He was identified by these activities. He pitched and was offered when he was eighteen to tryout for the Little Rock Travelers. His mother objected because the team played on Sundays, and he did not consider it further.

I could not carry a tune in a bucket of molasses, as my friends and family made sure I knew. In fifth grade I had to take public school music, which included not only singing but also singing solo.

I refused. The student teacher insisted; she offered me the opportunity to hide behind the piano and sing. I refused and continued to refuse. I was not going to sing alone no matter what she said or did. She finally gave up. I think she cried.

Another student teacher in fifth grade taught a lesson on Greek mythology. She went through the Greek pantheon and its various deities. I had never heard of such a thing. Then she explained Greeks believed their gods lived on top of Mount Olympus, but they were not real.

I can still vividly recall raising my hand to ask, "Why didn't the Greeks go to the top of Olympus? When they saw no gods there, they would have known their gods weren't real."

She seemed momentarily flustered and answered, "The Greeks were not very smart." When grown, I realized finding no deities on Olympus would have made no difference to the Greeks, because what a man does not reason himself into he cannot be reasoned out of. Besides that, students should not ask questions to teachers who do not know the answer. Bless her heart.

There was probably not a sport I cared less about than baseball, though I did reluctantly participate in the Monticello youth programs. If my total inability to sing and my disinterest in baseball ever disappointed Dad, he never showed it

I did play basketball, but my playing was lackluster at best. I was strong, coordinated, and fast enough to play but void of the slightest desire. I had no passion whatsoever for winning.

I had no interest in basketball beyond it being what everyone was doing. If Drew Central had only a baseball team, I would have as surely played baseball for the same reason I played basketball. Serious, passionate, and *artificial* competition has just never been part of who I am. I did not care for what others want me to compete.

To be successful in what I wanted to do, I did not need to compete. I barely needed to exert myself. A frequent conversation with my mother was about her notion that, if I only worked at what I enjoyed, I was lazy, a point of view I have never adopted.

Our coach was Leslie Beard, a good man, whom his friends, his wife and his colleagues called *Shorty*, a name of respect given to him by his teammates on the Arkansas A&M basketball team, on which he had been a star player.

Coach Beard tried to have a track team. To get boys to go out for it, he told us on the basketball team, if we did not participate in track, we could not play basketball next year.

In track I discovered something I was less interested in than baseball. My participation in track did not rise to the level of visible. Coach Beard never called upon me to prepare for an event until my pride and stupidity got the better of me.

We practiced at the Arkansas A&M field, where as a kid I had watched college meets. At a practice one afternoon, I was lying around with the rest of my fellow indifferentists, paying little attention to others practicing. I was in grade eleven.

The high-jump pits had overgrown vines, and the posts that hold the bar had fallen over. One post was so tangled in the vines that we could not get it upright. Coach Beard sent Fred Mousehart and me to the south end to fix the problem. Fred was a popular boy in our class who had a speech impediment that no one noticed, or at least never spoke of.

The posts were held upright by a large cement block on one end. While Fred and I were trying to remove vines, the post, suddenly freed from the vine, swung upright and smacked me on the left side of my head, knocking me out cold. I was awakened with Fred shaking me and saying, "Pig, Pig." His speech impediment kept him from saying *Peg*.

I was glad to hear *Pig*. I woke up. Fred had yelled for Coach Beard, who was present when I woke. He saw I was fine—no big deal.

Some of the boys at Drew Central assumed anything physical I could do they could do better. I never knew why they thought so. Maybe because I was the superintendent's son, I lived near town, I did not work on a farm, I was skinny and I did not try hard to be likeable. Who knows? Whatever the reasons, at track practice, out of the blue, several challenged me to a race.

Boys trying to goad me to do one thing or another had come up before, and I had successfully rejected each of their attempts. I always respectfully declined. Heck I respectfully refused. Albeit, I did it in a manner that was not obvious, and it worked because my challengers did not know what I was doing until the moment passed. On that day at the track, I did not want to race, but I could not get away from their more than usual unrelenting persistence.

They wanted us to "race around the track," referring to the 440-yard dash, the most difficult race in track. We lined up, someone started us, and we took off.

Before I had taken ten steps, it was apparent to me I would easily win. Obviously, none of my challengers had run a 440 dash, may not even have ever seen one run. Every one of them took off as if our race was a 100-yard dash, maybe only a 50-yard one. I began in a steady, fast trot that I continued as I passed the last of the others well before he was halfway around.

As I passed each challenger, he returned where we began and resumed his position on the ground. After I completed the 440 yards alone and returned to where our faux race began, I lay on the ground and said nothing, nor did they.

I do not recall any of them ever mentioning it afterward. At that time, I could name my incredulous friends, but have long since forgotten them all.

My satisfaction after the race was interrupted by the sudden appearance of a problem I should have foreseen. Coach Beard saw the race, came over, and told me to prepare to run the 440 in competition. I explained to him why I won so easily. He smiled and told me, "Well, I need someone to run the 440 who at least knows what it is." He had that kind of humor.

Fortunately for me, we only had a couple of home meets; they were on weekday afternoons. Almost no one was in the stands. In all our meets, I always made it all the way around the track. It seems as if I may not have come in last every race but do not recall finishing in the money.

Just before my senior year began, while trailing through some absence of mind or another, I told Dad I was not going to play basketball my senior year.

I expected my announcement to be of no importance to him; he never mentioned my playing. I was surprised when he sternly told me, "You can quit if you want to, but you will run five miles every day!" He explained it was not a punishment; it was taking the place of the exercise I got playing basketball.

I continued basketball my senior year. Whatever the reason, unconsciously or consciously, I probably played with less effort than before. As a senior, I had less playing time on the team, with the worst record ever at Drew Central.

If my dad had pressured me, no matter how subtly, to participate in baseball which could have happened, my life would have unfolded differently. I cannot stress too much how important my being who I am today is because my parents encouraged me to be *independent* in thought, speech, dress, action, and associations.

* I bought a bolt-action repeating .22 rifle when I was thirteen and frequently hiked off into the woods alone to kill what I could, mostly birds of the forest. I hiked in the woods surrounding the Drew Central and Arkansas A&M campuses and the ones across today's Highway 425, near a gravel pit at Scroughout, where Grandma Willis's childhood home had been.

I took good care of my rifle and kept it clean and in perfect working condition. I read books about shooting and sighting with a .22. I became a pretty good shot.

Buddy Barnett and his older brother James Shelton had moved into a house on the campus when their dad was the custodian for the school. James was two years younger than I; Buddy was three years younger.

In summer 1955, I had three 30.06 shells. I do not recall where or how I got them. Buddy and I were in the woods about fifty yards northeast behind Drew Central's old home economics building. We had found a place to build a fire and sit. It was late afternoon. The sun was low.

I got the idea of throwing the shells into the fire to see if they would shoot off, as I had seen in the westerns on Saturdays. I threw them in; Buddy and I got behind two separate trees within a few feet of the fire. After a while of nothing happening, I stuck my head out from behind my tree to see what was going on. I suddenly was engulfed in darkness.

When I awoke, I was on my back on the ground. My face and shirt were covered with blood, the fire had become embers, the afternoon had become twilight, and Buddy had become absent. He was nowhere to be seen; he did not answer when I several times loudly called his name.

The shell had exploded and hit me in my carelessly exposed head protruding from behind the tree. I was hit a glancing blow, striking me where my hairline begins, with enough force to knock me out cold. I walked home, washed my face and head well enough to hide everything but the noticeable scar, and changed my shirt.

Mother was pursuing her master's degree at Peabody College in Nashville. Dad and I went that evening to eat at the Anchor, today, a dentist office on the Highway 425 bypass. While we were eating, Dad stopped suddenly. He stared at my scar and asked what had happened. I told him the whole story.

Dad shook his head with incredulity; his expression changed until it bore the complexity of what had been lost and may never be regained. He was in full possession of dark knowledge—the hard melancholy resignation he had not yet plumed the depths of my stupidity.

His posture slumped. When he finally found his voice, he said quietly, "Son, I hope you have learned from this." I nodded silently.

Next morning, I went to Buddy Barnett's house to see what had happened to him. He answered the door and began crying from relief. He said he had tried to wake me but could not. He decided I was dead, ran home, went to bed, and told no one.

Thinking about the shell shooting in the fire, I realized when the powder ignites, what is thrown out of the fire is the light brass case; the heavy bullet remains in the fire. This means I was not in danger of being shot by a bullet.

If the brass case had hit me in the forehead flat on, instead of a glancing blow, or hit my eye, nose, lips, or face, I would have been hurt much worse, and the remainder of my life would have unfolded differently.

* School was easy for me, and I took advantage of this by being a lazy student, abysmally, appallingly, dreadfully lazy. I had a particular aversion to spelling. The teacher would give us the spelling words, and we were to memorize them and be tested on them. This made no sense to me. I believed if I memorized them, I would easily forget them later. I concluded learning what I was certain to forget made no sense.

Doing something only to get a grade may be sometimes what schooling is about, but I always thought it ought not to be any part of real learning.

My low spelling grades much bothered my mother. One week, I memorized the words and made one hundred percent on the test. I waited until just the right time to show her my paper so I could bask in her words of praise. I gave her the paper while she, Dad, and I were in the car driving home from town. She said, “This does not impress me; you should have been doing this all along.”

I made no reply and quietly returned to my old habits. My stubbornness that day has made me a bad speller all my life.

In the summer before my freshman year, I wrote on a sheet of clean white paper, “I will never again bring a book home from school.” I dated it and cut my finger sufficiently to bring enough blood to drip some on my contract and to make a large bloody *X* under my signature. I hid my contract with myself in a coffee can in the storage room of an old detached garage next to our house; I never showed it to anyone. I did not take a book home from freshman through junior year.

I thought to myself, if little learning is a dangerous thing, I was going to learn little and live dangerously. I laughed out loud at my silent joke.

At the end of my junior year, 1955, I was selected by the Monticello American Legion to go to Boys State. Going also were Ross, Stuckey, and Gunn from Monticello High School. Today, James Ross is an attorney in Monticello. I have lost track of Stuckey and Gunn and do not recall their first names.

I had never heard of Boys State. It was held at Camp Robinson near Little Rock, where we were put in huts with boys from other parts of the state. We were encouraged to organize campaigns and run for office. I successfully ran for city council and county commissioners' positions, but lost efforts at the state level. It was a great learning experience.

Forty-nine years later, my oldest stepdaughter Hayley was selected to Tennessee Girls State. When she arrived there, she knew not one person. Three days later she was elected president of more than 500 girls.

* During the three years I was following my contract not to take a school book home, I made mostly As but also A-s and some Bs. I managed to avoid Cs. Mother was beginning to adjust her life around the fact that I was not the student she had wished for.

After church on the Sunday before my senior year, a woman well known to the family, within hearing range of family, friends, and myself, challenged my mother, saying it was too bad I was not as smart as her daughter, as clearly evidenced by her daughter's superior grades.

I intended for my mother not to have to put up with the woman's condescending attitude. Without telling anyone my old plan, I made a new one; I regularly took my books home my senior year and, more importantly, studied. My grades in senior year were all

As; not one was an A-. Well, one was. Coach Beard in physical education gave an A- to most and an A to none.

Mother asked why I was suddenly interested in school and why the better grades. I recalled to her what the woman had said to her. I told her that I intended for her never to be talked to like that again. She nodded; neither she nor I mentioned it again.

* My parents were excellent role models for me. They offered the usual middle-class character stuff: faithful work, follow the rules and play nice with others. Perhaps, one of the most significant character traits I learned from their instructive lives was one they never mentioned; they modeled it every day, and I was impressed by its effect on me. They never complained or whined. And I mean never ever, ever . . .

When Dad was fourteen, a wagon fell off its blocks onto him while he was repairing it, and he suffered from a slipped disk that radiated excoriating pain in his legs and lower back. It was neither consistent nor constant, but it frequently occurred. People who knew him had no idea about his condition because the words *my back hurts* never came out of his mouth.

While shaving each morning, Dad sang, "You've got to accentuate the positive; eliminate the negative; and latch on to the affirmative; don't mess with Mister In-Between." This lyric is from a popular song form the forties sung by Bing Crosby and the Andrew Sisters, among others.

Another positive shaving song he sang, but not as often, was "Sentimental Journey" sung by Doris Day, also popular in the forties.

Mother had frequent headaches and was often ill. I never heard her complain.

When I complained or whined about one thing or another as a child, she rarely passed up an opportunity to tell me, "Why don't you just fuss about it. See if that helps." It never did help me and has not helped anyone who complains about their condition as far as I know.

No matter how hot or cold, wet or dry the weather was, they never complained, and never discussed what was evident to everyone. After all, it was only weather. Somewhere, Dad picked up the expression *It is cold enough to freeze the balls off a brass monkey*.

It impressed him enough sometimes to phone me, when he saw a weather report of where I was living, to say, "You had better bring in the brass monkey tonight, Son."

My relationship with my parents was not always ideal. The Bible does not reveal the age of Lucifer when he challenged Jehovah, but I think it was probably thirteen. I was this age for a whole year. Thirteen was followed by the rest of my adolescent years, a whole year in each. During each one, Mother explained I was just going through a phase.

During this period, she frequently told others, "I wouldn't take a million dollars for James William and I wouldn't give a nickel for another just like him."

I realized early my Dad and I were two separate people. My Mother and I were two separate people. They encouraged this realization—one some children never have, but one loving, knowledgeable parents encourage their children to have.

* The summer after I graduated high school, I asked Dad if I could use his car to visit Glenda Chambers. I had noticed her in my senior year, while I was dating Marilyn Reed, my first real girlfriend—very pretty. She and I had broken up by the time I graduated; I have no memory of our breaking up being hard to do, albeit I cannot imagine it was my idea.

With Marilyn no longer in my life, Glenda moved from the back of my mind to the front. Dad did not seem surprised I had noticed her. He loaned me his car and told me how to find her house. Glenda did not have a phone.

I found her place easily, but no Glenda. Her dad greeted me cordially said she was in the woods picking blackberries with her brothers. He invited me to sit on the porch with him and wait, assuring me, "Glenda won't be long."

I waited past what seemed *long*, making conversation with Mr. Chambers, any lack of which not being his fault. With no Glenda in sight, I finally, reluctantly bid him good-bye and disappointedly drove away.

Author with several of his graduating class on senior trip to Arkansas' Pettie Jean State Park, 1956. Author is left front. Next to him is Billy Lansdale who has remained a friend and helps to insure Booter is always OK at the Camp

Author's high school girl friend Marilyn Reed.

Author as high school senior with Glenda Chambers for whom he did not wait long enough while she was away picking blackberries.

Returning home through town, traveling west on East Gaines Street, I saw Mary Ann Lynn (also pretty), a friend of Glenda's; with her father pulling into Wolfe's Grocery on the east-end curve of Gaines Street.

Unhesitating, I excitedly I pulled in beside them on the passenger side of Mr. Lynn's truck, talked to Mary Ann for a moment, and asked her to the drive-in that coming Saturday, which is what I had intended to ask Glenda. Mary Ann quickly agreed without asking her dad, which she said later she had never before done.

Glenda not being at home when I visited and my spotting Mary Ann when looking for a date that weekend almost did not happen. If either had not, the rest of my life would have unfolded differently.

Author's high school senior picture.

FROM COLLEGE TO ARMY AND BACK
1956-1962

A throw of the dice never will abolish chance.
—Stéphane Mallarmé

##

When I graduated from high school in 1956, I wanted to join the army, go to Korea and kill communists. Dad said if I went to college two years, I could do as I please, but he did not want me to go into the army right out of high school.

I joined the National Guard unit at Arkansas A&M and was assigned the job of cook; my position was second cook. At summer camp, I was responsible for preparing everything except the entrée, for which the first cook was responsible, and baking, for which the third cook was responsible.

The first cook was an agreeable man named Sergeant Nuts. The eggs available for us to prepare for breakfast were powdered eggs, which he scrambled with water, milk, and butter. Adding butter and milk caused them to taste better, but they could not be made to taste real, if the person eating them knew they were not.

The men complained about the eggs each morning. After one morning, when they expressed more than usual discontent and unhappiness about the situation, Sergeant Nuts told me to take his car, go into town and buy a dozen eggs.

The next morning he dumped two eggs and their shells in with the powdered ones. The little amount of egg made no difference to the taste. The men, however, found pieces of shell and believed the eggs were real. They were appreciative Nuts had heard their complaints.

I don't know if I ever knew Sergeant Nuts's first name; everyone called him Fuzzy.

With any definition of *tried* one might imagine, I can in no way say I tried to go to college for two years as Dad and I had agreed. The first year, I earned five hours of F in college algebra

Author in National Guard uniform; insignia on collar is that of combat engineers, the branch of service to which the Monticello unit belonged.

Author in National Guard at Fort Polk.

Author, freshman at A&M campus, 1957.

I had taken two years of algebra in high school and figured how hard could college algebra be. I often missed class for no good reason but always showed up for tests. When I received my semester grade, I checked my test scores and saw I had passed just barely, but passed for sure. I took my scores to Professor Garrett in his office.

He carefully, silently looked them over, nodded and agreed my semester test grades did indeed average a D. Then he said in his low, slow, old man raspy voice, "I could have given you a D and I could have given you an F. I just decided to give you an F."

I also made a D in four hours of chemistry, taught by my dad's good friend and excellent teacher John McGinnis, and a C the other semester. I even made a C in a history course, my first and last one.

The explanation for my C in history is Bob Lynn's shenanigans. He was Mary Ann's brother, who had returned from the Korean War and enrolled at Arkansas A&M. The period before my history class, Bob had a class in a room next to the room where I was going to be. Consequently, before my class began, we would meet in the hall and chat.

Bob would say, "Lets skip our next class and go grab a coke." I would decline his offer.

To settle the question, Bob would suggest, "Let's flip a coin. You call it". As he was saying this, he flipped the coin before I could protest. Bob would catch the coin and turn it over on the back of his other hand, with his hand covering it. I always called it.

If I lost, we skipped our next class. I found out years later, Bob did not have a class the next period.

I was about worthless. No, I was totally worthless, without any academic value whatsoever. Dad told me to go to the army if I still wanted to.

I joined Tuesday, June 4, 1957.

* For basic training I was sent to Fort Polk, Louisiana, a hot, hot place in July and August, where my Guard unit went for two weeks of summer camp. I had been playing soldier since I was a child and had no trouble playing one as a young man during basic training, except that one time, that one night.

I went to the post movie every Sunday night until an obstacle arose that required effort to overcome. Our company had an unscheduled field exercise on Saturday, during which our company fouled up some way or another big time. Our drill instructor restricted us to the barracks all day Sunday. I had told no one of my intention to go to the movie and remained calm.

We could not even go to the Post Exchange to buy toothpaste. I am talking we were restricted to inside the four walls of the barracks; we were incarcerated. Our drill instructor had worked himself into a heavy duty, major snit.

I silently waited until after dark, when I was certain no one was in the yard or on the street, I stealthily slipped out of the barracks, alone, in time to make it the mile to the theater for the last movie.

(Writing my life's story, I have found a few occasions I have been over informed by my memory. My sneaking out of the barracks to go to a movie is one of them. I had remembered the movie I was going to see was *Bye-Bye Birdie, staring Ann Margret*; however, I recently discovered this movie was not released until 1963, I have been mistaken. I do not remember the name of the movie I was so anxious to see that I disobeyed orders and snuck out. Most likely, I just refused to be told I could not go a movie.)

Carefully returning to the barracks right after midnight and seeing no problem, I crept inside, where, unbeknownst to me, my problem was. It was waiting in my bed in the form of the one and only Raymond Yates. If you looked up *pretty good old boy* in the dictionary, you might find Raymond's picture.

Raymond, from Louisville, Kentucky, was my best friend in basic training. He had slipped out of the barracks as had I; only he had slipped out to go to the Post Exchange across the street for beer. He figured the sergeant of the guard would check who was at the Post Exchange, so Raymond bought his two six-packs and crawled under the PX to drink them alone. The building sat on blocks high enough off the ground that one could sit comfortably.

When the PX closed at eleven o'clock, he returned to the barracks having consumed twelve bottles of beer, desperately wanting to talk with me about something. When Raymond found I was not there, he decided to wait for me. To be sure he did not miss talking to me; he crawled into my bunk, where he promptly fell asleep.

Before I returned to the barracks, the sergeant of the guard made a bed check in our barracks at midnight. He counted me present; a sleeping body was in my bed. He counted Raymond absent without leave. No body of any kind was in his bed.

A couple of our comrades met me at the door and explained the situation, saying that Raymond was going to be in serious trouble, probably be put on report, if I did not go to the company office and explaine. I did not want Raymond in trouble. Our talking woke him up; he insisted on going with me.

When we went to the office to explain, the sergeant of the guard had to be awakened. Raymond perceived the whole incident as his fault and insisted on doing all the talking; the problem was he was still too inebriated to make any sense at all.

I tried to keep him straight, but that was not possible. The sleepy sergeant, who was not really a sergeant but a private first class acting as sergeant of the guard, became more and more confused. Raymond's story seemed to have no beginning, no middle, and especially troubling to the acting sergeant, no ending.

The sergeant of the guard became increasingly exasperated. Finally, pointing to each of us correctly, he said, "Okay, you are Yates and you are Willis?" We nodded. "And you are both back in the barracks?" "Yes, Sir," we answered in unison. He decided his problem was solved. He told us to go to sleep and keep our mouths shut; he would put nothing about the incident in his report.

If Raymond ever told me about what he wanted to talk about, I have forgotten it.

Raymond Yates

* I returned home on my post-basic leave, married Mary Ann, and took off for Fort Devens, Massachusetts. During basic training, I was asked to take a series of tests to be considered for acceptance into the Army Security Agency (ASA). This group is the army's branch of the National Security Agency. Fort Devens is where the army processed ASA recruits.

At Devens, after an additional battery of tests and interviews, I was selected to attend the army language school in Monterey, California, where the army flew me. I studied Russian six hours a day, five days a week, for 50 weeks.

The young lieutenant who approved the paperwork for my assignment was enjoying my Arkansas accent without making fun of it. He smiled, congratulated me, and said, "I guess the army needs some men who can speak Southern Russian."

The instructors at Army Language School were all native Russians; all well spoken, some well educated. One had commanded the Tsar's private guard during the revolution. The classes were small. Six students sat in a semicircle in front of the teacher, who, after a couple of weeks, spoke only Russian. The experience was intense.

Before I was finally accepted into the ASA, a couple of FBI agents visited people in Monticello to ask merchants, teachers, and neighbors about my background to see if I was eligible for a top-secret security clearance, required for ASA members. People with whom the FBI talked told Dad of the agency's interest.

If I had been put on company report for being absent during lockdown in basic training, which almost happened, I would not have been accepted into the ASA and the rest of my life would have unfolded significantly differently.

* Mary Ann came to live with me in Monterey. I rented a tiny furnished three-room house within walking distance of a grocery and the Presidio of Monterey, where the language school was. When I went to the grocery store, I placed the groceries I purchased in a cart, pushed it the few blocks home, and returned it. If it crossed my mind that I needed a car, I do not recall it.

Once, when I was returning the empty grocery cart, James Mason, a popular actor of that era, in a new Buick stopped to let me cross the street. I nodded and waved my thanks. He smiled and waved.

Gene Chapman, one of my closest friends in high school, who had moved to Dumas after his junior year, was stationed at nearby Fort Ord in the post hospital as a navy medic. If I remember correctly, one of us heard from home where the other was and contacted him.

Fort Ord, a large military installation, had regular bus service into Monterey. Gene sometimes came to my and Mary Ann's house on weekends.

The army and navy were vying with each other to get our first space satellite into orbit. The Soviet Union put up Sputnik on October 4, 1957.

Americans did not even know the Russians had rockets capable of this feat. It was an devastating shock to Americans in the Cold War. Gene, the navy guy, and I, the army one, managed to mention the subject when we got together.

When the navy's rocket put America into space after repeated army failures, Gene continued to have something to say. I had nothing more to say.

When Gene returned from the navy, he raised and trained foxhounds and became nationally recognized in that exclusive community. He had as many as thirty dogs and authored several articles in foxhunting magazines. His dogs won several tournaments.

Gene became a successful businessman in the medical-supply business, partly because of his superior intelligence and strong work ethic but mostly because he invented and patented a better way to preserve blood plasma, a method used everywhere today.

Author's high school friend, Gene Chapman, who often visited while he was in the navy at Fort Ord and author was at Army Language School in Monterey.

He lives in Del Rio, Texas, where he was chairman of the Val Verde County Republican Party in 2008. He spoke at a Del Rio Tea Party in July 2009. He and Anna, his beautiful, charming wife of Spanish decent, live in a rich man's house. They have visited me three times since I returned to Monticello, where his older brother Walter Stinson resides.

After Mary Ann's lengthy and difficult labor, my first son James Wesley was born in the hospital in Monterey on March 14, 1959, a Saturday. Before dawn that morning, Mary Ann, with Wes in her womb, and I walked to the hospital, which was about the same distance as the grocery.

I graduated in August, and Dad and Mother came to see their first grandson and drive us back to Monticello.

Dad made a tourist trip out of our journey home. We visited Hoover Dam, Grand Canyon, Painted Desert, Petrified Forest, and everything in between.

Wesley, home from Monterey in 1958, held by his Great Grandmother Willis, the same who held author in Willis Family picture,
Christmas. 1938.

* The next assignment of the 1958 army language school graduates in Russian was in one of two locations: a tiny remote village in Turkey whose name in Russian ironically translates as *nowhere* or Bad Aibling, a beautiful town in the Bavarian Alpine foothills, which had a small, ASA listening post where the United States monitored Russian radio spy traffic (Russian illicit communication speech in army parlance).

For reasons I do not know, I was assigned to Bad Aibling.

If I had been sent to Turkey, which could as well have happened, the rest of my life would have unfolded differently.

I sailed to Germany on a crowded troopship, the USS Rose, in late October. The North Atlantic was already stormy. I was seasick for four days and nights. I spent most of this time above the deck, eating soda crackers and drinking 7UP, thinking I was going to die. After a couple of days, I was afraid I was not going to.

One dayl was above decks. During the night, the water calmed and my seasickness immediately ended. When I awoke, it was day. We were in thick fog. Suddenly, the fog began to lift slowly, teasingly, as a beautiful woman raising her skirt, while I stopped breathing. Reveled off the port bow were the White Cliffs of Dover!

We were in the English Channel! The Cliffs were so close it seemed I could touch them. They were a totally unexpected, a thrilling sight. Often, movies I watch have scenes of these cliffs; I always recall when I saw them for the first time and how I felt—quiet sea, no sickness, land sighted and voyage nearly ended.

The sailors aboard the USS Rose said this trip was worse than usual. When we boarded, we piled our duffel bags in the hole. During the voyage, a comrade soldier with whom I had gone to the army language school disappeared. After a search of the ship, he was declared lost overboard; his parents were notified.

When we docked at Bremerhaven, Germany, we retrieved our bags and the "overboard" soldier was found. He had crawled down into the pile of bags in the hole to escape his seasickness. When he recovered, he was too weak from dehydration to move the bags out of his way to get out. He was alive!

While at Aibling, I ran across him on a ski trip in the Alps on the Austria border. He did not think the duffel-bag episode was humorous, but he seemed no worse from wear.

I became a part of the 180th ASA Battalion stationed at Bad Aibling. Aibling, as we cool Americans called it, except we pronounced it Abilene, like the Texas cow town, was a beautiful village in the Bavarian Alpine foothills, founded in 800.

Bad Aibling, Bavara where author was assigned 1958-60. Mountains in background are Bavarian Alps. Three peaks right are locally called "the sleeping woman."

Christmas, Plaza, Bad Aibling.

The ASA post at Bad Aibling was built in the 1930s to train German fighter pilots. There was an airfield where the ASA put its antennae. The living quarters were sturdy, made of brick and stone, and had a recreation building, cafeteria, and snack bar and wide streets and sidewalks. The hanger was transformed into a operations building. We language guys were called "Monterey Marys."

The radios were large transistor ones. We would monitor the Russians and type the codes while listening; most of them were six-digit numbers. After they were typed, they were sent to National Security Agency headquarters in Fort Meade, Maryland.

We also communicated with ASA posts in Turkey and France, attempting to triangulate the location of the Russian broadcast. Where our lines crossed was where the speaker was located. I remember we found one who communicated while driving on the Munich-Salzburg Autobahn, which passed three miles west of Bad Aibling. He continued this for some time. Suddenly his transmissions ceased.

On the highest hill in Bad Aibling were a Catholic church and a castle, both built by Charlemagne. The castle had evolved into Bad Aibling's city hall. The church was still in use as a church, unchanged for 1,158 years.

As the small town had grown, the people built a second church; therefore, the first one was not required to grow with the town and remained within its original construction. The newest item in it was the large ornate front door hung in 1776.

In 1995, my third wife Marilyn and I visited Bad Aibling and the 1,195-year old church, which was not a tourist attraction but a regular church in the town. When I told Marilyn the door was hung in1776, we took notice that this was the year of America's independence. After a moment of silence, she asked, "Why would anyone leave a place like this to travel 3,000 miles on a dangerous ocean voyage to live in the woods in America?"

She asked the fundamental question in the understanding of the founding of America, the exact same I used for discussions in my teaching of United States history at Lovington.

Before the founding of Bad Aibling, the area was known for its healing waters. *Bad* is German for *spa*; thus Bad Aibling.

* One thousand Volkswagen sedans were built in Germany in 1946; each had an air-cooled twenty-five-horsepower rear engine, a five-speed stick shift, a tiny split back window, pop-up turn signals, a roller for a gas peddle, and no chrome.

I bought number 556, according to its motor identification number, for $250. It met every single one of my requirements for a car at the time: it started, ran, and stopped.

I rented a tiny one-room apartment in a farming hamlet near town. Mary Ann and Wes flew into Munich, forty miles north of Bad Aibling; I went to the airport and picked them up.

The apartment I rented had one single-size bed, which the three of us became tired of quickly. I moved us to a more spacious apartment on the first floor of a grand three-story mansion-type home in town, designed by an Italian architect and built in 1898. This home belonged to the Dasch family, a father, mother, and fourteen-year-old daughter, named Traudi, who followed me around when I was home and she was not in school. They lived on the top floor. Renters occupied the other two.

Herr Dasch is what I called him; he called me Herr Willis. Herr Dasch had been in the *Wehrmacht* and invaded France on his eighteenth birthday, on May 10, 1940, and was one of the first German soldiers in Russia in June of 1941. He fought on the Eastern Front, until he was wounded in 1944, and was home on convalescent leave on June 6, 1944, when the Allies landed in Normandy. He spent the rest of the war in Serbia, where he surrendered to the Americans.

House in Bad Aibling of which author rented first floor.

In the first winter in Russia, he engaged in hand to hand combat; a Russian soldier struck him in the face with his rifle butt. Before the Russian could bayonet him, a comrade of Herr Dasch killed the Russian. The Russian's blow to his face broke Dasch's nose and the veins on his face. The blood under his skin froze and left a spider web wound covering his face.

The Dasch family and we became close friends. They spoke not a word of English, and I little German. We communicated comfortably enough because we liked each other and wanted to talk and because they were not put off with my bad grammar and pronunciation.

I was trying to learn to play chess. Herr Dasch and I played in his backyard. I loved chess but never learned to play it beyond beginner status. I kept hitting that chess-stupid ceiling, which was low for me, and never got beyond it.

I taught Wes to play and enjoyed games with him until he entered fourth grade and began beating me routinely. I lost interest. His interest continued. He joined the chess club at school and became club champion.

Fortunately for me, chess is not like life. As Isaac Asimov (1920-1992), Russian-born American and prolific science-fiction author, observed, "In life, unlike chess, the game continues after checkmate."

Before I went to Germany, I knew nothing of German food. I found it delicious. Frau Dasch was pleased I loved German food and often invited Mary Ann, Wes, and me to eat. I learned to cook what I liked the most: Wiener schnitzel, a breaded veal cutlet, or it can be a pork steak called *Jägerschnitzel*, and sauerbraten, specially prepared roast beef marinated in wine and spices for five days.

Jager (with umlaut over the a) is the German word for *hunter*. German Jews adopted Jaeger, without an umlaut, as the word for hunter. Jaeger is my great-grandson's name and his grandmother's maiden name.

I consider myself a connoisseur of potato salad and took favorable notice of the local Bavarian potato salad, a warm dish made with vinegar. A farmer near Bad Aibling was noted for his vinegar, which he sold in a small building on his farm, near where I first lived. I got the potato salad recipe but, after I returned home, found that without this special local vinegar, it did not taste as good.

*I was in the U.S. Army in Germany during the most frigid depths of the Cold War. The United States Army in Germany participated in maneuvers that included a mock invasion of Western Europe by the Soviet Union.

Because of the intelligence sensitivity of members of the 180th ASA Battalion in Bad Aibling and our not being a combat-trained outfit, if Russia invaded, we were to board trucks and hightail it toward France. Consequently, that procedure is what we practiced during these maneuvers.

The men of the 180th ASA Battalion called this *bugging out*—an accurate name for what we were doing that did not bother us.

These exercises were always at night. A *duce and a half* (two-and-a-half-ton truck) pulled up to my front door, motor running, lights on, and horn honking. I had ninety seconds to dress and to get out of the house and into the truck. At the post, we joined the convoy and roared off into the night toward France.

No plans were made for the evacuation of families. I never heard anyone mention this as a possible dilemma or morale problem. No one worried about this situation, because none of us believed the Soviet Union would attack Western Europe.

A common NATO exercise began with radio chatter on "secret frequencies" to which of course we knew the Soviets were listening. NATO chatter would indicate we were planning to invade the USSR immediately. Tanks and infantry divisions *seemed* to be on the move. B-52s *seemed* to be flying toward the Soviet border. Our job was to monitor the Russian counter mobilization to locate the various Soviet units and see how they would respond.

We normally worked three eight-hour shifts, 7:00 a.m. to 3:00 p.m. to 11:00 p.m. to 7:00 a.m. When my shift ended at 11:00 p.m., I usually went to the mess hall that had the same menu as the regular breakfast at 6:00 a.m. If it was what we called SOS (stuff on a shingle), ground beef and gravy over toast, I would go back at 6:00 a.m. Unlike my time in the National Guard, we got real eggs for breakfast.

* My best buddy at Bad Aibling was John Barry Bice, whom everyone called Bice. He was a member of the special police. I met him when I joined the force after my job in operations became overstaffed.

Sgt. John Bice holding Wes in front of the PX at ASA post in Bad Aibling, Germany, 1959.

Special police is what the military police was called on an ASA post. I was issued a 1911A-1 model World War II .45-caliber automatic sidearm and a billy club.

I fired Expert with the M1 Garand in basic training, thanks, I expect, to my many hours shooting my .22 rifle. My .45-caliber sidearm was so loosely constructed that I probably could not have hit the wall of a barn from the inside. Fortunately, accuracy was not what this weapon was about. Its purpose was to quickly and loudly fire slow-moving large soft lead bullets that could create an exit wound the size of a softball, a purpose for which it was well suited.

Bice was a tall, friendly, red-haired blue-eyed man who tended to freckle. When he got out of the army, he came to see Mary Ann and me in Monticello. We invited Dad and Mother over for supper to meet him. He is now a retired Presbyterian minister in North Carolina. We have exchanged infrequent e-mails.

John's wife died in March 2010, and he sent me a note. It read, "My Friend, Just lost my bride of 47 years. John." On January 1, 2011, I received a Christmas card from him with a nice letter and an up-to-date picture. As I had told him of my and Mary Ann's divorce, he included a sealed envelope with his desire I send it to Mary Ann.

The Dasch family was fond of Wes and took care of him when his mother and I wished to travel. Bice often went with us, sitting in the backseat of my tiny car. We spent time in Salzburg, Austria, and in the Bavarian Alps. We skied and hiked in the Alps and visited Hitler's Eagle's Nest and the castles of Mad King Ludwig, the one on the five-mark coin Skippy had given me for my worthless knife.

The Mad King's largest, most popular castle is the Neuschwanstein (New Swain Stone), the model for the castle at Disney World.

We visited Oberammergau, where the passion play had been performed every ten years since 1634, to acknowledge the Lord's grace for saving their town from the bubonic plague. We were there in 1959; the next play was in 1960. Many of the townspeople were already in character.

Oberammergau is a town of less than five thousand persons nestled in the Bavarian Alps on the small river Ammer. While driving to it on a winding two-lane mountain road, we experienced snow falling up! It was snowing in the valley below us, hidden by snow clouds, and the wind drove the snow up out of the cloud.

One probably has to be there to be impressed. The sensation is strange. You can stand on the side of the mountain and hold your hand out over the cliff, palm up, as if catching the snow; instead, snow collects on the back of your hand.

During my and Marilyn's 1995 trip to Bad Aibling, we visited Herr Dasch; Frau Dasch had died. Traudi, whom we also visited, was married and lived in a smaller town about ten miles west. It was a great time for great memories.

.

* The biggest trip Mary Ann and I took while in Germany was in 1959 to Italy. We went with another American couple in his Opel, which was old in 1959. (I don't recall the model, but think it was a Kadett.) The man's name was Mason; I do not recall his wife's name. We took cans of Sterno and beans, pup tents, camping equipment from post supply, and some blankets and camped every night.

We especially enjoyed eating fresh coconut in an outdoor market and taking a gondola ride in Venice and visiting Pizza and Florence. More importantly, we spent three days in Rome, a mecca of mine. The night of my twenty-first birthday, we camped on the beach at Ostia, the port of ancient Rome. It has a beautiful beach and great ruins.

Ostia was built at the mouth of the Tiber. (*Ostia* is Latin for "mouth.") Since then, the mouth has moved three miles toward the sea. Today, Ostia Beach, a nice one, is three miles from the ancient port.

On the beach, near sunset, a young man showed up with an olive-drab GI five-gallon can of gasoline. He slowly, slowly poured the contents into the sand. When the can was empty, the young man had created in the sand a gasoline wick the size of a silver dollar.

Several young Italians and Germans, most of them couples, began to arrive. At dark, someone lit the gas spot in the sand, and it burned well into the night. We had a spontaneous beach party, with a large sand-candle fire.

Two nights after we left Rome, while driving through an isolated part of the Italian Alps trying to find our campground where we had reservations, we were as lost as four blind pigs looking for acorns in a corn field. Worse, it was past eight o'clock and we were famished; I mean totally caved-in starving.

We arrived at a small building that would have looked as if it were an eatery, had it not been hanging on the cliff side of the narrow mountain road far away from any settlement. Fingers crossed, we found a place to park and went in.

The only people we saw were a half dozen or so Italian men of World War I and World War II veteran age, playing cards and drinking wine. Several empty bottles were on the table. One of the men called out, and a woman came from the back, nodded a welcome, and asked us what we wanted.

We had agreed we would ask for a steak, a word we decided would be the most likely understood. After the woman turned away, someone, I think it was Mary Ann, added loudly enough to be sure she was heard, "And iced tea."

When the card players heard "iced tea," they ceased playing, became completely silent, and fixed their eyes on us as if we had walked into the *Long Branch Saloon* off a long cattle drive with a dust-dry thirst and ordered from Miss Kitty's Barkeep Sam a glass of buttermilk.

If the men wondered where we were from when we arrived, our ordering iced tea convinced them we were not from around there or any place they wanted to visit.

The woman returned with four cooked-just-right, thick T-bones, a side order of spaghetti with marinara sauce, a quarter head of iceberg lettuce apiece with an olive oil-and-vinegar dressing, fresh chewy Italian bread, and iced tea.

Previous to my visiting Italy, I was unaware Italians routinely serve pasta as a side dish with meat, especially beef, as we do potatoes. In Italy, we did not see a place that served pizza or spaghetti with meatballs; albeit, we did not patronize places that catered to Americans.

I do not know where we were that lost night in the Alps, but that meal that evening was the best I had while I was in Italy.

We stumbled upon our campground after three o'clock; the office was closed. We discovered an unoccupied spot, put our sleeping bags on the ground, stretched out on them, and went straight to sleep. We did not undress or take the tents out of the car, nor discuss whether we should or wanted to.

On our Italy trip, we averaged spending five dollars a day per couple for fourteen days, including gas, food, lodging—all of it—though lodging was sleeping on the ground in tents we had checked out of post supply. Usually, food was beans cooked on Sterno cans. I think we did not sleep one night under a roof. This was the time a popular travel book was published titled *Europe on Five Dollars a Day*.

Mary Ann, Wesley and I would drive into the beautiful Bavarian country side, find a nice spot and picnic. Wes was walking very well; he like to explore and required watching.

*Mary Ann and Wes flew back to Arkansas in the early spring of 1960, I followed in May on a troop ship and found the North Atlantic more placid than in the fall, landed at New York, flew to Little Rock, took a bus to Monticello and a taxi to my parents' home. My attempt to surprise everyone succeeded.

Photo taken by Author of Wes picking a flower in Bavaria on a picnic with his shoe untied—one of author's favorite pictures of him.

I matriculated at A&M in a double major of history and English. With a freshman GPA of 1.00, I registered for twelve hours of college history that first summer.

My life was moving fast in a new direction, I was on a track that was going somewhere I had not been; I intended to remain on it until I arrive at a destination, wherever it turned out to be.

Mary Ann, Wes and I lived on campus in married, student housing near Weevil Lake on the east side where Weevil football tailgate parties are held today. The dwellings have been razed.

In the duplex with us was Downey Lee, with whom I graduated from high school, and his bride. Downey drowned a few years afterwards in a flash flood in Texas.

In the duplex next door were Hershel Gober and his wife Olivia DeArmond each with whom I had gone to high school. Hershel and Olivia had a beautiful dog named Denver.

Hershel went on to have a distinguished military career: he was recognized for bravery in Vietnam, received a battlefield promotion and served on General Westmoreland's staff. He was appointed by President Clinton to deputy secretary of veterans' affairs, and then secretary, wherein he earned a reputation of competence.

Hershel and Olivia divorced. She returned to Monticello, assumed her maiden name, and lives on the Saline River where she grew up. I count her among my better friends in Monticello.

The next duplex south lived Billy Webb, from Bowser, whom I have mentioned, with his wife Marilyn Reed, my previous girlfriend, also mentioned.

* The electric company did not read the kilowatts used each month by those of us living in campus housing. They made up the kilowatts on the meter for each duplex. They saved money by not sending a man to read the meter, or, perhaps, the meter man was lazy and made up the numbers on his own. Either way, we were getting the short end of the stick. The electric company would read it every several months or so and adjust the bill.

The problem was we were trying to save on our monthly electric bill, but we could not save on our monthly bill, because it was not read monthly.

Arkansas A&M had a new president, a man in his mid-thirties named Dr. Jack M. Mears, who had been dean of students at Eastern New Mexico University. I had occasions to talk with him; besides being young, likeable, and smart, he was interested in student life.

I thought he might like an opportunity to help married students, many of them veterans, against a faceless utility company that is always popular to oppose. I got an appointment with him, explained the students' problem, and told him I had painted over the meter glass on each duplex with black paint so no one could read it. He laughed and said to let him know how it worked.

I painted over the meters without asking him, because he needed to be able to deny he knew of our plan before it happened. I believe it was something he understood and appreciated.

Sure enough, next month we got our bills. The meter man could not have read the meter; the numbers were still painted over. Some of the guys collected their bills, and we took them to President Mears. He seemed tickled my idea worked. He said he would call the electric company.

A couple of days later, the paint was scraped off the meters, and as long as I was there, the meters were not painted and read each month. I heard no more about it. This bit of skullduggery helped me in a way I never anticipated.

When I returned to Arkansas A&M and enrolled, I rejoined the National Guard as cook; had a student-work job at the college for fifteen hours a week at fifty cents an hour; and worked all day Saturday in Magness Shoe Store on the square in Monticello, run by Olin Cockerel, a likeable, talented man. He shared with me his insightful philosophy for being a successful merchant, "James, if I could sell a pair of shoes to every person in Drew County, I would go broke."

Olin dropped out of college as a freshman. He was taking chemistry. He studied hard for the first test and missed the class when the papers were returned and discussed. He saw the professor on campus and asked him if he remembered his test score. The professor told him forty-seven. Olin thought if that is the best he could do, he may as well quit.

He did and took a job selling shoes for Mr. Magness. He found out two weeks later forty-seven was the second highest score.

After a few years, Mr. Magness sold his store to Olin, who became a successful businessman in Monticello. Today, the store carries his name.

Author, 1961, sophomore in college after leaving army.

I took speech under a Mr. Fletcher. Speech class to me was as natural as swimming is to a fish. I made an A. Aunt Clara was registrar at the college. She said Mr. Fletcher told her, "Your nephew could wake up out of a sound sleep and talk for an hour on why a board is flat." According to Aunt Clara, I was his second A since he had been at Arkansas A&M.

Mr. Fletcher, a bachelor, lived on campus with his married brother Dr. Fletcher, who taught English. They had been at the college since Mother was in school in the 1940s. Mother made her only B in college under Dr. Fletcher, a lapse of his judgment for which she never forgave him.

Dad told two of my wives, "James William needs an audience, you know." I wondered if he remembered my speaking to Grandma's chickens.

Robert William, my second son and last child, was born in Monticello on June 8, 1961. He was the sixth Willis generation named William to live in Drew County. The five others are William Jessie, William Alphus, John Milton (his older brother was named William Henry), William Earl, and James William. Robert named his son Richard William.

* John F. Kennedy was elected president of the United States in 1960. By summer 1961, the relationship between the United States and the USSR had started to focus on Berlin and was becoming heated. My news junkie habit that began with the death of FDR served me well. Following world events, I became convinced our military would be put on alert and National Guard units would be called up.

I had completed three years in the regular army and three years in the army reserve, a total of six years, which completed was the military obligation then.

I went to see the warrant officer of our unit Childs Martin and asked him to begin processing papers for me to get out of the military, as my obligation had been fulfilled.

He said, "It is too late; by the time I get the papers ready, send them to Little Rock and got them back, our unit will be activated."

I told him, "Dad is out front in his car with the motor running, and we will take the papers to Little Rock and bring them back. I will wait until you complete them." I sat down in the chair by his desk and crossed my arms.

My bluff impressed Mr. Martin more than I had thought it would. After a moment of exchanging stares, he waved his hand in resignation and said, "Okay, you are out. I will take care of the paper work. Don't worry about it."

He was as good as his word. My discharge from the National Guard came through just a couple of days before the unit was called up, in August 1961. My guard buddies spent a year at Fort

Chaffee near Fort Smith, Arkansas. I remained in Monticello and continued my last year of college.

My getting out of the guard when I did almost did not happen. If it had not, my life would have unfolded significantly differently.

* Since I was a child, I knew what I wanted to do was history. Albeit, the situation with majoring in history, about which I was aware but had not yet internalized, is history is not like accounting or engineering. One can *do* history with a bachelor's degree only by teaching it.

The first day of the rest of my life was Wednesday, May 16, 1962. That afternoon, a student came from the superintendent's office into my class at Drew Central where I was student teaching to tell me I had a long distance call and asked if I would come to the office and take it.

As quick as were my steps down the hall to take the call, my mind was moving faster. I knew Don's plan was afoot, and I must concentrate my mind to be ready.

The man with the plan was Don Fleming. We were friendly acquaintances in high school, though he was six years ahead of me. When he graduated in 1950, he joined the army to go to Korea and kill communists. We went our separate ways.

In 1960, when I returned from the army, Don had graduated from Arkansas A&M and was teaching history at Monticello High School. He had married Wanda Bowden, whom Mary Ann knew in high school. Wanda was teaching elementary school.

By a series of serendipitous happenstances, he and I became closest of friends. Don Fleming was my first, close, adult friend, and he played a significant part in my life, none more than the one he played that culminated with that phone call.

In 1961, Don left Monticello to go to Lovington, New Mexico, to teach United States history at a high school for a considerably higher salary than he was making in Monticello. He and I continued our friendship that school year through letters that commented on the news, politics, and cultural scene in the United States and world, which were the bulk of the topics of our conversations when we were together. We visited when he and Wanda came home Christmas.

Earlier that May of 1962, before Wednesday the sixteenth, Don called me from Lovington to say he was going to Bremerhaven, Germany, to teach at the American high school and his United States history teaching job at Lovington would be vacant.

I knew Don's plan was coming to fruition that afternoon as I was hurrying to the superintendent's office. His plan was he would resign on Wednesday, May 16, right after Lovington's Superintendent H.C. Pannell had opened his mail. I would send my letter of application for a history teaching job to Mr. Pannell so it would arrive in that morning's mail.

The piece de resistance of Don's plan was Mr. Pannell would ask him about me, as he would think Don probably knew me, since we were from the same town in Arkansas.

Lovington's superintendent picked up the phone on his desk that first day of the rest of my life and called me at Drew Central.

My and Don's friendship, his going to Lovington and then leaving there the year I graduated from Arkansas A&M almost did not happen. If any of these had not, the rest of my life would have unfolded significantly differently.

* New Mexico colleges did not produce enough of teachers to fill the schools in the state, and Mr. Pannell went to Oklahoma and Arkansas to find teachers for Lovington's high school. Don was one of those he hired from Arkansas in 1961.

While teaching in Monticello, Don read in the *Arkansas Gazette*, now *Arkansas Democrat-Gazette*, an advertisement for teachers in Lovington. He contacted the superintendent who met him on the steps of the post office, then located on West Gaines on the corner across from Commercial Bank today. They interviewed standing on the post office steps. Mr. Pannell had teaching contracts with him; Don and he signed one. It was that quick, that simple.

After Don's call, I made my application personal for Mr. Pannell and did not send him a generic copy. For his copy, I included my letter of application, an official copy of my transcript, and an extended vita, including education, travel, and military experience, with letters of recommendation, instead of names of persons he could contact.

One of these was from Arkansas A&M's President Mears via' New Mexico. Before he telephoned me, Mr. Pannell read my vita and called some persons who had written letters of recommendation.

At the bottom of President Mears' letter to Superintendent Pannell, he scrawled, "H.C., he is our kind of people." I had no idea the two men knew each other, until I learned Pannell was a member of the board of regents at Eastern New Mexico University, the same college Mears had been dean of students!

After Mr. Pannell and I had talked by phone a few minutes, he felt he knew enough about me for him to know he wanted me to meet the high school principal. He proposed I fly there to continue the interview, for which he would reimburse me. I agreed.

The episode of my painting over the gas meters is an example of occasions in my life that turned out well but that could have just as easily come back to haunt me.

Author's great friend and boon companion Don Fleming who was directly responsible for author going to New Mexico his first year to teach.

* I had never heard of Lovington before Don went there and knew no one there except Don and Wanda, who were leaving. It never occurred to me that I would not be offered the job. I knew I would take it, as the salary was $5,200 a year, an amount $1,600 more than any other offer I had received for teaching and only $3,500 a year less than Dad, who was making for twelve months as superintendent at Drew Central after twenty-four years!

New Mexico ranked sixth among the states in teachers' salaries in 1962, and Lovington was the county seat of Lea County, the wealthiest county in the state. The best offer I had from schools in Arkansas and one in Kentucky, the name of which I have forgotten, was $3,600.

Mr. Clyde Ross had offered me $3,450. Actually, he offered $3,400 and said he was pretty sure he could get me another

$50. He helped me get my driver's license; I figured he could do what he said.

It never occurred to me I would be anything other than successful in Lovington. Not the remotest possibility of failure ever entered my mind. Because I had heard my dad sing each morning 365 days a year, "You've got to accentuate the positive; eliminate the negative; latch on to the affirmative; don't mess with Mister In-Between."

Today, I cannot imagine I ever had such complete absence of doubt. Several things breed confidence—ignorance the primary cause of my confidence being not the least among them. I had not yet learned ignorance coupled with unbridled enthusiasm provides all one needs to act beyond an iota of good sense and be driven over a rational precipice.

The phone on which I was speaking to Mr. Pannell was on Dad's desk. Through Mr. Pannell's call, Dad learned about the possibility of my going to New Mexico to teach. Mary Ann knew of Don's plan; I told her when I returned home that day it had worked; we were going to New Mexico.

* Don picked me up at the airport in Hobbs, New Mexico, at ten thirty in the evening and drove me to his house. As I exited his car, a scrawny otherwise nondescript bush was blocking my way. I effortlessly pushed it aside. With exaggerated mockery, Don said, "Be careful with my tree; you might break it".

I exclaimed, "You call this thing a tree!"

He replied, "After you have been in Lovington a few days, you will too." His answer was a portent of what I would see the next morning; miles and miles of flat, dry, brown empty.

The next day, Don drove me to the high school, introduced me to the principal Larry Crouse and I interviewed with him and some faculty the rest of the day.

Robert Frost wrote a profound poem about a road diverging in a yellow wood. He said, "I took the one least traveled, and that made all the difference."

During my professional life, every road I took was not just the one least traveled, it was the one never traveled by me. At every place I lived and worked, I had never been there and knew not one person there before I arrived for an interview.

Chance influences everyone's life. In my professional life, it was master. What happened in my life that almost did not happen decided everything.

TEACHER AT LOVINGTON HIGH SCHOOL, LOVINGTON, NEW MEXICO

(1962-1966)

Sir Thomas More (1478-1535) asked his young friend Richard Rich, "Why not be a teacher? You would be a fine teacher, perhaps a great one."

Richard asked, "If I was, who would know it?"

More answered, "You, your pupils, your friends, God. Not a bad public, that."

* * *

British comic Ricky Gervais quoted Winston Churchill as saying, "If you find a job you really love, you'll never work again."
—NPR, January 16, 2011

##

Several of my parents' friends learned I was going to New Mexico. They warned me not to drink the water and to get immunization shots.

Each spot in the world is equal distance from the horizon, albeit by their advice, I was surprised to learn the extent persons can be successful in their spot in the world they live and remain ignorant of what is beyond its horizon.

I lacked six specific college hours being eligible for a New Mexico teaching certificate. I took those hours in the summer of 1962, after I had graduated in May.

* Mary Ann and I loaded *everything* we owned in a six-by-ten-foot U-Haul trailer, and hooked it on a U-Haul bumper hitch behind a 1960 Impala with six cylinders, standard shift, AM radio, and heater. Noticeably absent among its accessories was air-conditioning. We pulled out of Monticello late afternoon in August and drove through the night. Mary Ann slept much of the way. Wes and Robb, in the backseat on pillows, piled up like puppies, slept all the way.

I rented a house at 607 West Adams Avenue with two bedrooms, bath, kitchen, dining and living rooms, and a stucco facade. Air was cooled in the living area by a window fan that moved air over evaporating water. The air did not reach the bedrooms. Heat was a floor furnace.

The buffalo-grass lawn, never green in the wettest of times, was crispy dry from a long drought and full of horse briars, called so because it was believed one of them could cripple a horse that stepped on it. In the yard was not one tree, shrub, or flower; nothing green was to be seen. I recalled Don predicting what scrawny vegetation I would begin to call a tree.

The house was the worst one in a nice neighborhood, which is more advantageous than having the best one in a bad neighborhood. Living on the east side was the city attorney with whom I became well acquainted; living on the west was a business man dying of cancer, whom I never met. Their son I had in class my first year.

Across the street from us were Rusty and Louise Woodward. He was Lovington's fire chief. I had their only child Glenn in class my first year. They and we became good friends.

Before school began in Lovington, I attended a three-day preschool workshop; the first of the three days was for new teachers only. I was acquainted with none of them, as none were present the day I interviewed in May, except for the principal, Larry Crouse. The next two days, I knew the few I had briefly met the day I interviewed. Everyone at the workshop was friendly and welcoming.

The night before classes began, I lay awake anxiously contemplating my new responsibilities. The next morning, I would be *alone* in a room of 25 to 30 high school juniors, sixteen-year-olds. I would meet 130 to 150 of them in the five classes of the day. With none would I be acquainted. They expected me to know what I was doing with little tolerance for me if I did not.

That night, I could remember nothing helpful I had learned in my education classes. However, I had forty-five college credit hours of history, including three from the University of Maryland I took while in Germany. To complement my history knowledge, I had nine hours of geography and government and thirty hours of English. I was confident of my subject.

I also had the advice of Jeff Moore, an education professor who was longtime superintendent at Fountain Hill, a small town twenty miles south of Monticello. At the end of each class, he admonished us, "Remember; be fair, firm, and consistent, and do not smile before thanksgiving."

Deciding I was as ready as I was going to be, I went to sleep and dreamed in color for the first time. (Since this dream, I have dreamed more often than not in color, including flesh tones.) In my dream, I was the confident luminary wearing a bright red shirt in front of a classroom of adoring students, dressed in many colors but red. It was going to be just like preaching to chickens.

The next morning, certain of my knowledge of history and its academic environs, determined to be fair, firm, and consistent, and not to smile as long as I could keep from it, I walked confidently onto my stage to meet my audience.

* When I arrived in Lovington, New Mexico, I had been three years in the regular army and three in the National Guard; for a year I had attended the army language school in Monterey, California, studying Russian six hours a day, five days a week; and for twenty months I was in Germany, living with a German family, monitoring Russian spy traffic, and serving in the base's special police force. I had graduated college with a bachelor of liberal arts with a double major in history and English. I was married and had two children. I had traveled in Europe and the United States. I was age twenty-three and appeared much younger.

I was five feet ten inches and skinny, not slim, with a twenty-two-inch waist and thirty-eight-inch chest, and I weighed 120 pounds. I had weighed the same since I was fifteen and a sophomore in high school, after I recovered from an extraordinary rough bout of intestinal flu, the plain, old fashioned regular sickest I have ever been, congestive heart, diabetes, and spinal stenosis included.

With this flu, I was in bed or bathroom for eleven days. For a few days, I had fever above 103 degrees and was heavily medicated and so weak that I exhausted myself turning over in bed.

After two weeks and without fever for three days, my parents believed I was no longer contagious. I returned to school, looking like death warmed over but feeling better because I had recently felt so bad.

My normal ravenous appetite returned, I ate each meal until I was as full as a goat, but I gained no weight for eight years. Dad's youngest sibling, Uncle Hugh, who witnessed my gluttony, suspected I had a hollow leg because all the food I ate was not going anywhere it could be seen.

After I fully recovered from the flu, I was glad to find neither my strength nor stamina had been effected. I continued to play basketball and run track (though, as I have mentioned, never enough to be noticed in either sport). I walked for miles in the woods surrounding my house, camped in them, and spent hours riding my bicycle without rest. All of this I did alone, except for Spot.

I made it through army basic training with high scores. One day, our drill instructor ordered our platoon to race back to the barracks when returning from a lengthy field exercise. To my surprise, I won the race. I was probably the only one trying. I was gung ho.

For my victory, I was ordered to attend a base-wide meeting that turned out to be a recruiting effort for men to join the airborne. My being sufficiently gung ho to win an ad-hoc race in basic training did not extend to jumping out of a perfectly good airplane.

At the Lovington High School cafeteria, teachers were allowed to go to the front of the line and have double entrée and milk portions. Everything went to my satisfaction for three days. On the fourth day, a serving lady who had not seen me before refused to give me a faculty portion; she declared I was too young to be a teacher. My cheerful protestations did not thaw her cold heart.

When my assertions became less cheerful and I began noticeably to refuse to respond to her increasingly less jovial hints that I take my tray and continue along the line, Chester Hamzy, a fellow history teacher, stepped up and explained, "He really is a teacher, even if he does look like a kid."

Several students and faculty in the cafeteria witnessed this episode, and from then on, I was referred to as *The Kid*, though no one addressed me with that title.

My colleagues never called me anything other than James. Students addressed me as Mr. Willis, except when the James

Bond movies became popular, some girls thought calling me James in an exaggerated flirting manner was tons of fun.

* One afternoon, during my first semester, I was sitting among my students on the front row in the auditorium at a school assembly called by the superintendent to listen to a man he brought from his noon Rotary meeting who had spoken on what was wrong with America, Pannell thought we teachers needed to hear what he had to say.

The man knew what was wrong with America: its youth knew so little United States history. And he knew why: "Our teachers have been seduced by Hollywood culture."

He continued, "America's youth is going to hell in a hand basket." He pointed to me, obviously thinking I was a student, ignoring my white shirt and tie teacher uniform, and asked, "When did the Pilgrims land at Plymouth?" His tone clearly implied he thought this question fundamental to understanding United States history and he did not expect me, a student, to know its answer.

"December 22, 1620, a Tuesday, at ten o'clock in the morning," I responded. He became visibly shaken when his audience burst into laughter. He was not in on the joke that I was not a student, but a teacher and a history teacher at that.

After he recovered and kept going, I began thinking how people have been committing inhumane violence against each other, usually in the name of a deity, for millennia without access to anything remotely resembling Hollywood culture. I wondered on what we used to blame man's inhumanity to man. I considered asking our speaker, but did not.

* Lovington school district was wealthy and its facilities and equipment were modern but it did not encourage teachers to adopt progressive pedagogy. Teachers were expected to know their subject, teach it and test for it. Students were expected to learn it, or earnestly attempt to.

The best modern technology and money notwithstanding, assumptions about teaching and learning at Lovington had not changed since the schools of seventeenth-century colonial New England.

The high school was organized and run efficiently by its principal, Larry Crouse, a wiry, intense, hard-bodied World War II veteran, who had been prisoner in a German POW camp for two years. If he was afraid of anything or anyone, I never found out what or who it was and never knew anyone who did. I liked him immensely; we developed a rapport built on mutual respect.

I was completely devoted and dedicated to teaching history. Before I graduated from Drew Central in 1956, I had read every history book in the library, which was not a large number but all available to me to read. Most of the books were old texts, including ancient history. Except for magazines in my home, I read only history for enjoyment.

I have authored a history book on the Civil War that received awards and a historical novel, both of which I will speak later. After my novel was published, I was interviewed by a television reporter at a Little Rock station, who asked me how long I had loved history. Without thought, Ianswered, “Maybe all my life; I don’t recall when I didn’t.”

* People of all cultures, including liberal democracies, as the United States and European countries, cherish their national myths too much to allow mere historical facts or even assertions of historical doubt to besmirch them. The better historians believe their proper role is to challenge cultural myths; a culture’s sustaining society believes the historians’ proper role is to perpetuate these myths. Therein lies the rub.

The usual approach to teaching high school history in public high schools has emphasized those parts of America’s past that are believed to best encourage patriotism among America’s youth. To wit, the founding fathers’ motives were pure and their actions were heroic; our nation was founded by Christian, God-fearing people seeking democracy and religious freedom. America has an exceptionality granted by God who quickly forgives any occasional American misstep. American missteps are always unintended and, therefore, excusable. "Real Americans" *know* this.

I taught American history as it was researched and written by learned historians, who followed proper historiography procedures. I never intended to teach it any other way; it did not occur to me any serious person could want me to. Diluting any nation's history to make its youth patriotic eventually comes back to bite that nation in its backside.

Senator Daniel Patrick Moynihan (1927-2003), New York Democrat said, "Everyone is entitled to his own opinion, but not his own facts." Others have been credited with similar remarks.

* At the end of the first nine-week grading period of my first semester, several students had earned an A. However, thirty percent of my students were failing and twelve percent more had earned Ds. A chorus of complaints from parents was heard. Larry sent them to me; I talked to every one of them.

My records were in order; all parents left understanding how their children earned what they did. It became obvious from my students' behavior that afterward many parents had told their children to work harder and focus on studying.

It was also obvious to me that my expectations of their children were too high. With the students' increased efforts and my becoming enlightened my expectations were too high, by the semester's end, the percentage failing and almost failing was about ten percent total. All my time at Lovington my grades continued at this level and remained among the largest, if not the largest, percentage of Ds and Fs in the school.

Part of what saved my job was Larry Crouse liked me; I made his job easier. I kept order in my classroom, turned in all my reports correctly and on time, and rarely, if ever, missed a school day. Principals admire these qualities in a teacher to the extent that they rarely find important fault with one who does these things. Further, I kept order wherever I went on campus, another teacher's quality principals admire and seldom find.

Primarily, my job was saved because after my first year, when the schedule was completed for the next year and students registered for classes in the summer before school began, all sections of my history class filled before all other classes of every kind for juniors.

After I cut my percentage of failures by two thirds and the students clamored to get into my classes during registration, criticism of me lessened. Somewhat analogous to criticism of a coach is inverse to his winning record.

Author, first year teacher at Lovington High School

Author, first year teacher (in uniform), taking a stretch.

* During my first year at Lovington, my Uncle Wesley, Dad's oldest brother, died unexpectedly of a heart attack. I did not know about his passing until a few days after his funeral, when Dad called to tell me. I told him I considered his tardiness a serious neglect; he explained he knew I would insist on coming home for the funeral but had no money to come home, and he had none to lend me.

In fall 1963, the beginning of my second year, Mary Ann was hired by the superintendent as secretary for Mr. Glenn Teskie, principal of one of the elementary schools within walking distance of our house.

Her education was high school, without secretarial training, but she ran the principal's office effectively. Her salary was a little less than a teacher's in Arkansas; our combined income was about the same as that of two Arkansas teachers.

Mr. Pannell told Mary Ann one of the reasons he hired her was he was impressed by her asking for a 7:00 a.m. appointment. What impressed me about her being hired was my superintendent and principal were encouraging me to continue teaching in Lovington.

Her desire to work helped ensure I could skip an experience common among male teachers in Arkansas: a second job to supplement their teaching salary. I never was an assistant coach, never drove a bus, worked in the post office during the holidays, clerked in a store on weekends, followed the wheat harvest to Canada or roped calves in rodeos. I was free to teach school and pursue a master's degree in history.

* When school ended in Lovington in May 1963, Mary Ann, the boys, and I began a routine that we continued until we returned to Arkansas to live. On the Friday that school ended, we drove to Monticello. On Sunday I drove or rode with someone to the University of Arkansas in Fayetteville to take twelve semester hours toward my master's degree in history.

When the university ended its twelve-week summer school on a Friday, I returned to Monticello that afternoon, picked up Mary Ann and the boys, left Saturday morning for the thirteen-hour trip to Lovington, and began teaching on Monday.

Mr. Crouse gave me leave to miss the preschool orientation each fall. I took his decision for granted at the time. Having since been high school principal, junior college dean, superintendent of schools, and university department chair, I realize what a difficult and unusual decision he had made to allow a faculty member to be absent from preschool orientation every year and what heat from other teachers he must have taken for it.

Preschool orientations and workshops are not enjoyed by most teachers. I am sure Larry was questioned as to why I was not required to be there. I do not know his explanation and never heard a word from anyone about it, except from some friendly colleagues who would grin at me like mules eating saw briars and make some comment about their being glad I finally decided to return from my holiday and join them in the salt mines.

* Mary Ann, the boys, and I also returned to Monticello each year for the Christmas holidays. Early morning on Christmas

Day 1963, snow began to fall at my parents' home three miles south of Monticello. We had told Mary Ann's mother that we would come to her house for dinner that day. With snow falling, we started out. The snow began to fall harder and accumulate faster.

By the time we got to Monticello, snow was falling so thickly, I did not consider it prudent to continue to Cominto, the community southeast of Monticello, where her family lived. I pulled into Grandma McKinstry's on Jefferson Street in Monticello and called Mary Ann's mother to tell her we were not coming and also called Dad and Mother to tell them we were at Grandma's.

They cautiously drove into Monticello, and we enjoyed a fine, spontaneous Christmas dinner, immediately after which we six crept home in two cars. The snow continued until twelve inches had accumulated the highest snowfall in Monticello in the twentieth century. Dad said old-timers remembered a two feet of snow in 1877.

It was a pleasurable experience, with a fire in the fireplace, to look out my parents' picture window, across the highway to the old Arkansas A&M airfield, watching the snow falling. The moon was three-quarters full and showed brightly after sundown.

* Before we left Grandma's that day, it became apparent I should have asked Mary Ann to call her mother, as her parents were looking forward to seeing her and the boys and Mary Ann's mother had cooked for two days. When I called her and finally convinced her no matter what she said we were not coming, she hung up.

After she had hung up, she thought about it a while and called Grandma and asked to talk to her daughter. Mary Ann convinced her mother I really loved them and wanted to see them but I was doing the right thing, considering the road conditions and lives of her daughter and grandchildren.

The most difficult problem Mary Ann had was convincing her brother, Curtis, who feared nothing, we would not come even if he came to get us in his log truck. A couple of days later, we arrived at Mary Ann's parents' to spend a day and night. All was as well among us, as if it had never been otherwise.

Author's Grandpa Willis with Wesley and Robert, his two great grandsons in Monticello, Christmas, 1963. He would die May 2, 1964.

* On that 1963 Christmas vacation in Monticello, I bought a new 1964 Ford Galaxie 500 from Bennie Rayburn Jr. It had an automatic transmission, eight cylinders, air-conditioning, AM/FM radio, power steering, and breaks. It had what at that time would pass for *the works* on a Ford automobile.

Previously, in summer 1963, I began my master's degree in history at the University of Arkansas in Fayetteville. Mary Ann and the boys remained in Monticello with my parents. Except passing through when I was twelve with my parents on a vacation, I had never been to Fayetteville and knew no one in town or at the university. I found a boarding house I could afford two blocks from Old Main Street, where all of my classes would be held. The house was the rambling three-story Farrar House at 612 Storer Avenue.

Except Saturday evenings and Sundays, Mr. and Mrs. Farrar prepared three meals a day that could feed a gang of starving farmhands. I was at the table on time for every meal and was usually among the last to leave it. For dessert, I often stacked up several slices of light bread over which I ladled Mr. Farrar's fine brown beef gravy.

I napped after dinner and awoke in time to study an hour or so before supper, which I never missed; I set an alarm.

A new hamburger restaurant no one had heard of opened in Fayetteville. It advertised a cheeseburger and shake for twenty-five cents. A fellow boarder from New York City, working on his master's degree in psychology, had a car. He and I went almost every night at ten thirty, after an evening of study, to eat at McDonald's before it closed at eleven.

Besides the fond memories of that summer, taking twelve hours graduate history, making new friends, and eating good food four times a day, I gained 15 pounds to 135. Until that time, I had not gained one ounce since I had the flu when I was fifteen. My waist size grew from twenty-two to twenty-four inches, my chest size from thirty-eight to forty inches, and my neck size from fourteen and a half inches to fifteen, which is not significant, unless one has to button one's shirt collar every day to wear a tie. I had become slim; no longer was I skinny.

* My best two buddies in Lovington were Chester Hamzy, from Clarksville, Arkansas, who taught senior government, and Russell Harrison, from a small town in eastern Oklahoma, who taught sophomore world history. Both were World War II veterans. Chester had been in the Aleutians protecting Alaska from the Japanese Empire. Russell fought in Europe under George S. Patton and escaped from two burning tanks; some of his comrades did not.

Author at Lovington High School speaking with students.

Russell did not finish high school. He made the dust bowl *Grapes of Wrath* scene to California, where he was living when he was drafted in 1942. After the war, he went to college on the GI bill. Before he matriculated at the University of Oklahoma, he went to the library there and read encyclopedias for two weeks to help overcome his lack of high school education.

We three taught in the same building, same hall, across from each other. These two and the guidance counselor Darwin Crockett, a descendent of Davy's brother, who decided I was okay, after he had told Larry he wanted me fired because the number of my low grades the first nine weeks, and Seth Adams, a popular teacher of sophomore biology, became my group of friends.

When Seth left Lovington, he obtained his doctorate and taught biology at Western Colorado University. He built a cabin in the Rocky Mountains and lived there. We kept up with each other for several years. Russell came to see me once in Oklahoma and again in Arkansas.

In 1997, my wife Dawn prepared a paper on teaching Shakespeare to eighth-graders. She was selected to present at the National Council of Teachers of English Conference in Albuquerque, where Chester had moved. I accompanied her, and we visited with him and his second wife. Darwin and I exchanged e-mails in later years.

Wesley and Robert, 1963.

* Lea County, of which Lovington is the seat, is a large county in the southeast corner of New Mexico. It is part of a geographical feature called *Llano Estacado*, Staked Plains, located in southeast New Mexico and southwest Texas. New Mexico's name *Land of Enchantment* very well fits much of this beautiful state. However, nothing about the Staked Plains is enchanted.

The geographical feature was named Llano Estacado by the Spaniards because it was so flat they had to drive stakes into the ground to avoid traveling in circles. It is as flat as a stiffly starched shirt ironed without a wrinkle. The only bridge in Lea County spanned a small manmade trickle that was a part of the landscaping in the backyard of a house in Hobbs, the largest town in the county.

Wesley and Robert, 1966.

Rainfall averaged nine inches a year. (Arkansas averages fifty-five inches; in 2009, it was a record eighty-one inches.) These nine inches of rain were few and far between and, therefore, heavy when they fell. The joke was: "What do you think of last year's rain?" Answer: "I don't know; I was out of town that day."

I was driving Robert to his day care one morning, and a few drops of rain began to hit the windshield. He did not recognize the water drops as rain and exclaimed, "Daddy, look. It's a sandstorm!"

Agriculture in Llano Estacado was ranching; it did not include irrigation or crops. Russell, Chester, Seth, Darwin, and I liked to go jackrabbit hunting. Lea County ranchers believed three jackrabbits eat as much grass as a cow, and were glad to let us hunt them on their land.

To hunt them, we got in Russell's pickup at night, two in the front and three in the back, with our .22 rifles, and roared across the Staked Plains, chasing rabbits. The rabbit while running would turn first one way and then another. When the truck lights hit its eye just right, it froze and was caught in the headlights.

When it froze, we shot it, except when Russell got out of his truck, walked up behind the animal, and kicked it. The startled rabbit ran away. Russell would laugh uproariously, as if remembering a joke from his Oklahoma boyhood. It is impossible to kill in the dark a recently kicked jackrabbit with a .22 rifle. After Russell kicked one, the jackrabbit was safe.

When other hunters joined us, we had two trucks. During one two-truck hunt, our truck ran up on a skunk, which frightened it just in time for it to spray the other truck. Two new guys were in the bed of that truck, one near the cab, the other near the rear; they were recipients of the skunk's liquid wrath. When the skunk sprayed, we in the back of our truck could see droplets in the lights. They fell more heavily on the man in the rear; on the one in front not so much.

The doused guy collapsed as if he were a shot rabbit, became too weak to stand, and began to gag uncontrollably. All of us were country boys with enough skunk experience of varying amounts not to worry about what might seem serious to the one too sick to stand.

To get rid of the stunk stink, he had to burn his clothes, including his cherished broken-in-just-right boots, and sit repeatedly and at length in a tub of hot water scrubbing with lye soap, vinegar, and baking soda. He decided scrubbing with tomato juice lessened the smell the most.

Fortunately, for the rest of us that night, these two had come together in the same truck and went home together. The doused one rode in the back. His skunk juice soaking was the best story in the teachers' lounge.

There was not much competition for best story. Fifty years ago in a small New Mexico town, surrounded by cows and oil wells, scattered over miles and miles of dry empty, a tale did not have to be particularly tall to provide excitement among a room of middle-class, church-going, school-teaching white folks who did not curse in public, talk loud, or stay up late at night, and were entertained at home by a black-and-white seventeen-inch television with one available channel.

As sure as Woody Guthrie's train was bound for glory, in Lovington High School teachers' lounge, were no jokers or cigar smokers.

On one hunt, Russell, Chester, Seth, and I were in Russell's truck. Russ ran out of gas. We were miles from a dwelling and would not know which direction to walk, as ranch houses did not have mercury lights then. It was nearly midnight; the sky was overcast; the night was dark and cold; and we four adult men sat in the cramped cab of the truck that was decade old. As the dark and cold became deeper, our huddled knot became smaller.

Our nourishment depended on Russell's and Seth's beer supply—liquid bread the Germans call it—that was soon depleted. Our wives were the only ones who knew we were out that night and knew only generally where we were. If we were to have a timely rescue, it would be in their collective hands.

After we had told every funny and clean joke we knew, Seth asked us, "How much life insurance do you each have?" After we answered, he said, "My wife will find us before daylight."

"Why," Russ and I asked?

"I have the most insurance," he replied. It was three o'clock.

Two hours later, during the darkest hour before dawn, we saw vehicle lights moving slowly, searching first one way and then another. We discussed whether to turn on our lights and decided not to; the show was too much fun to watch to ruin the suspense.

Seth's wife found us and had thought to bring water and a gallon can of gas. We marveled at Seth's insight into the incomprehensive soul of women and his worldly acumen in general. When I got home, Mary Ann was not awake. Neither was Chester's or Russell's wife. This story provided more lounge entertainment.

This group was a gang of great male camaraderie, a belonging the like of which I had never been part of, nor have I since.

Author and family, 1964.

One day at Lovington, a new student came to my class with a registration card she was to fill out and return it to me to turn into the office. After she had worked with it a while at her desk, she brought her card to me. I held my hand out to take it and asked her in an attempt to project interest, "Got it finished?"

"No sir," she replied, "I have a question here I do not understand." She showed it to me. The blank space was for her to provide her Church denomination.

I told her, "Church denomination means the kind of church you attend." She thanked me and returned to her seat.

When she turned in her card, I noticed she had answered, "Red Brick." Bless her heart; after several weeks, she left for another place, another school. I remember thinking that I hoped she found another red brick church to attend.

Another thing I enjoyed doing while living in Lovington was sand surfing on a board, not unlike a skateboard without wheels. Sand dunes in large numbers covering several acres were a few miles outside town on a farm road east of town. Mary Ann and the boys joined this activity that I participated in with my students. We would stand on the board and go down a sand dune for as much as 60 feet. Then we had to climb back up in the soft sand. I don't remember ever being ready to go home when it became dark. It was great, tiring fun.

* In fall 1963, I was invited to teach a course in American Southwest history for Lea County Community College at night in Lovington. I agreed. I had never had a course in this subject specifically, but I had a couple of American West history courses and figured no problem.

The text book was excellent, and I learned a lot preparing for the course; one thing I learned was about Juan de Onate's attack on Acoma Pueblo, a place about which I had heard nothing.

Acoma is a 367-foot-high mesa with sheer sides. Its top is an area of seventy acres, on which is the oldest continually occupied site in the United States, dating from circa1100; archeological digs provide some evidence of an additional five hundred years. Some archeologists think artifact evidence of humans exists on the site from two thousand years ago.

Its inhabitants maintain subsistence farming, utilizing a spring and small river a short distance from the mesa. They call their home *Enchanted Mesa.* It is a sacred place for them.

When Onate and his group came through the area looking for the Seven Cities of Gold, a member of the scouting party raped the chief's daughter on top of Acoma after the friendly natives had welcomed the visitors, the likes of whom they had never imagined, much less seen.

Some Spaniards were killed instantly by the Acoma who pitched others over the mesa's side. In retaliation, Onete organized a superior heavily armed force to return to Acoma and subdue it. The year was 1560.

An important part of the Spanish armament was a cannon capable of firing shells into the pueblo on top of the mesa.

After three days, the Spanish conquistadores vanquished the Stone Age natives. It took that long because the only way to the top was steps carved into the steep side of the mesa that could be climbed only one person at a time.

I determined I would visit Acoma.

* In late spring 1964, while I was attending an education conference in Albuquerque, I drove the seventy miles to Acoma, including the last twelve miles on an unmarked, unimproved gravel/dirt road that appeared likely to be going nowhere at all, much less a place that generates exhilaration.

I could see the mesa and the pueblo atop several miles away. I parked at its base, found the carved steps to the top, and climbed them. The village was there. All buildings were adobe, some of them three stories tall. I saw and heard no one. None of its reportedly estimated 2,000 inhabitants were to be seen or heard. I began to walk about.

Only a few buildings had ground-level doors, all built by the Spanish for storage. The entry to the houses and buildings was through the roof that one accessed by a ladder, common pueblo architecture built for defense.

All I heard was silence; all I saw were adobe buildings that looked like they had grown out of the dirt on which they were erected. There were no people, no animals, and no plants. No lights were visible; nothing was stirring, not even an ant, lizard, or spider—a silent universe. I imagined I was witnessing the end of the flicker of time, until I realized Acoma had been unchanged since the sixteenth century or the eleventh century, perhaps before.

Faye Chandler asked me if I had been frightened. I was taken aback by the question of one of my more discerning friends and in a thoughtless, glib manner, replied I was not. Reflecting on her question, I believe I was so filled with curiosity no space inside me remained for apprehension.

After maybe ten minutes of strolling about, hearing and seeing nothing living, I came upon a building with a screen door that had across it an aged sign reading "Colonial is Good Bread." When I was a child, these signs were seen on screen doors to a grocery. I opened it and walked in.

The room had no windows; it took a moment for my eyes to adjust to the darkness. Inside were an icebox (not a refrigerator), a few narrow shelves with cans of food, and two Native American women. One was middle-aged and obese; the second young and beautiful.

My sudden appearance startled both women and badly frightened the older one; she screamed and began yelling at me in a language I had not heard before. I assume was Acoma. I could not understand her words, but that she desired me to leave immediately she communicated perfectly.

As I began backing out the door I had just entered, the younger one stood, calmed the fearful one, smiled at me, and asked in impeccable English, "How may I help you, Sir?"

After I explained why I was there, she enthusiastically said she would be glad to be my guide. I was excited; nothing in Acoma had changed for hundreds of years, and I had an Acoma native who wanted to show it to me!

I learned my beautiful guide was eighteen and had only recently returned to her home from the American Indian school in Pueblo, Colorado, where she had been since taken from her home, family, and tribe by the United States Department of the Interior, when she was six.

Separating Native American children from their tribes and parents and placing them in an Indian School to Americanize them, which included changing their names and making them speak English and become Christians, began in 1880s and continued, with few changes until well into the Twentieth Century.

When I asked to see various sites important to the story of the Spanish conquest of her home, her answer was the same, "I can show you what you have asked to see, but what you learned happened is not what happened."

I soon discovered the Acoma story I had learned from American history texts, taken from Spanish records and archives, told only the Spanish side of the fight.

I had heard a truth about history that I had superficially learned; therefore, easily forgotten. Since that day, I have viscerally understood the significance of an unforgettable truth of history: it is written by winners.

My guide explained parts of the village were off limits to outsiders; the natives held religious ceremonies in them. While walking about with her, I found in the dust a drumstick used to beat the Acoma shaman drums. Though obviously recently made, equally obviously, it was made exactly as they had been for a thousand years, perhaps more.

She saw how excited I was and gave it to me. Today it is on a shelf in my library.

I descended the stone steps. Thirty minutes later, I was on my way home, driving on a paved highway in my air-conditioned Ford Galaxie 500, listening to stereo FM music and news of the twentieth century.

This abrupt change increased the illusion I had been caught in a time warp under the spell of a powerful sorcerer. Everything about that day on the Enchanted Mesa was surreal.

* Since my visit, I have learned the Acoma consider themselves a sovereign nation. Visitors are not welcome; one must gain permission to visit.

In 1972, Alistair Cooke's *America*, a thirteen-week television series, began with scenes atop Acoma. After the camera panned around various places in the pueblo, Cooke appeared. With a somber expression, he whispered directly into the camera, "We are among the first white people allowed to visit here. This mesa is considered sacred by the natives. We must be quiet and reverent."

In 1997, on the trip with Dawn to Albuquerque to present her English paper, as already mentioned, we visited Acoma. The twentieth century had definitely arrived.

The first change I noticed was a large sign on the highway advertising Acoma the Enchanted Mesa. The next thing was the unimproved gravel road to the mesa had become a paved highway.

When we arrived at the sacred mesa, we parked on a paved, marked-off parking lot among a tour bus, several automobiles, and campers. Next to the parking lot was a tourist center that housed a restaurant, a tourist shop with central heating and air conditioning, and a booth to buy tickets for fifteen dollars each to take a van ride to the top of the mesa for a group guided tour. We were not allowed to climb the carved steps.

We rode the van to the top on a paved road built by the BBC as part of the deal made with the Acoma to film Cooke's television series.

The pueblo structures were unchanged, albeit most of the population had moved into the desert below into air-conditioned mobile homes, complete with color television and running water. As everyone else in America, they drove daily to work that just happened to be atop the Enchanted Mesa, the longest continually occupied site in North America.

I asked the guide where the carved steps were. He said he was unaware of any such steps. However, as the tour ended, the guide announced to everyone, while looking directly at me, "You may get down any way you want." Probably everyone but I interpreted his remark to mean we could walk back on the road and not have to wait for the van. Dawn made a video of our descent.

* On Friday, November 22, 1963, during the regular morning announcements over the school address system, everyone learned, "The Lovington High School Student Association of Future Teachers has elected James Willis the best teacher in Lovington High School." The announcement was at 11:55 a.m.

Mountain Standard Time, 12:55 p.m. in Dallas. My class cheered and applauded.

The lunch bell rang at noon; I was walking across campus to the cafeteria, expecting good-natured teasing from my colleagues in the lounge after eating, when a thoroughly delighted student of mine bounded up to me, put his hands on my shoulders, looked into my eyes and gleefully exclaimed, "*Your* president has been shot!"

For *almost* everyone at Lovington High School, the Friday President Kennedy was killed in Dallas was a joyless day. Without discussion or word from Larry's office, no one attempted to teach that afternoon. The students moved as the soulless living dead from room to room, responding as zombies to ringing bells.

Silently, we listened to the uninterrupted news reports over the school address system.

That day, in the lounge, all of us were grimly silent. I received no teasing or congratulations from my colleagues for being named by students the best teacher. Except for a few friends' congratulatory remarks to me days afterward, my honor dissolved into the evanescence of morning dew.

The effect of Kennedy's assassination on Americans surprised people in Lovington, who were among those proud to be living in the John Birch Society's belt buckle, a belt that stretched from the old Confederacy into Arizona, with pieces of it scattered about hither and yon in Southern California.

The Birchers were much surprised to learn how beloved and popular the president was. Before the president was killed, when I was in a barbershop in Lovington, a customer came in and, with exaggerated excitement, asked if anyone had heard the latest news: "We have captured Castro, shaved his beard, and found another Kennedy!"

The shop filled with raucous laughter. Anti-Kennedy sentiment spawned humor akin to the more demeaning jokes that were then told in the white, Anglo-Saxon, Protestant male cultural mainstream. *When alone among themselves,* they told demeaning jokes about women, blacks, Mexicans, Jews, Catholics, homosexuals, handicapped, and other persons deemed marginal by real Americans, namely those who were white, Anglo-Saxon, Protestant and male.

And I mean white, Anglo-Saxon, Protestant and male.

A Bircher wag during that period explained how to tell if someone was a communist: "If he waddles like a duck and quacks like a duck, he is a duck." Some of the Birch bunch had already decided I was waddling and quacking when I ordered *Time* for my students and tested them on it as part of their class grade.

Time was ordered for every student in all my classes; Crouse put the cost in the school budget. The weekly issues came in a package to the high school. When they arrived on Monday, I took my copy home and read it through that night. The next day, I distributed the issues to my students and assigned articles from it, and on Friday I tested them. It was an open-book, timed, ten-question, and short-answer test.

I assigned *Time* and tested on it because I was startled at how little the students knew of the nation, world, and current events. I recalled the good people of Monticello who, when they learned I was going to New Mexico, confused it with Mexico, and warned me not to drink the water and to get my shots.

Some Birchers in Lovington complained to Crouse that *Time* was a socialist magazine and I was trying to indoctrinate my students to become socialist. He asked me about it.

I explained *Time* had the highest circulation of weekly newsmagazines in the nation. I reminded him the magazine had supported Richard Nixon in the 1960 election, and Dewey and

Eisenhower in presidential elections of the 1940s and 1950s. Larry smiled, nodded and said not to worry about it.

He said later he figured the problem was that the Birchers did not consider Dewey and Eisenhower real Republicans and Nixon was Eisenhower's vice president and not to be trusted by real Americans. I was not worrying; I always did what Larry Crouse said.

A few years back, I got a letter from a student I had at LHS, now a state judge in New Mexico. He had children who had gone through Lovington High School and were in college. He said he wished his children could have had me as their teacher for American history. He specifically mentioned the values of *Time* that he had continued to read.

After the conservative Republican presidential candidate Barry Goldwater's overwhelming defeat in 1964, the John Birch Society's rhetoric quieted. Under the radar, with little attention from the public, the Birchers melded with the radical Christian cultural conservatives to become part of the authoritarian culture of the right wing of today's Republicans.

* Don and I exchanged letters while he was in Germany. He often typed letters of up to ten pages; all were several pages, single spaced in a small font. I remember very well that he wrote about President Kennedy's assassination. He felt isolated in Germany when the biggest news was in the United States. His isolation was compounded by not having a soul-mate/friend with whom to share his feelings.

I placed his letters about President Kennedy in the Drew County Museum archives. The more personal letters I have kept.

After a year in Germany, Don and his family returned to the United States in 1964 and moved to El Paso, Texas that fall. We began occasional weekend visits.

One night, we went to a club in Juarez; Jerry Van Dike, the brother of Dick, was doing a stand up there. His stick was extremely funny. Until then, I had never heard of him. He went on to career in TV, most notable on the long running *Coach,* during which he was nominated four times for an Emmy as Best supporting actor. Today he lives on an 800 acre ranch near Malvern, Arkansas.

* Besides trips to El Paso to visit Don and Wanda, Mary Ann, the boys, and I took three major tourist trips while at Lovington.

We toured Carlsbad Caverns. The park was only eighty-five miles away, but like my obliviousness participating in extracurricular activities, I had never before considered going there. During trips to Monticello, several people asked if we had seen the caverns, expressed surprise that we had not, and talked about how much they wished to see them.

I did not want to continue having to explain to people why we had not gone there, so we went one weekend. It was worth it, and I am glad I visited them. We took the longest tour. Robb was too young to walk much of the way, and rode asleep on my shoulders most of the hike through them. Wes managed to tough it out without complaint.

We four went with Chester and his wife, Mary, on a day trip to Lincoln, site of the Lincoln County War from 1878 to 1881. It was a most interesting trip. The original jail from which Billy the Kid escaped was unchanged, as was much of the tiny town. To make the day perfect for recreating the old west, blowing wind tumbled weeds across the land.

Mary Ann, the boys, and I spent a day in Columbus, New Mexico, on the border with Mexico, site of the Poncho Villa raid March 9, 1916, the first armed invasion of the continental United States since the War of 1812 and the only one in the twentieth century. Eighteen Americans were killed.

The town is small and interesting; it includes the Poncho Villa State Park and a museum. This raid prompted the invasion of a large American force led by General John J. "Black Jack" Pershing that chased the Mexican for a year in Mexico, fighting two skirmishes with some of his soldiers without ever seeing him.

* I did something as a teacher at Lovington for which I am ashamed. No student ever slept in any of my classes, high school or college, ever—except one. What was he thinking? I could not believe it! Shaking him or nudging him was to no avail. I hit on a surefire plan to keep him awake, the one of which I am ashamed.

He was in the second period and remained sound asleep the whole time. As class ended, I indicated to the students to leave quietly and told those entering to enter quietly. I told the student who usually sits in the sleeper's seat to sit elsewhere and began the third-period class as normal. The student continued sleeping for most of the period.

When he awoke and realized what had happened, he left embarrassed amid laughter. I was so cute, I could hardly stand myself. He remained awake after that; I thought nothing more about it. Who did he think he was anyway, sleeping in my class?

On parents' night at Lovington, the students' parents came to their children's classrooms and visited the teachers. Almost all the parents who came were those of the better students, who enjoyed hearing their children bragged on and being told how much the teachers enjoyed having them in class.

At the next parents' night after the sleeping-boy incident, a woman arrived and lingered in the back of the room; she listened to my conversations with each parent.

After all parents had left, she approached me, smiled expressively and said that she was the mother of the sleeping student and wanted to meet me to thank me personally for letting her son sleep in my class. She took my hand.

She explained he worked two jobs to help feed the family and pay the rent and his need to study often kept him from sleeping at home. "Some days," she said, "the only sleep he gets is in your class." Continuing to hold my hand and look into my eyes with a level gaze, she added, "Thank you, Sir. I pray our holy Savior walks with you always, Mr. Willis."

Her sardonic cleverness was so sharp that I did not know I had been cut until I tried to walk. What is a man called who feels lower than one who can walk under a snake's belly with a high hat on? Whatever such man is called, that night I was he.

On Saturday, May 2, 1964, Dad called to say his father, my beloved grandpa, was dead. Mary Ann and I did not discuss whether to go home for his funeral. Within seconds after Dad called, I called Mr. Crouse to tell him my grandpa had died and I would not be in class for a while, and Mary Ann called Mr. Teskie with the same information.

Lovington schools had a personnel leave policy that did not include time off for death of grandparents. I explained to Larry I was going anyway and why; he said he understood but was required to deduct a day's salary for each day I was absent. Both of us knew what we had to do.

We four drove to Monticello. The funeral was Tuesday morning. We left from the cemetery immediately afterward. I was in the classroom the next morning, and Mary Ann was in her office. Crouse welcomed me back and commented he did not expect me for a few more days. He said nothing else, I recall.

We had driven eight hundred miles to Monticello and returned, missing only two days of school. He did not deduct any pay for

May, though the personnel policies clearly said he was required to. I never asked him about it. If I remember correctly, Glenn did not deduct anything from Mary Ann's pay. Grandpa was buried at Scroughout.

When he died, found among his possessions was a receipt of his payment of the 1900 poll tax that he had saved from the first presidential election in which he voted. It is framed along with a picture of him taken in 1900. It hangs in the wall in my living room, as it has since 1964.

A singular peculiarity of his keeping his first pole tax until his death was I never heard him offer a word on any moment of the passing political scene. Albeit, he did subscribe to the *Arkansas Gazette* when the biannual legislature was in session.

Students saved my hide on occasions of which I knew or only heard about. A preacher of one of the largest congregations in town told a youth group of his church he believed I was not a Christian and wondered if I ought to be teaching America's youth. Several of my students were among the group and told him in so many words to let me alone. They also called other students in my classes who talked to others and to parents. The whole affair was done and finished before I knew anything was going on.

Simply stated, students liked me. Incongruous is the fact that I was also considered the most difficult teacher in the school. How could the most difficult teacher be popular? When I began teaching, my being either popular or difficult never entered my mind.

My only intention was to teach history as accurately and interestingly as I could. I was surprised as anyone that being a hard teacher and a popular one was not mutually exclusive. I wondered about it.

I was fair, firm and consistent, I knew my subject cold; I was organized and always had something ready when every class began and for every minute during class. These behaviors brought me to the level of a competent teacher in a school filled with competent teachers. These teaching qualities were certainly not enough for me to be recognized among that faculty as the most anything, difficult or popular or whatever else.

Part of my popularity was my approach to teaching history, one the students were unaccustomed to. They had been spoon-fed stories of patriotic mush in fifth grade and eighth grade *Social Studies* that presented our forefathers as unblemished persons without human frailty.

I did not teach this history gobbledygook fed to public high school students on the false notion they could become patriots only if they were taught watered-down and false notions of our past.

My students learned that heroes in America's past were as real as men and women living today, as human as they were, their friends, their parents, and modern politicians, with whose feet of clay they were familiar. They loved the subject when they discovered the real history of America. An accurate history is important because a people become the story they believe about themselves.

I attempted to make my lectures, which I took largely from the Hicks college freshman American history text, exciting and entertaining. I never passed up an opportunity to make my lecture humorous. My idea was students will not learn if they do not pay attention, and they will not pay attention if I am boring. The description of a teacher I studiously avoided is that of the aptly named Mr. Gradgrind, the tyrant of the schoolroom in Dickens' *Hard Times,* described as "a kind of cannon loaded to the muzzle with facts."

My effort was much appreciated by students. School is often the most boring portion of their lives. I lectured without notes. But mostly they liked me because they knew I liked them, every one of them; not to say every one of them liked me.

* Whatever the cause of my popularity, it was hardly unanimous. A female student began to come to my classroom door the first period after lunch and could physically, literally not enter the room. The very sight of me made her sick. She would stand in the hall, look at me, throw up and flee to the bathroom, where she would remain. I would call the building janitor to clean up the hall.

I told Mr. Crouse about her situation and persuaded him to transfer her. I say *persuaded him* because one of his cardinal rules was a student never transfers from a teacher's class because of a conflict between the student and teacher. His notions were, if the student does what the teacher directs, there is no conflict and, if the student does not do what the teacher directs, there is no conflict.

To me the most incredulous aspect of my popularity is that I did not attend a single solitary student sporting event in four years—except two to which I was assigned, one football game and one basketball game. And I attended only the other student functions I was required as sponsor to attend.

I would have understood if my students believed I materialized in the classroom each morning out of chalk dust and returned to dust each afternoon.

Crouse asked me to coach the junior debate team two years. I did, and we beat the seniors, coached by Chester Hamzy, each year. Also, I was a junior class sponsor; therefore I had to be involved in something, such as a dance or a mum sale, but this was with all the other sponsors.

Two years as a junior sponsor, I alone was placed in charge of the junior class homecoming float. The theme for homecoming one year was *Fairy Tales*. My bunch named their float "I Love My Pussy; Her Fur Is So Warm."

I don't remember the theme of the other year I was in charge of the juniors' float; but my bunch ignored it. They nailed chicken wire on the sides of a trailer, stuffed some crepe paper in the wire, set a couple of wooden boxes on it, with some planks lying promiscuously around.

On the day of the parade, the girls rode on the float dressed in jeans and T-shirts and were frantically stuffing the crepe paper into the chicken wire; the boys in overalls were anxiously sawing and hammering the wood. The title of our float was, "We Thought It Was Next Week."

Probably neither float won anything, as I do not remember if either did.

* After the second homecoming float event, I and the students returned the float and trailer to its designated place at a barn in a field several miles from town and unhooked it from the tractor. The man who owned the tractor drove away. My students with the float dwindled away until I was alone in the darkness except for arguably the most stunning girl in the school, an eighteen-year-old, mature, confident senior, whom I had not had in class and, therefore, knew superficially.

I do not recall why she was among my juniors that night but did not find her presence curious at the time.

I thought she ought not be left alone in the country in the darkness and offered to drive her home. She said her mother was not home and her dad was coming to pick her up; we would probably pass him on the way and he would show up with no one here. In that day, the closest thing to communicating by a phone not plugged into a wall was on Dick Tracy's wrist.

I knew her father Mr. Franklin by repute as one of the leading ranchers and largest landholders in the county, with a reputation of being used to having his way; and she was his only daughter if not his only child. After a period of awkward silence, she said, "I was disappointed I did not have you for my teacher. I registered too late. I had looked forward to being in your class."

A fan wanting to talk with me about me is a great conversation starter. The moon set in a couple of hours. The sky was clear; no ground lights impeded our view of the stars. We lay on our backs on the trailer looking at the cloudless canopy of stars in the big New Mexico sky until we fell asleep.

I was startled awake when I heard her exclaim, "Daddy!"

The sun was coming up; striding toward us was a lanky, graceful, sunburned, chisel-faced man in expensive hat, boots and suit in a western cut. I was trying to figure out how to explain the situation he was seeing without beginning with, "This is not what it looks like." I have never known anything beginning with these words that end well.

Exacerbating the situation, I was dressed in jeans and sweatshirt, suitable for float work but not for meeting at sunrise the father of a beautiful eighteen-year-old female student with whom I had been alone most of the night.

Before I could speak, she excitedly, smilingly, grabbed her Dad's arm and introduced me to her father as "The Mr. Willis I have been telling you and Mother about," and in the manner natural to a father's beautiful, only daughter, she gently reproved him for being late.

Properly chastised, Mr. Franklin shook my hand, apologized for being late, and told me, "I am so glad to finally get to meet you. Thank you very much for not leaving my daughter alone during the night." They drove away. The episode ended before my life had finished flashing before my eyes.

Alone, I looked at the clear sky, filled with sunlight, void of stars, and wondered which among the shinning canopy above us that night my lucky one was.

* My students were more than a little curious about where I was from in Arkansas. I told them I was from Scroughout. They were justifiably suspicious, but I insisted I was telling the truth. Some of them looked unsuccessfully for Scroughout on a map of Arkansas. The local postmaster told them there was no post office in Arkansas by that name. Some of them called people they knew in Arkansas who told them they had never heard of such a place. My students' incredulity grew.

The attitude I assumed with them was I did not have to take their guff; I guess I knew where I was from. If none of them had heard of Scroughout that was their personal problem.

Periodically, the question of where I was from continued to come up; I answered the same. In my third year the subject came up, a student on the front row said with some excitement, "I was born in Scroughout, Arkansas!" I thought he was joking, but unlike me, he was telling the truth.

His father had worked for Ashley, Drew and Northern Railroad. My student was born in the caboose that was pulled over at the Scroughout switch and disconnected so his mother could deliver him. He had never been back and knew absolutely nothing about the place except the name and that he was born there in a caboose. The young man was pleased to share his hometown with me.

Because I never told anyone differently, everyone either believed I was from Scroughout or gave up asking. Now that the question was "settled," the junior boy's intramural volleyball team proudly called themselves "The Willis Scroughouts" and printed T-shirts they wore when playing.

* I find my deliberate lack of participation in students' extracurricular activities inexcusable, unacceptable and beyond incredulous. I would not believe it except I was there. I did not witness it; I participated in my nonparticipation. The only explanation I have

is it never entered my mind that extracurricular activities were something I ought to do or should want to do.

As were the false gods in Psalm 82; I knew nothing and understood nothing. I "walked about in the darkness." I did not know I was in darkness because I did not stumble over nor bump into anything. I was not unconscious of the rest of a teacher's school responsibilities; I was non-conscious of them. I was not as much self-absorbed as I was self-absent.

I followed this path day after day with the complete confidence of a sleepwalker.

My somnambulism continued regarding going to church. It never crossed my mind whether I ought to or whether I wanted to. I just never thought about it. I did not attend church at all, as I remember.

Lovington was a town of ten thousand; it had public places to eat. I never visited one. We began buying most of our groceries at a small one-room grocery owned by a nice, little, old lady, who gave me credit until the end of the month and was in easy walking distance from our house.

As our finances increased, a new supermarket opened in town and our choices of food improved. It had a deli where we bought fruit, fresh items for sandwiches, and banana pudding, of which Wes never tired.

One of my favorite dishes that Mary Ann prepared was a tuna casserole served warm with sweet corn. On Sundays, I cooked a beef pot roast with cabbage, potatoes, and carrots and the four of us watched a newly franchised, professional football team called the Dallas Cowboys on our seventeen-inch, black-and-white television set. The Cowboys and their opponents was the only professional football game available on our only channel.

* Cowboy quarterback Don Meredith struggled. His usual play was to take the snap and three steps back before becoming buried under several hundred pounds of defensive linemen, if he had not fallen down before they got to him. I became a dyed-in-the-wool Cowboy fan and have continued so for forty-nine years.

Soon, they began to win with their same quarterback and became the most popular team in America, according to sales of team paraphernalia. A friend of mine several years later said I was the longest-time Cowboy fan he knew. Quarterback Meredith became widely acclaimed as "Dandy Don."

Some friends thought I resembled Don Meredith. I could see why they thought so, albeit never considered I resembled him enough to be mistaken for him. One night while Meredith was still quarterback for the Cowboys, I was driving alone through Oklahoma City and stopped at a restaurant-bar near closing time. The place was about empty; lights were dim.

I could hear a few busboys and waitresses talking about whether I was Don Meredith. I ignored them, until one approached my table and asked for my autograph without asking my name. I graciously complied. He said he was proud to shake my hand.

In 1980, before it was common to own professional football team jerseys, I called the Cowboys home office and purchased a Cowboy jersey with Don Meredith's number and my name on it. I wore it for an unofficial visit to J.T. Toy, a teacher friend of mine in Paducah, Kentucky, when on my way to see Alan Detrich, a friend in Great Bend, Kansas.

When I walked into J.T.'s class unexpectedly, he saw me and spontaneously introduced me to the class as a friend of his who was running back for the Cowboys. A couple of boys wanted autographs. They said the Cowboys were their team.

* During our first couple of years in Lovington, Robert ate sitting in his highchair at the table with Mary Ann, Wes, and me. One

evening, after he finished, he slammed both fists on the highchair tray and demanded loudly, “Get me down.”

I told him he had to ask to get down and had to say *please*. He became quiet. I worked at the table that evening on my lessons for the next day; Robert sat within two feet of me. He did not say another word. Eventually, he fell asleep in his chair.

Mary Ann said that at least we knew from whom he got his stubborn streak, which caused me to recall my throwing the tuna salad sandwich three times and refusing to sing solo in grade five. I carried him to his bed, put him into his pajamas and tucked him in.

The incident was not mentioned again. Robb began to ask to be taken from his highchair.

* I began to drive to Chester’s house Fridays after school to celebrate the weekend’s arrival. Chester poured two glasses of Scotch neat, each a double-double. We would click our glasses together, Chester would exclaim, “Thank God it’s Friday,” which was the first time I ever heard this expression, and we would take a drink. He drank his glass easily. In the beginning, I could drink no more than two or three swallows, sips actually.

Not the least insulted, Chester finished my glass. Weeks of Fridays became months of them, and I learned to appreciate the taste of good Scotch. When I am introducing someone to the joys of this whisky, I explain Scotch is like olives, an acquired taste, and how I learned to appreciate it.

Chester’s parents were Lebanese immigrants. He was a big man of swarthy complexion and with a large nose. He was sometimes mistaken for Jewish, which amused him no end.

* Among the faculty, I was either popular or not. Few seemed to be neutral. I imagine some thought I was a disgrace, though

I was always considerate, gracious and respectful to everyone. Mother believed no one ever has an excuse for being rude.

Dad was a conventional man. He thought conventionally and supported conventional thinking. He rarely, if ever, questioned communal thought. Mother often did not consider conventional wisdom to be the wisest and encouraged me to question the question.

Her attitude encouraged me to conclude that a person's opinion about what I think about anything is of little importance.

* In 1964, Russell and I were active in local Democratic politics and elected precinct captains. We attended the state Democratic Convention that year to select delegates to the National Convention to nominate the Democratic candidate.

Lyndon Baines Johnson was the incumbent and a Democrat; therefore, it was not a question who our delegates would support for president. The question was who among those desiring to go we would select. Our choice was not easy. We were scrumptiously wined and dined; the mighty sought our favor.

At a fine dinner in the evening, a woman in an expensive gown and jewels at our table asked Russell where we were from and what we did. Russell and I had never eaten truffles and caviar and were paying more attention to our food than to our table partners' conversations. Without looking up, Russell told her we were from Lovington and were teachers.

The woman asked Russell what he taught. He looked at her for the first time. "Boys and girls," he answered with a tone and smile that may allow one who knew him to believe he thought the answer to her question was too obvious to be asked.

I enjoyed Russell's humor and respected him for his viewpoint. It is a humane one and, for him, a natural one. I, however, unabashedly continued to teach history, not boys and girls. My emphasis on subject rather than students bothered some of my colleagues. Once, in the lounge, a colleague asked me. "What are you going to be doing in your class week?"

I answered, "I am going to cover the Reconstruction."

Intending to show everyone in the lounge my ignorance of proper pedagogy, a senior science teacher, not a fan, asked me, "What do you think your students are going to do while you are *covering* the Reconstruction?" He emphasized I did not say *teaching* the Reconstruction.

I replied, "Learn it, if they want to pass. I am not a good enough teacher to do my job and theirs too." I heard those words for the first time when they came out of my mouth, just like he did. It was a spontaneous expression of my lifelong teaching philosophy.

On the last night of the convention in Santa Fe, my mouth got my tail in a serious crack. A labor organizer from Albuquerque and I got into a hypothetical discussion about the difficulty of organizing teachers into a union. During the course of it, I told him, "You could begin by scheduling the community room at one of the banks in Lovington and call an organization meeting." I never thought another second about it.

Unknown to me, our conversation was overheard and I had ceased being a competent, interesting young man, mildly weird to some and irritating to others. I had become a reckless one, the sort to whom bad things happen. My ignorance coupled with my unbridled enthusiasm had taken me beyond good sense one time too many.

The following Monday afternoon, the superintendent called an assembly of high school faculty in the auditorium. I learned later that earlier that day, H.C. Pannell had attended a regents' meeting at Eastern New Mexico University. At the meeting, while he was holding forth, another regent told him, "You did not even know what is going on in his own school. One of your teachers and a state labor leader are planning to undo all you have done."

At that faculty assembly, H.C. told us, "A young man, not even thirty years old, is trying to destroy the public schools of Lovington." He continued, "This boy, instead of putting his shoulder to the wheel to push it forward, is like grit in the machinery of progress."

He firmly announced he intended "to put a stop to this foolishness." He was angry. He was a determined man who was not known for listening to others, perhaps a reason many faculty referred to H.C. Pannell as Hairy Chest.

When he finished, quietness filled the auditorium until one could have heard a snowfall gathering on an overripe peach. Several teachers went forward to swear their allegiance to him as would feudal surfs to their liege. Others of us walked out in small groups, wondering aloud what in the heck the old man was talking about this time and who could possibly be the foolish young man who got the superintendent so upset.

About ten o'clock that night, Russell called me at home to say he had been thinking about what the superintendent said and he believed he was talking about me, and reminded me of my conversation with the labor organizer from Albuquerque.

I realized he was probably correct and called Mr. Crouse, who lived close by. I told him I needed to see him right then. He was already dressed for bed; he said he would see me in the morning at school. I insisted. He relented.

I walked over and sat with him in his living room. He was in his pajamas, robe, and slippers, and I explained what had gone down in Santa Fe. He said he would see Mr. Pannell first thing the next morning and explain everything to him. When Crouse arrived at school the next day, he came to my room and told me everything would be all right.

I didn't know what Mr. Crouse said to Pannell to settle him down that much. During their meeting, Larry had to have totally supported me. He probably put some words into my mouth that had me apologizing, saying something like, "He was just joshing with the silly old labor guy; the whole incident has been overblown." And so on.

By noon that day, the high school faculty knew the superintendent had been talking about me. To some, I had become more interesting. To some, I had become more irritating.

* The next morning, on the table in the lounge was a framed certificate with gold lettering reading "GRITS boy of the year award to James Willis—who has put his shoulders to the wheel and pushed with vigor in the wrong direction consistently," for which, according to the certificate, I was named Champion Gear Clogger.

Mr. Crouse witnessed this ceremony without expression, assuming the air of Sergeant Schultz in *Hogan's Heroes*, a television show set in a German POW camp: "I know nu zang."

The certificate had been prepared by Armor Lee Marchbanks, a fan, Korean War widow and mother, who taught sophomore English. I had her son in class my first year. I enjoyed our many stimulating conversations on a wide range of subjects. Whatever my reputation had been among the faculty, it had become more so.

The framed certificate she gave me has hung on a wall in every office and home I have occupied. It has faded to the point where the words are barely legible. It is among my more precious stuff.

* Lovington had a two-nine-week grading system each semester. At the end of week five of each nine-week period, every student who was failing or may fail was to be given a "down slip" to take home to parents. The slip was in duplicate form, and the student

signed it; the teacher kept the second copy for a record of having notified the student, whose responsibility it was to inform the parents.

During roll call on the appointed day, I called forward each student who had a slip for him to sign. It was routine and never a problem. As insensitive as I now realize I was, most teachers did it pretty much the same way.

On the fifth week of the first nine-week period of the spring semester in 1965, I called a boy to come forward. He said he was not going to do it. No student had ever failed to do what I said; his defiance so startled me that all I could think of as a response was, “Okay, sit there,” which he did.

When I finished taking the roll, I asked him, again, to sign the down slip; he continued to refuse. I told him to follow me and strode out of the room. We walked together to the principal’s office.

Mr. Crouse was absent; his assistant “Chub” Howell was there. To say the least, Chub was not Larry but knew how principals were supposed to act; he took the slip and said he would sign it for the student. The student defiantly, loudly said, “You are committing forgery!”

I left them yelling back and forth and returned to my class; the student did not. He never did. Before this incident, he had not been a troublemaker in the least; he had been pleasant to have in class. His behavior puzzled me.

Later, I learned the cause of his defiance; he had received a down slip in every class that day; mine was the fifth period, and he was not going to sign another one. His protestation caused me to realize how such an experience was demeaning for students, and I questioned myself why I did it that way. I did not do it that way again.

After that incident, I began to hand the slip quietly to the students when they came in and they quietly returned them at end of class. Everyone knew what was going on, but it allowed some face-saving and showed more understanding from me of their feelings.

Late in the spring of that school year, on a Saturday, I was getting my hair cut at a shop owned by a Mr. Williams, whose daughter Kathy I had in class my second year. The shop was *not* the one I was in when the Birchers found another Kennedy in Castro's beard.

Mr. Williams' shop was a long narrow one-room shop on the northeast corner of Court Square. On the east wall was a row of windows, with chairs for customers to sit while waiting; along the other wall were three barber chairs. At the south end, opening toward the square, was the only door.

I was sitting in the last chair, with Mr. Williams cutting my hair, when a strong, confident male voice declared, "I am looking for Willis." The voice was that of the student I had taken to the principal months before. He was twenty pounds heavier, filling the doorway in a marine uniform. He had gone to my house; Mary Ann told him where I was.

Before I could say anything, Mr. Williams announced, "Here he's back here." The youth began walking toward me not smiling. I had nowhere to go. I wondered, if I poked the tip of my finger up under the barber towel covering me, would he believe I had a gun. I recalled having seen that ploy work in a Glenn Ford or, perhaps, Gregory Peck western.

He came to my chair, smiled, and extended his hand. He began to talk, going on and on, how I was the best teacher he ever had and that he would still be in school if others were like me and understood him like I did. He had enjoyed my class so much, sometimes he came to school just to attend my class. He said he wanted to be sure I knew how he felt.

I thanked him and wished him well. We shook again. He apologized to Mr. Williams for the interruption and left. I sat wondering how frail the wisdom of the wise is.

Years later, I recalled my action with new regret when I read a profoundly insightful quote of Dr. Haim Ginott, educator and child psychologist (1922-1973):

> I have come to the frightening conclusion that I am the decisive element in the class room. It is my personal approach that creates the climate. It is my daily mood that makes the weather. As a teacher, I possess a tremendous power to make a child's life miserable or joyous. I can be a tool of torture or an instrument of inspiration. I can humiliate or humor, hurt or heal. In all situations, it is my response that decides whether a crisis will be escalated or deescalated, and a child humanized or dehumanized.

* In spring 1966, I received a tenured contract for the next and subsequent years. I had taught four years and received excellent evaluations from Mr. Crouse and the supervisor of instruction from the central office each year. Tenure means I would never be out of contract and could be fired only for a specific *legal* cause the school must prove.

Before tenure, I had a one-year contract each year, during which I had no assumption of another contract. I could simply not be offered a contract for the following year; no reason had to be given, and I would have had no recourse. Even with my reputation as an excellent teacher and the aid of Mr. Crouse, I had been lucky.

For instance, all the superintendent had to do in 1964, after the labor leader's and my discussion, was send me a letter telling me I would not have a contract for the following year, and that would have been that. He did not have to discuss his decision with Mr. Crouse, the board, or anyone else, including with me. Nor did he have to give a cause for not retaining me.

I was not saved by dumb luck as much as by luck of the dumb. Or as some wag put it, "Fortune can not save all the fools, so she makes some of them lucky,"

A few days after I received my tenure contract, I was watching my students come in for my next class when the realization came over me that I was twenty-six and did not want to be telling high school students about George Washington when I was forty.

This large epiphany created in me a second, equally important, lesser one: if I wanted to do something besides teaching high school history by the time I was forty, I needed to begin doing something else soon. I could not wait until I was thirty-nine to make my change.

I think my realization originated with my becoming tenured and nearing the end of my master's degree. Whatever the origin of these thoughts, I did not try to dispute them. If I believed deities directed the affairs of man, I would have been certain a deity was directing me to leave Lovington, as surely as one had originally directed me to come.

One must focus and have an objective. If he does not, he will focus and have an objective but it will not be his own.

I did not have a plan and had not thought about what else I wanted to do. Clarity of vision has never been my long suit. If I had considered it, I would have known my new job would have to be something to do with education. I had no other saleable skill.

On my eighteenth birthday, I picked cotton for Uncle Wesley, who had assumed ownership of Grandpa's farm. I worked from could see to could not see, using both hands. My sack of cotton weighed 186 pounds. A few years before my cotton picking birthday, my seventy-two-year-old Grandpa Willis had picked more than 500 pounds in one day, in fewer hours.

That night Uncle Wesley and Aunt Mary drove to my house to pay me for my work. The amount was way short of enough to live on if I had picked 186 pounds every day of the year.

* In 1966, on our way to Monticello, we stopped at Alvin, Texas, where Aunt Artie, who had let Spot in my bed, lived. I always enjoyed her company. When I was about five, Aunt Artie was staying with me. Out of the clear blue she said, "James William, when a soldier sticks a bayonet into an enemy; sometimes it gets stuck so tight he cannot get it out. Did you know that?" I shook my head. "Yea," she continued, "He has to fire into the rib cage to soften the body up enough to pull the bayonet out."

Alvin was a pleasant suburb halfway between Galveston and Houston. It was a rich and fast-growing town, with a flourishing junior college.

I visited the dean there for an interview. He liked me for a job, and the school was growing so fast he was sure there would be an opening in the fall, but advised me I needed to finish my master's degree, which I intended to do that summer.

I had taken the comprehensive exam to complete the master's degree in summer 1965 but had failed it! What I failed were the questions about bibliography. I was somewhat at a disadvantage because bibliography had not been mentioned in summer classes, which were the only classes I took.

A larger disadvantage was I had made almost all, if not all, I do not remember, As in the course work and was confident I could pass a comprehensive exam without studying—exactly the same reason I flunked the written portion of my driving test.

My largest disadvantage was the fact that I was still an abysmally lazy student. I thought I had only to learn what I wanted to learn and could get by with only the effort I wanted to make.

This failure was not getting by; it required me to face up to my problem and fix it. I obtained an annotated bibliography that was part of each class syllabus; I memorized it not unlike I did the list of spelling words to impress Mother in grade school. I was confident I would be ready. Unlike many other times I was confident, this time I had a reason to be. My confidence was based on preparation, not ignorance or arrogance.

We continued to Little Rock, where my parents had moved, and then to Fayetteville, with Alvin Junior College on my mind.

* Dad came to Fayetteville that summer to take some courses. He had resigned from Drew Central the year before and was working at the Arkansas State Department of Education in Little Rock; where Mother taught English in Park View High School.

In June, Dad and I were standing in a line to enter a banquet room for a dinner and a speaker. Behind us was a man I had never seen. He asked Dad if he knew anyone he could recommend for high school principal, explaining his principal had suddenly resigned. Dad said he did not, but would keep the man's personnel problem in mind.

After we had been seated, Dad told me that the man who talked to him about a principal for his high school was Tommy Venters, superintendent of Prairie Grove Schools, "probably the best small school near the university and would be a good place for a young man to start who is looking for a high school principal's job." I nodded. He and I said nothing else about Tommy or Prairie Grove.

Being a principal had not crossed my mind.

Tommy talking to Dad with me present about his needing a principal almost did not happen. If it had not, all that followed in my life would have unfolded significantly differently.

PRINCIPAL OF PRAIRIE GROVE HIGH SCHOOL, PRAIRIE GROVE, ARKANSAS

(1966-1968)

Endurance is frequently a form of indecision.
—Elizabeth Bibesco

##

As I had not been to Lovington before I interviewed, Prairie Grove I had never heard of, nor did I know anyone there, though it was only twelve miles from Fayetteville and had a Civil War battlefield! The best explanation I can offer for this incongruity is I studied several hours each weekday and went to Monticello almost each weekend.

Mary Ann and the boys were staying with me in Fayetteville in 1966. Mother was with her mother in Monticello.

When I returned to our apartment that afternoon after Tommy asked Dad if he knew of a high school principal prospect, I told Mary Ann and the boys we were going for a ride. We drove to Prairie Grove. After driving around the town, we were impressed with its beauty and serenity.

I told them about the conversations between Tommy and Dad and Dad and me. I asked them if they would like to live there. They were delighted at the prospect. I told them I was going to call Tommy the next morning about the job. I did, and he asked me to come over for an interview. Tommy had been the high school principal until two years before, when he became superintendent. He had been at Prairie Grove several years.

He and I visited for most of the rest of the day. Sometime during the interview, Tommy began to say *When you come*, rather than *If you come*. I knew to become principal of Prairie Grove High School, all I had to do was say yes and obtain an Arkansas principal's certificate, toward which I had not one college hour.

Then, in Arkansas, one could qualify for a provisional principal's certificate with a minimum of three years successful teaching experience and a master's degree in any subject for which one was certified. I passed easily the comprehensive exam for the master's degree in history that summer and applied for and obtained a provisional principal's certificate.

The provisional certificate was good for two years, at the end of which I had to have completed all requirements for the regular certificate or have an extension for one year. I received the regular certificate in two years by attending classes two nights a week, three hours each night, each semester for two years and attending summer classes.

When I was awarded the provisional principal's certificate, no other impediment to my taking the job remained. Tommy took me to visit each of the eight board members, not to get their permission to hire me but to introduce me to them. Tommy was a good superintendent and smart about school boards. He retired many years later as the commissioner of education for the state of Arkansas, following Dad, who retired as acting commissioner.

The salary for principal was $6,000 for twelve months, less than I was making in Lovington for nine months after four years of teaching, and MaryAnn was not employed. My approach to money has always been nonchalant; maybe I cannot overemphasize Dad's singing *accentuate the positive* with loud enthusiasm every morning. Perhaps my somnambulism accounts more for my non-consciousness. Or maybe it was because I never heard my parents discuss money in any of its aspects and I never considered it important.

Shortly after I began working at Prairie Grove, Tommy hired Mary Ann as secretary to the new elementary principal.

* In July, we drove to Lovington. I resigned to Mr. Crouse, who had become the superintendent. He expressed genuine, I believe, regret for my leaving. We rented a U-Haul trailer a little larger than the one in which we moved there. Some of the high school faculty had a small party for my leaving. Some students attended.

At the party, Glenn Teskie had been watching me intently, strangely I thought. When the chair next to me became vacant, he filled it and said, “So you’re going to be a principal?” I nodded with a smile. “Well, don’t let them run over you,” he replied.

Puzzled at his admonition, I responded, “I have never had trouble with students.”

He studied me for a moment with a vacant amazement that he quickly filled with disappointment and then pity. He said slowly, emphasizing each word separately with equal spacing, “I . . . am . . . not . . . talking . . . about . . . students.”

If not students, of whom could he be speaking, I silently wondered. Then it hit me: *Teachers! But . . . but I am a teacher . . . Have I gone over to the dark side?*

Glenn was watching my expressions and accurately reading my thoughts. Without my saying anything, he smiled and said, “Teachers, yes. Don’t let them run over you.”

* I have thought about how easily we left Lovington after four good, fruitful, friend-filled years. We were never there in the summer and missed the bonding that families and friends do in

the summer; the boys were not involved in the youth programs and swimming pool and park activities in the summer. The paramount reason for wanting to leave was the barren, stark landscape, so unlike the lush green one we had grown up in.

More disconcerting was the wind that blew frequently, often for days. An undisputed fact among the faculty was, when the wind blew incessantly for three days, the students developed a restless edge that affected the temper and mood of the classroom. It was as if the witless winds of Lovington contained the power to cause students to become monsters, as surely as the clueless full moon of Transylvania causes its people to become werewolves.

Recently, I googled Lovington and found a city map that provides videos of street scenes of the town. The bleakness is starker than I remember. The high school complex appears unchanged.

* On the way to Prairie Grove on a hot, hot Fourth of July, 1966, directly in front of the main gate of Fort Sill, I had a flat on the right back tire of the Galaxie. It was the hottest part of a hot day. I had to unload the entire trunk to get the spare out.

I had to unhitch the trailer to take weight off the car to jack it up. I found a blanket in the trailer and folded it to insulate me from the pavement that was much too hot on which to sit or lay to change the tire.

Changing the tire was not a problem. I had many times changed flat tires with inner tubes on my dad's car, when driving over Drew County's nail-strewn gravel roads, usually at night and alone.

With the tire changed, I had to re-hitch the loaded trailer to the car—no mean feat. Everyone stayed calm. The boys and Mary Ann remained in the car with the motor running periodically to keep the air-conditioning going without the motor overheating.

At Prairie Grove, I assumed the duties of principal immediately, as the position was already vacant. I had two important conflicting tasks. I had to create a class schedule for the school within six weeks and had to *actively, patiently* listen to everyone who wanted to talk to me, which I could hardly do simultaneously.

I had never made a class schedule before and had never thought about creating one; it was more difficult than I, in my ignorance, had imagined. Not only did it have to work, but it had to have no room for improvement if I was to achieve the school beginning I intended to have.

The previous two principals were not effective. The first one did not have a schedule until two weeks after school began. At the end of his first year, he was asked not to return. Now it was my turn. Many people in Prairie Grove looked doubtfully at *The Kid* who showed up from somewhere in Mexico or wherever, without any administrative experience, about whom no one had ever heard a mumbling word nor heard of anyone who had.

The school counselor Mrs. Billy Yates, a competent professional, was working some weeks that summer, and she assisted me. She, my secretary Mrs. Giles and I were the only staff in the building. Computers were years away. The schedule was built by hand, piece by tiny, important piece.

After Mrs. Yates and I carefully checked the schedule for conflicts and omissions, I took it to Tommy, whose office was in the elementary school, for him to look it over for mistakes or suggestions. He ignored the schedule completely, refused to look at it!

I was taken aback by his response. The single most important thing that would help me, and him, ensure a successful beginning of school was the schedule. He said, with a smile, words I shall never forget: "If it works, you don't have any problems. If it doesn't work, I don't have any problems."

His response brought home how much in charge of the high school I was. It was mine; I was in the deep water alone to swim, sink, float, drown, or walk on it. I alone was responsible. This sudden realization filled me with a vigorous, enthusiastic determination fueled by cold comfort. My life was no longer a dress rehearsal.

I began viscerally to understand I had entered a new world fraught with possibilities of greater failures than at Lovington. Instead of having 150 students who expected me to know my subject and know how to teach, I had a school filled with students, and teachers, who I had been warned not to let give me a hard time.

Each student had parents and extended family. Each teacher had a spouse, family, friends and neighbors. All were part of a community that was proud of its school and interested in its success.

I was no longer one ant on a hill of ants. First impressions are important, and I had only one chance to make it and a one-year contract. I could no longer hide behind Mr. Crouse. Suddenly, I had become Mr. Crouse!

* Lovington had the best grading system I had ever seen or heard of. At my first meeting with the Prairie Grove faculty, I explained to them the method they would use to determine grades, which was the Lovington method. They all listened, took notes, and asked informed questions.

I gave them the faculty and student handbooks that I had adopted, with necessary changes, from the Lovington High School and went over the handouts with the faculty. All this we did in one day.

I had enough student handbooks made for each student to have a copy. I instructed the faculty to go over the handbook sentence by sentence with students during homeroom, continuing each day until the handbook was completed. The teachers instantly saw the value of this; everybody would know what to do; everyone would literally be on the same page.

Prairie Grove High School faculty had never experienced this kind of organization before—something that would have been beyond my ability, had I not had the experience at Lovington with Larry Crouse as a model.

No one seemed to be concerned I had made all these decisions that affected their work without any input from them. It was a different world back in the day. They had rather I do all the work and leave them alone to teach, as long as I knew what I was doing.

* On the first day of class, I was walking to lunch at the cafeteria that was in the elementary school and fell in step with a sophomore. I noticed he had a pack of cigarettes in his shirt pocket. No tobacco had been allowed on campus for several years.

Aware I was being watched and that my measure was being taken, I kept my cool. I casually tapped his shirt pocket and pleasantly, quietly said, "Leave those home tomorrow, Son." I figured I pulled that off brilliantly; no fuss, no muss and no bother.

He gutturally growled, "I go where my smokes go."

I replied, "You can go home with them." He abruptly turned and walked away. I never knew who he was; he never came back to school; I have never seen him since. Today, he would be a man in his sixties who dropped out of school on the first day of his sophomore year 45 years ago to smoke cigarettes.

* Except for this incident, the first days went smoothly. The schedule worked perfectly; the halls and classrooms were quiet. I gained the confidence of the faculty and students, most of them, anyway. I had not yet impressed one young man called

"Peewee" Shelton, whom I was always careful to call by his first name James.

He began to show up in my office regularly sent there by one teacher or another for causing a disturbance of some kind or another in some class or another. I talked sternly to him and called his parents; neither approach worked at all. I escalated his punishment into giving him sentences to write and keeping him in at noon, the usual stuff of inconveniencing students to change their behavior, none of which worked.

James showing up in my office in trouble became more frequent. I searched my mind for a solution. What was the reason James wanted to be in my office, as unwelcome as he knew he was, and as surely as he knew he would be punished by me? What was the draw for him; why did he want to be there so badly?

In a moment of clarity, I decided I would go straight to the horse's mouth. On one of his visits, I asked James why he wanted to be in my office. He seemed surprised that I would ask a question with such an obvious answer, "Why, Mr. Willis, you are the man. Everybody wants to be in here with you. Besides, everybody knows you ain't gonna spank."

A light bulb appeared over my head! On a shelf behind me was a large wooden paddle left by a previous principal. When I stood and picked it up, James became pale and quiet. I told him to stand up and bend over my desk. I hit him four times with the paddle as hard and quickly as I could and tried to place each lick in the same place. After the first lick, he began to scream, cry, and beg me to stop.

When I finished, I asked him if he thought he could stay out of my office for a while. He sobbingly nodded strong assurance he could. I sent him out into the hall crowded with students changing classes. James did not return, nor did others begin to come.

I gave no thought of paddling as punishment probably because the Lovington faculty never used a paddle, and while there, I never heard corporal punishment of students mentioned, much less discussed.

I had thoughtlessly paddled my sons. My father had paddled me, therefore, I without thought assumed paddling was what a father did, if I were to be a good one. I ceased the practice when my boys reached elementary. I have since much regretted that I paddled them at all.

Previous to paddling James, I had not considered spanking at Prairie Grove. At that time, in that culture, spanking children was not only allowed; it was expected. After I spanked James, more than a few parents, some of whom I had not met, told me people in town had been wondering if I knew what a paddle was for.

Prairie Grove also had a history of spanking girls, which I knew I was not going to do, a decision I decided best never to let be known; none of the girls tried to find out.

Since James wanted my attention, I tried to not let a day pass that I did not talk with him, when he was with other students. He became one of my bigger fans.

* A few days after my session with James, I was walking across campus to the football field to watch the practice of the last period of the day when I was literally almost run over by a car with four senior girls in it, all drinking from Dixie cups. They did not see me. They continued into the parking lot and remained in the car, waiting for the school day to end.

I returned to the main building, found in which class they were supposed to be, went to that class, and asked the teacher where the four girls were. "I wonder that myself," he said.

I spoke not a word to anyone about the incident. Next morning I called over the school address system for the four girls to come to my office. Mrs. Giles asked why I was calling them. When I told her, she whispered with eyes wide, “One is a daughter of a longtime board member, and the other three are children of well-established families.”

She clearly was trying to keep me out of trouble by warning me to go easy. I nodded my understanding and appreciation.

When the four arrived, I asked them about their absence. They had no idea I had seen them the afternoon before. After some hemming and hawing, one offered that the home economics teacher had them on an errand. Without any further conversation, I handed them a paper that suspended them from school and all extracurricular activities for ten days, the longest time a principal can legally suspend a student from school without school board approval.

One uninitiated to ways of schooling may think suspending students from school because they had missed school is analogous to throwing Br’er Rabbit into the briar patch. However, a ten-day suspension meant they had to explain to their parents why they were out of school and they would miss all class work for ten days. Since their absence was unexcused, they could not make up grades they missed. As the suspension included extracurricular activities, they could not attend school functions.

As I thought he might, within fifteen minutes, Tommy called and said a board member had called him to ask what I thought I was doing suspending four seniors for ten days. I told him. He asked if I knew who the daddy of one of them was. I told him. He chuckled and said, “Well, one thing is for sure. You have taken care of any student problems for a long time.”

I had also taken care of any faculty problems before they got started. By my suspending seniors of prominent families, they knew I would back them one hundred percent against all comers *if* they were where they were supposed to be, doing what they were supposed to. For one of them, that small *if* was more than he could manage.

* Later that same fall during football homecoming week, three cheerleaders came into the office during the last period to ask if they could go to the field to decorate the goal posts. I asked them what class they were in. They told me and said the teacher had given them permission to ask me, saying to them, "Tell Mr. Willis I am not going to be doing anything today, anyway."

I told them to go ahead and walked down to the teacher's room. Sure enough, best I could tell neither he nor anyone else in the room were doing anything remotely resembling teaching or learning.

I asked him, "Did you tell your class you were not going to be doing anything that day?" He said he had. I told him, "If you are not going to be doing anything, you need to go home." It took a moment for him to understand I was not kidding and left.

I taught his class that period and docked the teacher one-sixth of one day's pay that month. The teacher had a well-earned reputation for being lazy. I got no blowback from anyone. More importantly, his teaching improved. Interestingly, he was the same teacher who had the four girls skip his class to go down town.

Everyone knew who was running the place.

* A principal routinely meeting with the school board was not practiced in any school of which I was familiar. Albeit, I met with the board routinely and remained in the room with the board, including executive sessions, except when my and Tommy's contracts were discussed. If they had a question about the high school, they asked me. I evaluated the high school faculty for them.

Author principal at Prairie Grove High School, standing by his office door, watching hall traffic.

Tommy and I would go over the board agenda in detail before the meetings. I cannot stress too much how unusual this practice was and how beneficial it was to my growth and understanding of how things work in a school and community. The board was eight white men.

The board evaluated me for contract renewal in the spring my first year and gave me a thousand-dollar raise, a seventeen-percent increase! It was the largest percentage raise without changing jobs I received forty-three years in the profession.

The next year, I had a conflict with a board member during a closed executive session. Stella Cash taught biology and was an excellent teacher, and biology teachers, much less excellent ones, were difficult to find. She became pregnant, and by second semester, her grow began to show.

A board member asked me to persuade her to resign. "She is becoming an embarrassment," he said.

I responded, "She is a married woman carrying her husband's child. I don't understand why someone is embarrassed."

The board member insisted, and a couple of others began to nod their silent support, until our conversation was becoming extended and warm. Tommy said nothing. Finally, I said, "I will do as you wish, if you make a motion for me to do that in open session and your motion is seconded and passed by the board."

As I expected, he refused. I never spoke of the incident to anyone, but the word got out. Mrs. Cash continued growing and teaching biology.

* Prairie Grove had a tradition of taking the graduating seniors to Washington, DC, and environs in the spring just before graduation. In 1967, the end of my first year as principal, Mary Ann and I went along. Football coach Ed Staggs and his wife Wanda, and another teacher couple, named Higgins, went also, six adults in all. The school chartered a bus with a professional driver.

We stopped our first night in Chattanooga, Tennessee, at a motel. Lo and behold! A dozen boys who had been my students at Lovington when juniors were there! They had graduated in 1967and were in Chattanooga to become orientated in a program to sell Bibles in Appalachia for the summer.

After they and I recovered from our total surprise, we had a grand reunion. The Prairie Grove seniors were very curious about my work at Lovington. Many stories were exchanged.

As we neared DC, we drove across Manassas National Battlefield Park. I had never visited the park, but recognized immediately the stone bridge over the creek, called *a run* in Virginia, and told the driver to park. Half the students, the two male teachers, Mary Ann, and the bus driver tromped over the battlefield with me as their enthusiastic guide.

When we returned to the bus after two hours, much displeasure toward me was shown by the students who had remained on the bus.

Before I had stopped the bus, they figured they would be at our motel in DC in time for a good swim and they were hot and irritated about being delayed. They were not in school and did not intend to learn anything. The students with me had such a good time that they began to tell the others what they had missed, and complainers got all right, or at least they shut up, which suited me just as well.

In DC, besides the museums on the mall, we toured the White House, Arlington National Cemetery, Ford's Theatre, and Mount Vernon. Ed and I raced up the steps to the top of the Washington Monument. I must not have won, as I do not recall who did

While there, some of the seniors skipped bed check and were out after curfew, albeit when we started back, everyone was on the bus, on time, and unhurt, if one does not include seriously hangover as being hurt.

For reasons I do not recall, the board decided to discontinue senior trips to DC after that one. They instituted a senior day, in which the seniors collectively decided where within a day's travel they wanted to go.

* On the DC trip, I coordinated everything through the chief of staff of John Paul Hammerschmidt, newly elected Republican representative. He did us a great job.

The next year's graduating class asked me to ask Congressman Hammerschmidt to be their graduation speaker. I called his chief of staff, expecting nothing to come of it, but he immediately knew who I was and said he would see what he could do. The congressman agreed to come.

The kids spread the word; local northwest Arkansas papers called me. Everyone assumed I knew a United States congressman. I smiled and remained silent.

On graduation night, I rose to introduce warmly Congressman Hammerschmidt. He went to the podium in front of graduating seniors, the faculty, and half the adult population of Prairie Grove and began his address with, "Thank you, Mr. *Lewis*."

* When Mary Ann, the boys, and I first arrived in Prairie Grove, we lived in a house rented to us by Rusty and Louise Woodward, the same couple living across the street from us in Lovington, who had moved by happenstance to Prairie Grove the previous year.

They had purchased a forty-thousand-chicken ranch located on the side of a mountain overlooking beautiful Prairie Grove Valley. They had a nice, large, stone house. On their land was a nice, smaller, stone house; it we rented.

The view was great; life was good. The fly in our buttermilk was I had to be in town both early and late. My schedule rarely fit Mary Ann's and the boys' schedules. After a year, we moved into town. We lived in three different houses, all within easy walking distance of the campus.

At our second house in town, two boys, approximately the same ages as my sons, came into the yard. Shortly afterward, Wes came inside and said, "I have to change my shirt." He quickly did and went back outside.

I looked out and saw Robb and the younger boy were fighting. The two boys had challenged Wes and Robb to a fight, not unlike dogs welcoming new ones to their neighborhood.

When Wes went back outside, he and the larger boy began to fight. I watched the four to make sure no one would be hurt. After rolling around on the ground, several blows were struck;

the two visiting boys had all they wanted of the Willis brothers and hauled out.

My sons came into the house with big grins. I asked Robb, "Why didn't you wait on your brother to change his shirt and help you?"

"I didn't have to change *my* shirt."

* In February 1965, while Don was in El Paso, Dr. Claude Babin, professor of history at Arkansas A&M, had become president and asked Don to join the faculty at the college. I was the first person Don told about the offer. Before Claude's offer, Don had called previously to say he had received a probable offer for more money at Odessa Junior College, at which he would not need a doctor's degree and avoided the expense of more graduate work.

Claude wanted an answer for his official offer, and the offer at Odessa remained probable. Don returned to Arkansas A&M that summer and began his PhD in history at the University of Mississippi at Oxford. When Mary Ann and I went to Monticello, we visited Don and Wanda. They visited us in Prairie Grove.

Two years later, on May 5, 1967, a beautiful Friday in late afternoon, I took a call at home from Dorothy Lynn, Mary Ann's sister-in-law, who was married to Curtis; the same who insisted he come and get us Christmas of 1963 in his log truck. Dorothy grew up with Don in the community of Enon.

She told me Don had been killed that day in an automobile accident. I was too numb to breathe and mumbled a thank you for calling. Dad called moments later; same news, same mumble.

Don was killed driving to Memphis to a meeting of history professors. He had a head cold and got some over-the-counter cold medicine. He went to sleep at the wheel south of Pine Bluff on what is today Highway 63 and drove into a tree. He died at the scene. I was a pallbearer at his funeral at the Enon church.

He had written me a letter of several pages from A&M three weeks before he was killed. It was full of campus and Drew Central gossip. He and Wanda were considering going to New York to meet some air force friends they had met in Germany to go to the World's Fair in Montreal. All his letters were so long, they occasionally arrived with postage due.

In the age of Enlightenment, Don would have been honored among the enlightened as a freethinker. He was not sure a deity existed; but if one did, he was certain it was not the one that woke up Abraham near Ur during Mesopotamia's Bronze Age.

Don's considered Christians atheists because they do not believe in any gods men have believed in since the dawn of religion, except their own, which is what all people do with their gods.

Looking back at my life, as one must when writing his self reflection, I realize the concept that doubting is thinking began in early conversations with my friend.

His family selected a military stone without a cross to mark his grave. He was the first man I loved, besides my father and grandfather. In 2011 he has been dead for forty-five years. I still miss him.

He had two daughters, Sonya, named by Don for a character in Tolstoy's *War and Peace*, and Bird, for Lady Bird Johnson.

* Two of my favorite teachers at Arkansas A&M were Claude Babin and Robert Kirchman. When Claude became president, he asked Robert to be dean. They asked me to visit with them while I was in Monticello for the funeral. At this visit, they offered me Don's vacant position. I was tempted, much tempted. There was a time in my life such offer would have epitomized the pinnacle

of my ambition. I seriously considered their offer before I turned them down.

I was in the middle of my administration certificate program. If I joined the Arkansas A&M faculty, I would have to get a PhD in history, probably from the University of Mississippi at Oxford. I had only been one year at Prairie Grove and did not want to leave Tommy, the students and faculty with another vacancy after one year.

Had I gone to Arkansas A&M, Mary Ann would not have had a job, and the best she could have gotten was another secretary position. My salary as professor at Arkansas A&M would be the same or less, probably less, than I would be making with my second contract as principal at Prairie Grove. Don had started at six thousand dollars, and Don said Claude had told him he had to stretch the budget to get him that amount. I had signed a seven-thousand-dollar contract for 1967-1968.

* I was building a good reputation among faculty of the College of Education at the University of Arkansas. The University of Arkansas did not have a PhD program in history. It looked as if school administration was my future, and my immediate future would be at Prairie Grove.

I knew I would never have the money to go further in a post-master's program, except to obtain a superintendent's certificate, which I could remaining home and finish by attending classes nights and summers at the University of Arkansas.

Tommy suspected I would be offered Don's job. When I returned to Prairie Grove, he asked me about it and seemed genuinely relieved I had turned Claude down.

My family and I loved Prairie Grove. I enjoyed my job; Mary Ann did hers. We were much a part of the community. My position as high school principal gave us community visibility and entry into the town's society. We were well received and well liked. Mary Ann, the boys and I had many friends.

A visiting school photographer took a picture of Wes and Robb standing together against the front hall wall in the elementary school. They had on blue jeans and jackets; shoes untied, jackets opened. Both had huge grins; Robert had a tooth or two missing. They had just come inside after a bout of hard playing after school and looked like it. It is another of my favorite pictures and hangs on the wall of my bedroom with other family pictures.

Prairie Grove had a football, a basketball, and a track team for boys. Girls had a basketball team composed of six girls playing half-court. (This was before Title IX.) I never missed an athletic event, home or away; we often attended as a family. I attended *all* student social events.

Author's boys standing next to the wall in the Prairie Grove Elementary, having come in from playing after school.

Author and wife Mary Ann at a Prairie Grove student dance.

We joined the Baptist church where I taught a Sunday school class for teenage boys. Mary Ann and I joined a bridge club and played regularly. The boys were active in the neighborhood and community activities. They joined a square dance group.

I was popular among the students and became close to some, with whom I have remained in touch over the years. Two of them got into trouble, and I had to deal sternly with them.

In my experience as a high school teacher and principal, I have seen a pattern: if the principal or teacher fairly, without rancor, punishes students, as adults they look back on it with appreciation.

One such student was Glenda. She was cheerleader captain, senior class president, student council president, National Honor

Society president, and girls' basketball team captain. As one may imagine, we were often together on some project or another and became friends.

In her senior year, she allowed some friends to cheat off her during an English final. I removed her from the honor society and prohibited her from going on the senior day. Probably, I hurt me more that than I did her.

After Glenda graduated, she went to Arkansas Tech University, married a Prairie Grove boy and became president of the school board as one of the first, if not the first female member, and she raised a family. She has remained in touch over the years.

Another was Stan. He showed up his junior year from California and was absolutely certain he knew more about everything than anyone in Arkansas knew about anything, especially people in a hamlet with the bucolic name of Prairie Grove.

It took a while, including a paddling, for him to find out he needed to rethink some ideas he had. Before I paddled him, I told him I would not administer the punishment until the next day and he should go home and think about it. He had a strong mother and stepfather who appreciated my efforts.

He was waiting for me at seven o'clock the next morning; he was a completely changed young man. That incident was the beginning of his turnaround. He played basketball and used his natural gifts of intelligence, leadership, and personality to become an important leader among students in the school and on the basketball team.

He married one of the prettiest girls in school and went to college in Texas and became an electrical engineer. He returned to Prairie Grove when he retired. He has remained in touch over the years.

* As at Lovington, some students at Prairie Grove were immune to my charms. One morning at seven o'clock, the postmaster called me and asked that I come to the post office to get the school's mail. This was an unusual request, and I asked him what the mail was. He said I had to see it. I knew the post office was not open until eight o'clock, but he insisted I come immediately.

When I got there, I saw painted in large neat green letters on the sidewalk in front of the post office: WILLIS EATS GREEN DONKEY DICKS.

When the postmaster saw I thought it was hilarious, he laughed too and said he would get rid of it before he opened. I thanked him and left. I never mentioned it to anyone and never heard more about it. He got rid of it by painting over it. Forty years later, the stain of the paint was still on the sidewalk.

When a bus driver was unable to drive and no substitute could be found, I drove a bus. One dark rainy morning, wearing my army poncho for protection from the weather, I crawled into the driver's seat of a bus that needed a driver and began its route.

As I began to drive, I noticed a stink. I drove to the end of the line, picked up the kids, returned to school, unloaded them and took the bus to the parking area. When I got up from the seat, I found the cause of the smell; I had been sitting in a sizeable pile of human excrement. Much of it was now on my poncho.

The rain had ceased. I took off my poncho, walked to my car, left it in the trunk, and returned to my office, never saying a word to anyone about it. I was puzzled.

Who was the target; the regular driver, a regular substitute, or I? How did the culprit know I would be driving? Human excrement is a personal message. A big pile of dog poop is the familiar excrement for this common practical joke. I never tried to find out more about it and never heard a whisper or saw a glance from anyone who may know about it.

* I had no thought of leaving Prairie Grove; however, my job had become so easy I was running on automatic pilot and had difficulty finding something to do. I still enjoyed being principal, but underneath my contentment, I began vaguely to recognize a familiar restlessness.

In January 1968, I was at the university registering for spring semester classes, sitting at a library table talking with some of my professors. Dr. Roy B. Allan, the Department of Educational Administration chairman, was sitting at an adjacent table. I did not know him well, but I was aware he was listening to my exchanges with my professors.

Out of the blue, he asked me if I did not think it was time to come on campus with them and get my doctorate. I was unaware I had previously thought about such a thing at all.

Professor Allan's department contained a division that gave a doctor of education degree in higher education. This degree, with my master's in history, would provide me the necessary academic credentials to teach history at a junior college or small four-year college, such as Arkansas A&M. The head of the division was Professor Donald Ray Miller, with whom I had established an enjoyable acquaintance in a previous course.

* On April 4, 1968, at 6:01 p.m., Martin Luther King Jr. was assassinated in a Memphis motel. I saw it on the evening news. I believe Dr. King led the largest most far-reaching, profound, *bloodless* societal transformation in the history of the United States. He was an eminent, great American whom I much admired.

Without talking to anyone, when I got to school the next morning, I took the school's United States flag outside, raised it to the top of the pole, and lowered it to half-mast.

Tommy called when he got to work and asked me about the flag. He was okay with it and was glad I had thought of it. Right after noon that day, Mrs. Giles told me a man had called to say he was coming to school with a gun and "shoot that nigger-loving, dumb, SOB principal." She told me the man's name. I did not know him. I asked her if he serious?

"He is serious about doing something; I don't think he will shoot you, but he sure does hate colored people," she responded.

I told her, "I have planned to go to the bus garage this afternoon. Tell anyone who comes to the office to see me where they can find me". I went to the bus garage to take care of whatever I needed to do. When I returned to the office, the man was not there and had not shown up. He never did.

Make no mistake; I did not remain at school because I was brave. I was decidedly not and never have been. I remained because I had put myself in a position where I had no choice. I had to assume others knew the man had threatened to kill me for honoring a black American. I could not suddenly decide I was ill and needed to go home and lock the door, or go sit with the superintendent in his office, or go out of town on school business. If I hid, the man and his cohorts would know I was not serious that the American flag should fly at half-mast for a black American.

The flag at Prairie Grove High School remained at half-mast until Dr. King's funeral.

* Previously that spring, I had written by hand a three-page letter, misspellings and all, to Arkansas Senator James William Fulbright, asking him to support a GI bill for the Cold War servicemen as the one Congress had passed for the World War II veterans.

I received a courteous, routine response from his office, providing no reason to believe my letter had any effect. That spring, the senator proposed and Congress passed the Cold War GI bill, for which I was eligible. I decided I could continue my education.

I had passed the Graduate Record Examinations with a sufficiently high score to qualify as a candidate in the doctorate program in higher education.

I told Tommy of my plans and resigned at a board meeting that April. I called a short assembly the next morning after the meeting and told the students and teachers of my decision. It was a complete surprise to them all. Many teachers expressed sincere sadness; some of the students wept. I expected nothing like this and was touched.

If Roy Allen had not been at the faculty table when I was and not said what he did, and if Senator Fulbright had not got the Cold War GI bill passed that same year, either of *which almost did not happen,* the rest of my life would have unfolded significantly differently.

If the bigot had shot me, the rest of my life would have unfolded differently; albeit I believe my being shot was not something that almost happened.

RESIDENCY AT UNIVERSITY OF ARKANSAS AT FAYETTEVILLE (1968-1970)

You cannot fully understand your own life without knowing and thinking beyond your own life, you own neighborhood, and even your own nation.
—Johnnetta B. Cole

Man is condemned to be free; because once thrown into the world, he is responsible for every thing he does.
—Jean-Paul Sartre

##

Professor Jack U. Williams, head of the Secondary Department, with whom I had a previous class, awarded me a teaching assistantship. After my contract ended at Prairie Grove, on June 30, 1968, I enrolled at the university the second summer semester.

That semester, I took Philosophy of Education with Professor Don Miller. The experience was better than I had expected, and I had expected it to be excellent. I presented in the class one day; my topic was existentialism. I selected this philosophy because I had not heard of it until I enrolled in the course and I was interested in knowing more.

After researching it, for probably one hundred hours over two weeks, I found existentialism put a name to and best explained my view of the world and my place in it, which made my presentation more articulate and passionate than the usual student class appearance. My fellow students had many questions, all of which I answered. I knew I had done well when my classmates spontaneously applauded when I finished.

* Existentialism does not attempt to objectively contemplate traditional philosophic questions; rather it seeks a passionate encounter with the perennial problems of life and, in particular, with the inevitability of death, the agony and joy of love, the reality of choice, the experience of freedom and the futility or fruitfulness of personal relationships.

Existentialism proposes that by itself the universe is without meaning or purpose. Man does not form part of a single cosmic design, because design is no more than a concept of mind, and the universe is indifferent to mind. If a man asks what his purpose is, he can as well ask what the purpose of a daffodil is. The purposes we think we detect in the universe are only a projection of our own desire for order.

Man is cast into an alien world, for which we are not especially created but within which we must die. Our *Angst* or "dread arises from our awareness of the "absurdity" of this condition that we are free and yet finite, in the world, yet not of the world, and withal condemned to death. Man who knows meaning must live and die is a world without meaning.

Existentialism emphasizes the individual's power to choose a purpose, a value system, while living in a purposeless universe. People are individually responsible for their lives because their lives are no more and no less than the consequences of their choices, all of which they freely make.

Clearly, people's power to choose is not to say they have the power always to choose what they want. For instance, they would not choose for their children to die or their love to be unrequited or their parents to divorce. Stuff happens; their choices often become not whether things happen; their choices *become* how these things that happen affect them.

However, among choices available to people, they shall select the choice they want. How can they do otherwise? Also, they cannot not choose. Choosing not to choose is a choice. They cannot blame their choice on someone else. If someone chooses for them, it is their choice to give up their choice.

No Exit is a play written in 1944 by Jean-Paul Sartre, leading French existentialist of the twentieth century (1905-1980), that clearly explains the impossibility of one escaping choice. Sartre was recognized as a leader among the existentialist philosophers in France between the wars. His experience in the French underground solidified his thinking about the existential emphasis on choice making.

Sartre was awarded the Nobel Prize in Literature in 1964. He refused it.

After World War II, in the Nuremberg trials for war crimes, the court would not accept being ordered to commit an atrocity by a superior as an excuse. It was still an individual's choice. Choosing their death was their alternative to killing innocent others. Their *choice* was to kill others.

I told the class that when we ask people to do something they do not want to, most of them excuse themselves explaining they do not have the time, money or space required to do what ever we asked them to do. But, everyone has some money and space; all have the same amount of time. What they mean, but do not admit, is they have made their choice to use their time, money and space for something more important to them than what they are being asked to do.

* The afternoon following my presentation that morning, Professor Miller stopped me on the stairwell to say, "You gave a brilliant performance and demonstrated many of the talents you

need to be a successful college professor." I have never before or since had my ears tickled so much by one person with one sentence at one time. I did not even try my "aw-shucks, 'tweren't nothing" ploy to maintain my reputation for humility, which was fast disappearing.

The most important thing he told me was he wanted to hire me as his graduate assistant. I told him, "I am Chairman Williams' teaching assistant."

He said, "I have talked to Jack. He told me I could hire you as long as you also remain his teaching assistant."

I suddenly had two graduate assistantships! No other student I knew had more than one; some had none. With Mary Ann's salary, the GI bill, and two graduate assistantships, more money was coming into the Willis house in Prairie Grove while I was a resident doctoral student at the University of Arkansas than when I was principal.

* Don's office was one in a three-office, windowless suite, with a central area for a secretary. Professor Martin W. Schoppmeyer was in another, and a student secretary, a work-study student, was in the central space for fifteen hours a week. I was in the third office.

Most graduate students were housed in large single rooms all together; consequently, often two or three were in my office for stories, jokes and gossip. After I had been with Don for a while, the dean told me Professor Miller had never had a graduate assistant before. "He had never found anyone he wanted."

Don Miller, a Jew, became one of the three most influential men in my life; the other two, as mentioned, were my father and his father. Each man's influence on me was different. Without either of the three, I would have become a decidedly different person in almost every important way.

* Some wag has observed, "We grow what we know." Coming of age in Drew County when I did, I grew into what I knew. I never met an educated black person, much less conversed with one; I had heard of Republicans, but had never laid eyes on one that I knew of. I was vaguely aware of people called Catholics and Jews, but what I heard of them was largely negative stereotypes, which I had to unlearn before I could know about them in any helpful way.

Prior knowledge influences future learning. If one's prior knowledge is filled with lies and misconceptions, future learning is poisoned. Erroneous beliefs are enormously difficult to change. One must know what one's misconceptions are and then *consciously*, *deliberately* work to correct them. I still find prejudices tucked around, scattered about and hidden among my character flaws.

Unlearning is more difficult than learning.

* Don helped me perceive I could learn differently. He helped my heart and mind become receptive to seeds of change, new thought and new way to see the world.

Haim Ginott, quoted above, presented a graphic word picture of the classic *tabula rasa* (blank slate) description of a child's mind offered by John Locke (1632-1704). Ginott said, "A child's mind is like wet cement; whatever falls on it leaves a permanent impression." If one continues this analogy; an adult mind would be like cement hardened into whatever has impressed it. I realized I needed to soften my hard cement.

With Don's guidance, I opened my mind to learning, to changing.

Don and I would often stay late into the evening talking alone and long about matters of the mind. From these conversations, I began to understand why and how I came to believe as I did and why and how I came to know what I thought I knew. He gently encouraged me to question everything and then question my questions.

When one becomes an adult, he can no longer believe his parents/ raising responsible for his thoughts and actions. By definition an adult alone is responsible for his thoughts and actions,

(When writing this last sentence, it occurred to me that I am unable to recall a single time I ever explained what I did be referencing my parents' influence or that of my childhood environment.)

I began to understand I believed as I did and what I did, not because it was true, but entirely and only because of where and when I came of age. If I had been born and raised in different circumstances, I would have believed differently. How differently would depended on how different the circumstances.

It takes no imagination to grasp this concept if one tries to think about it; I could as well be a Hindu as a Baptist. For instance, if Earl Willis had been born in 1914 in Bad Aibling, Germany, instead of Drew County, Arkansas, he would have been a soldier in Hitler's *Whermacht*, killing enemies of the fatherland, which included boys from Drew County.

In World War I, German soldiers went into combat with GOTT MIT UNS on their belt buckles, which means: "God is wirh us." God being on their side was a belief equally held by Germany's World War I enemies, namely, England, France, America, and the most Christian country in Europe in 1914, Russia.

The world is full of gods. Computation shows hundreds of religions have existed since homo-sapiens began to feel the need for a deity about 40,000 years ago when we first buried our dead with tools and weapons needed in the next life. In this accounting of religions, all of Christianity's denominations are counted as one religion among these hundreds. This number includes religions that are no longer practiced such as those of primitive, prehistoric and early cultures.

It is obvious each culture believes in its god(s), and these ancient faiths were as real and enduring as any today. Among the classical Greeks, who are revered today as the triumph of the rational mind, the Athenians expended a gigantic amount of their time, energy and money over fifteen years to build the iconic Parthenon to show their faith and dedication to Athena, Goddess of learning. The same my fifth grade student teacher said was not real.

Similar examples of faith and dedication are abundant throughout ancient human history. One must only observe the extent the ancient Egyptians went to preserve bodies for after life, the several huge pyramids in Meso-America, Native American structures in North America, Stonehenge structures in the British Islands. These cultures believed their deities real without an iota of doubt as surely as the most ardent of today's people believe theirs is.

From its beginnings as a small village of subsistence farmers in 10th Century B.C. until its demise in 5th Century A.D., Rome became the super power of the world. Its religion was borrowed mostly from the Greeks and was never central to their culture beyond holidays and ceremonies. If the U.S. had such history, the pilgrims would have had to arrive in 511, rather than 1620. We have hardly existed long enough to claim for our nation a manifest destiny, much less a manifest exceptionalism.

From the earliest religions to the current day, which deities people worship depends entirely on when, where and to whom they were born and in what culture they came of age

The single most profound, obvious, inescapable discovery of my reading was the inevitable fact that individuals of these *different* religions or philosophies believe the truths of their ways as surely as others believe the truths of their ways. My reading placed me in the throes of a new spiritual awareness. This was not an ordinary sort of epiphany. It changed the core of who I am.

This discovery was not aha! It was a slow passage of change, a digestion of this idea over years. It informed the remainder o my life. It informed the remainder o my life.. First, I was a nondenominational Protestant, and then a nondenominational Christian. In my mind, I continued threading around and through my doubts, until I could not ignore the obvious, unyielding truth. I became and remain a religious skeptic, which eased my tormented mind.

> *Hail, skeptic ease! When errors' waves are past,*
> *How sweet to reach thy tranquil port at last,*
> *And, gently rocked in undulating doubt,*
> *Smile at the sturdy winds which war without!*
>
> —Thomas Moore.

Once aware, one cannot become unaware.

My decision was slow, determined and visceral. I eventually realized if anything is sacred to me it is truth. What is sacred cannot be compromised. To do less than live as a skeptic, my life would be a lie. My conscience would not allow me to do that. Hypocrisy summons man's worst angels. Feeling morally superior is an unhealthy concept.

I especially enjoyed reading Lao-Tzu, Sixth Century B.C. Chinese philosopher, founder of the interesting Tao philosophy. It is followed today by hundreds of millions of Chinese.

If one defines atheism as believing there is not an anthropomorphic and personal deity—a theist deity, which is the literal meaning of atheism—I am an atheist. If one defines atheism as believing no deities of any sort exist, I am not an atheist. Thinking about religions in a broader sense, I prefer to identify myself as an agnostic secular *humanist*. Lao Tzu said, "I do not concern myself with gods and spirits either good or evil nor do I serve any."

Of the religions I have studied, the one I find most compatible to my thought is Hinduism. An important tenet of Hinduism is *all* religions are true, all of them no matter their name or beliefs. From the Hindu perspective, a Methodist is a Hindu. And in Hinduism, service to man is the most effective worship of all deities.

Also, while reading about Hinduism, I found my favorite religious concept: "It is as if God were on top of a mountain, and to its top are many paths. It is indeed a foolish man who goes to the other side of the mountain to tell those there, 'Come follow me; I have found *the* path to the top of the mountain.'"

A religion I read about was Methodism, whose Hindu compatible tenet is one with which I also agree: "Open minds, open hearts, and open doors." I enjoyed being part of the inclusivity of the Methodist church community in Monticello more than any other church with which I have associated.

Most religions have some rule similar to the Golden Rule that translates as "Harm not others." Among them only Jesus said, "Do unto others as you would have them do unto you." Only Jesus says, "*Do,*" take an action to help. His philosophy of actively loving others sets him apart.

The concept of truth being relative has never been a popular one among enlightened societies; they know *the* truth—the very knowledge, they believe makes them enlightened. Therefore, they are the least likely to think among themselves a heretofore unheard-of idea has merit and is worth being examined further; though, every idea today accepted as true was strange when first introduced.

The sophist philosopher Protagoras (circa 490-420 BC), living in Athens, wrote, "Man is the measure of all things." Prevailing western thought then held to the concept that truth was something objective in the universe, outside human influence. Athenians rejected his notion of truth being relative to the individual and charged him with heresy and impiety. He drowned in the sea while fleeing for his life to the colony of Sicily.

Two thousand years later, Shakespeare, without censorship and little notice, wrote, "There is nothing either good or bad but our thinking makes it so." (*Hamlet*, Act II, scene ii). Putting revolutionary words in the speech of actors playing fictional characters in script can better disguise subversive thought from a culture's sustaining society.

When Professor Don Miller arrived one morning, without any antecedents or conversation, he placed in my hand an old, rusty railroad spike that he had electronically gold-plated! I don't know why he gave it to me; I don't know where he got it; I don't know why he had it gold-plated; I don't know what its significance was to him. He never said anything about it. I am unaware of him giving anything at all to another student.

It is another item among my precious pieces of stuff.

Each day, when Dr. Miller saw me the first time, no matter whom he was with or what he was doing, he stopped and exclaimed, "James, my boy!"

* For Professor Williams, I taught each semester a senior class of students the semester before they began student teaching and I supervised four student teachers. The class was held in the old original Peabody Hall, which was mine alone. It was crowded with more than forty senior college students in a room hardly big enough for twenty-five. It was a great learning experience.

Once, I had to drive to Springdale High School, where one of my student teachers was assigned. I had to put him in my car and drive him back to the university. He could not stop saying the F-word in class, every time he became irritated or upset, which was frequently.

Previously, I had encouraged him to find another word to substitute for the queen mother of all curse words, but he continued to say it. He explained no other word could sufficiently express the profound depths of his feeling.

I told him, “Honest, observant, thoughtful youth occasionally want to say no to the world. Some may contemplate doing so by stripping naked, painting their favorite word on their forehead, and strolling through the town square.” His knowing smile and nod allowed me to believe he was not unfamiliar with such thought.

I continued, “You decided to say no to the world by using your favorite expression aloud in a class room,one of our world’s sacred places. You, therefore, must be prepared for the world to say no to you in return. And the world has done so by refusing you a teaching certificate.”

I told him he could reapply in one year. I do not know if he did. He was a smart, good-looking, personable young man who could have made a good teacher or be good at whatever he wanted to do.

* During my second year of residency, I frequently taught graduate classes for Professor Miller in his absence. When he first asked me to, I went through the same protestation as Old Testament prophets called by God to some awesome task: “I am unworthy; I am unworthy.”

He insisted I was worthy and that I must enter the room with confidence; if I did, no one would question my assuming his position. He was correct; the students took notes, joined into discussions and asked me questions as if I knew what I was doing. It was a thrilling learning experience for me and a confidence builder.

At the end of my first year, graduate students and faculty in the College of Education elected me president of University of Arkansas Phi Delta Kappa, an organization of professional educators.

* I took nine hours a semester, a full load in a doctoral program that allowed me to qualify for the assistantships and GI bill. At the end of my first semester, I took qualifying exams, which consisted of four questions. I had one hour to write on each of them. If I passed, I would be accepted as a doctoral candidate. These were not generic questions. They were developed by my professors on my graduate committee exclusively for me.

I was fortunate Professor Miller was my committee chair; he was a well-respected by his colleagues. In addition, I selected James Hudson, a World War II fighter pilot veteran and graduate dean, who had been my favorite professor in history and chaired my 1966 master's committee, and Jack Williams, chair of the Secondary Department, with whom I had a class and for whom I was a teaching assistant. I selected R. M. Roelfs, assistant dean of the College of Education and my favorite education professor, second to Professor Miller, and Martin Schoppmeyer, suite colleague, with whom I had a class. They graded my written responses and followed up with an oral session.

The oral session opened with Dr. Hudson, as visiting team member, invited by Chairman Miller to begin. He went to the board and freehandedly drew a nearly perfect outline of Italy. As I watched him, I began to think of all the questions he could ask about Italy, anything about the 1,500 years of Roman history, the Renaissance, Italy's unification—anything.

When he finished, he pitched me the chalk and told me, "Locate Anzio beachhead before the breakout, draw the winter line of 1943, locate Monte Casino, and thoroughly explain the situation facing the Fifth United States Army that winter."

I nearly laughed from decompression of tension. The question was easy. He told me later, we were probably the only two men in the room who could answer that question. I passed the orals and was assigned only three additional hours. The average number of hours assigned was nine. It was another successful milestone in my program and another confidence builder.

I wrote a dissertation prospectus that the committee evaluated with me and made what changes they felt would make it stronger. During this meeting, they challenged each other and disputed which changes to make, the kind of dialogue that passes for friendly conversation among academia. Professor Miller was a master at academic dialogue and helpful in these proceedings.

I discovered after I had completed my course work, I was only halfway through the program as far as energy and time expended on work was concerned; the dissertation was a large and important part of my degree. When I completed my dissertation, I defend it before my committee.

Afterward, each member shook my hand and said, "Congratulations, Doctor Willis." I had only to wait until graduation that spring to receive my diploma that read James William Willis, Ed.D, with emphasis in school administration and foundations.

That night, Professor Miller took me to dinner and we returned to campus to attend a lecture, presented by a nationally known physics professor, whose name I have forgotten. His first words were, "No one today can call himself educated who does not know fundamental concepts of physics."

The same day, five professors called me *Doctor Willis*; another stated confidently and publicly I was not educated. Dr. Miller leaned over and said, "James, my boy, I know nothing about physics." Whew!

During the process of obtaining my doctorate, I gathered enough hours to receive a superintendent's certificate, which would become important.

I graduated in May 1970 from the University of Arkansas. From May 1960, when I returned from Germany and reenrolled at Arkansas A&M, to May 1970, I had been in school as a student or teacher or principal every single semester: summer, winter, fall and spring. During that time I had not read a single book of fiction, except, as I mentioned, *Advise and Consent*, while waiting for Robert to be born. It was a political novel, from which a movie was made.

Other than a couple of weekly newsmagazines and daily newspapers, all my reading was history, averaging three books a week, plus material for my classes. Don Fleming had observed of me in a letter years before, "James, you are a self made slave."

* Other than within the relatively narrow confines of academia, I have never referred to myself or introduced myself as *Doctor Willis*, though some people, even in Monticello, call me *Doctor Willis*. I have learned to hesitate correcting them because I have not found a way without embarrassing them or their having to suffer through a laborious explanation that does not really interest them and may cause me to appear supercilious.

A story apropos to this subject made the rounds among my cohorts about a colleague who graduated with a doctorate and went to a community as a superintendent of schools. He was seen sitting with his wife in the stands at a little league game that summer and was persuaded to call balls and strikes. Several in the audience did not know who he was.

Two women were sitting behind his wife, and she heard one ask who was the man calling balls and strikes. The second explained he was Dr. So-and-So, the new superintendent. "Well," harrumphed the first woman, "he can't be a very good doctor if he has to take a job as a school teacher to get by."

* My best friend at the University of Arkansas at Fayetteville was Robert Skelton from Tahlequah, Oklahoma. He and I began our masters' in history together and remained friends through our masters and doctorial programs and continued after we graduated. We, with our wives, often visited in each other's homes.

After we graduated, Bob went to Southeast Missouri State University at Cape Girardeau to teach history and became the acknowledged History Department expert in Native American history. Though Bob was sandy haired and prone to freckles, his ancestors were among the Cherokees, whom Andrew Jackson had removed to Oklahoma from Georgia along the infamous Trail of Tears. He was officially listed as a member of the Cherokee tribe.

Bob was much in love with his vivacious, lovely wife Kathy, which did not keep her from leaving him, after he found her in his kitchen passionately kissing a Cape Girardeau insurance salesman.

When she left Bob, she took with her his only child, a precocious daughter. Kathy's sole explanation for leaving Bob was she liked the way the salesman smelled. Bob was not the same afterwards. He remarried a few times. Last time I saw him, he was retired and living on a farm in Missouri with a wife, who I expect is his last, as she loved him, and he was in bad health.

* In spring 1970, I was faced with the need for a job.

Tommy was moving from Prairie Grove to Eudora as superintendent of schools. I was approached by town people and faculty asking me to become his successor. I successfully discouraged that idea.

I took a call from a physician in Bastrop, Louisiana, who introduced himself as chairman of the board of the newly founded Bastrop Academy. He was ready to hire me sight unseen for twenty-five thousand dollars, considerably more dollars than any graduate I knew was being offered.

I asked him what did a private school offer children of Bastrop not offered by the public schools. He mumbled and stumbled a no answer.

I knew the Bastrop Academy was founded solely because of racial integration in Louisiana public schools and blacks would not be allowed in the private school. He denied that. It was easy to turn him down and his twenty-five thousand dollars. I did not consider it a moment.

* College teaching jobs were scarce in 1970. I applied to several colleges in a geographical area generally south of St. Louis and east of Dallas that offered master programs and to the University of Montana. I received no encouraging response.

After graduation, Arkansas State University at Jonesboro offered me the position of visiting lecturer for a summer semester, a job I was glad to get. I lived in a dorm, ate in the student cafeteria, and enjoyed teaching college. I also read my second fiction in eleven years, *Catch-22*, which I highly recommend.

One hot afternoon on the campus, without a job prospect on the horizon, I was playing tennis with some colleagues when the secretary from the dean's office approached me, after walking at least three hundred yards in the heat, to tell me I had a call from the dean of the College of Education at Eastern Kentucky University in Richmond. She said, "He wants to talk with you about a job."

This university was among those I contacted. I thanked her and asked for the dean's number, promising her I would call him back. She did not have his number; she explained, "He's waiting on the phone."

I exclaimed, "He's waiting for me on the phone?!"

"Yea, I think he really wants to talk to you," she responded.

With this news, I hurried ahead of her to the dean's office. After a few minutes of conversation, the dean said his office would pay my expenses to come for a look.

Before I went to Eastern Kentucky University, after my summer lecturer job ended and I had returned to Prairie Grove, the dean of the School of Education at Fort Hays State University at Hays, Kansas, called saying he wished to interview me, expenses paid. I agreed.

I had not contacted Fort Hays. They had contacted the University of Arkansas Placement Office, where my vita, with letters and transcript, were on file. As at Lovington, Prairie Grove, and the University of Arkansas, I knew not one person at either university or town and had never been there.

* Mary Ann and I drove to Richmond, visiting Abraham Lincoln's and Jefferson Davis's birthplaces on the way. Eastern Kentucky wanted to hire me to be principal of its teacher training high school. The salary was already acceptable, and when I interviewed with the president, he offered me an additional $2,500. I was impressed with the salary they offered and by their desire to hire me.

We returned to Prairie Grove overnight and drove to Hays, Kansas. On the way, we noticed biscuits and gravy was not a breakfast menu item at public eating establishments and wondered what part of America we were in. This was no small thing and consumed considerable conversation time between us. We suspected a Yankee plot. After we had been there a while, this suspicion grew because we began to notice people in Kansas were able to speak ill of others without first saying, "Bless their heart."

Fort Hays wanted to hire me as a regular faculty in its College of Education and for less salary than at Eastern Kentucky. We both liked Richmond better than Hays but I liked the job at Fort Hays more than the one at Eastern Kentucky. Being principal of a university school was too much like the job I already had, but without a community of support. I remembered Robert Kirchman at Arkansas A&M had advised me when I went to Lovington: "Go for the job; everything else will come." His advice made sense.

I signed the contract with Fort Hays, called Eastern Kentucky to say I was not coming, and returned home to Prairie Grove. The day I arrived, I received a call from the University of Montana!

The University of Montana is located in western Montana on the Pacific side of the Continental Divide, near Glacier National Park, a Mecca of mine I had not yet seen but was definitely on my list.

The dean of the College of Education offered me sight unseen the assistant dean's job, including the task to teach one three-hour course of my choice. If I had not signed a contract, I would have gone there gladly with the intention of taking the job.

If one has signed a contract to teach in one state, one may refuse to honor that contract and sign with another school in another state without any legal repercussions. I knew the dean knew this also. I was tempted, thanked him and regretfully declined.

The call from Fort Hays State University almost did not happen; if it had not, the rest of my life would have unfolded significantly differently.

If the University of Montana had called before I signed a contract with another university, which almost happened, my life would have unfolded significantly differently.

The University of Montana is the only road I chose not to go down in my forty-three years between leaving Monticello and returning, about which I still wonder from time to time. The long arm of coincidence that made so many important choices for me in my unplanned life failed to reach me in time from the University of Montana.

ON FACULTY AT FORT HAYS STATE UNIVERSITY, HAYS, KANSAS (1970-1972)

Your work is to discover the world and then with all
your heart give yourself to it.
—The Buddha.

##

Mary Ann and I returned to Hays without the boys to look for a house. We made the realtor rounds without success. A bank owned a new house and, for reasons I do not remember, if I ever knew, was willing to lend me one hundred percent, including down payment and closing cost to buy it.

It was a new house in a nice neighborhood and included three bedrooms, living room, dining room, kitchen, and a full basement, which most houses in Hays had. It was a block from the school both boys would attend. We came back to Prairie Grove, loaded another U-Haul trailer, hitched it behind the seven-year old Galaxie 500, and moved to Kansas.

The new house was void of any landscaping, and I took the opportunity to learn how to put in a yard. The experience was successful. Almost everyone in Hays had Bermuda grass. An old grass man talked me into putting in all fescue, Kentucky 31, Tall. It had to be planted very thickly, or it would clump.

I followed his directions, and it grew thick, lush and crowded Bermuda out of my neighbors' yards. On one side of us was an optometrist, and on the other side was the local television weatherman.

While we lived there, my cousin John, who lived with my grandparents when I did, his wife Lois and their son Mike stopped for a visit, returning from Estes Park, Colorado, on the way to their home in Springfield, Missouri, where John taught high school math.

* I went right to work. My classes were senior teacher preparation, student teaching supervision, and a graduate class in History of Education. As I was the new faculty member and not present when the schedule was made, I was assigned a late afternoon class, including Fridays. The schedule listed the teacher of this class as "Staff."

A late afternoon class, including Fridays, taught by "Staff" dissuaded students to the extent I had less than ten in the class. Most of them were in it because they did not get around to scheduling their class until more favorable choices for them were not available.

All went smoothly, until I assigned the students to present to the class a lesson they might expect to teach during their student teaching next semester. Alan Detrich made his presentation while his blood contained tetrahydrocannabinol, the active ingredient in the cannabis plant, otherwise known as marijuana or pot. Tetrahydrocannabinol is a muscle relaxer and a mild hallucinogenic. Alan had puffed enough that he was stoned out of his gourd.

Alan was an art major, a sculptor, and his lesson was how to prepare clay to form objects for the kiln. He began to knead the clay and tell us what he was doing. After a while, he fixated on the feel, smell and color of the clay oozing between his fingers and became lost in that thought and continued lost while his mind wondered among the labyrinth of the marijuana inspired.

I summarily dismissed the class and asked Alan to sit with me. We watched the video I had made of his presentation. What we were seeing was obvious to both of us. I made no judgment about his drugs and what he had done. However, I stressed on him that if he student taught while under the influence of even a common and harmless drug, which I agreed with him pot was, he would be taken out of student teaching and not allowed to obtain a teacher's certificate.

He said he understood what I was saying. I wondered how long his understanding me would stick.

It stuck. He came to my office Monday morning and asked to redo his presentation. I also carefully supervised his successful student teaching, during which we continued to talk. He finished the class in good order. He mentioned more than once how much he appreciated my not judging him.

He continued to remain free of drugs except pot, and his consumption of it he cut way down. He had been a die-hard druggie. He started on LSD as a freshman at Wichita State University, where he was introduced to it by a high school friend! He never paid a great deal of attention to pot; he smoked it and enjoyed it but did not consider it a real drug. He equated puffing pot to downing a cold brewsky.

Alan was successful in his student teaching, though he did not enjoy teaching. He returned to Fort Hays and obtained his master's degree in art. We talked almost daily, and he visited in my home frequently, including Thanksgiving, and New Year's, to eat black-eyed peas, which were mostly purple hulls with a few black eyes in the pot for luck.

It was interesting to have him around. His is the most creative and interesting mind I have encountered. He was twenty-one years old when I first met him. When we visited in summer 2009, he recalled our early relationship and told me I was his first real friend.

Alan has given me four of his art pieces. Three of them he created while he was gaining his three degrees in art. The first was his piece for his bachelor degree in art; the second was the piece for his master's degree. It is quite an honor to be given art pieces by students for which they have been awarded degrees. The third one is among several he did for his master's degree in fine arts at Wichita State. He told me to pick the one I fancied.

I much regret that I broke the first piece he had given me, which was done in ceramic; it was a wise man on a donkey that he said he had made for me especially.

During his master's, he began using the method known in the art world as the *Lost Egyptian* or the *Lost African Process*. It was a process practiced by the ancients to make three-dimensional figures from bronze; the method had only recently been rediscovered by modern artists. The piece for his master's degree he gave me had been done with that process.

It is one of the, if not the, strangest art objects, or any object, I have seen. I asked him what he called it. "*Synapse*," he said.

I asked, "Is this *Synapse* the same one that carries messages between nerve endings?" He nodded, seemingly pleased and a little surprised, I knew such things.

His *Synapse* is on roller skates. I asked him, "How do you know what a synapse looks like?"

He said without any shade of tone or demeanor or affectation whatsoever, "When I was in my stomach, I saw one."

Guests visiting my home ask about *Synapse*. The thing I like most about it is it contains Alan's finger prints in bronze because of the method used to make it.

He used the Lost Egyptian Process, which is fascinating and much more intricately difficult than my telling about it would make it seem. The artist molds the piece with a special artist's wax and places it into a hollow container, such as a coffee can, into which a plaster of paris-like substance is poured, filling up the space surrounding the wax figure with liquid plaster. When it dries, the artist puts the whole thing into the kiln. The heat melts the wax and leaves the form of the object molded. The artist then fills this hollow space with liquid bronze; it becomes hardened into a solid in the shape of the space left by the melted wax.

Alan's *Synapse* has long skinny fingers and toes, legs, feet, a tail, and teeth, all intricately made and delicately fired. It contains his finger prints where he formed the wax. He was among the first to practice at Fort Hays State University successfully the Lost Egyptian Process.

Synapse sits atop my antique grandfather clock and observes its domain.

Alan owned an antique store in Great Bend, Kansas. By the time he graduated with his master's degree in fine arts, both his parents were dead, and he took up full ownership of the store. In 1980, a picture of his store was on the cover of the Sunday magazine of the *Hutchinson News*, a daily paper covering western Kansas. Since 1980, it has hung, framed, in my house. In 2009, I discovered Alan did not have a copy, and sent him mine.

He specialized in what is known among antique folk as *primitives*, one-of-a-kind antiques, often made by earnest working men, for whom talent of the craftsman was not a priority. Interestingly, those were the antiques I liked best because they were objects I was familiar with from my childhood, they were comparatively cheap, and no two were alike.

While he owned this store for sixteen years, he stayed at the Travellodge hotel across the street from his store for two hundred dollars a month, which included utilities, maid service, and coffee. He also successfully speculated in oil in Great Bend.

While a student at Fort Hays State University, Alan lived in the most humble of conditions in a concrete-block single-story apartment house. If these were not the least expensive apartments in Hays, I knew of none as cheap. In one small room and a tiny three-quarter bath, he had a cotton mattress on the concrete floor, blankets, a hot plate, and a small refrigerator. He had no telephone, no television, no radio, no newspapers and few books.

He prepared his art pieces for the kiln sitting Buddha-like on his floor, always smiling. The single word that defines Alan, if there is such a thing as a single word to describe a person, is *smiling*. I have seen him disappointed, distressed, depressed, sad and broke. I have never seen him angry, revengeful, jealous or not smiling

When Alan had his antique store, he would let his younger brother or some temporary employee greet customers and answer the phone, while he traveled around rural Kansas in his old pickup and knocked on doors to get permission to look in barns, garages, attics or fields.

If he found something he thought he could sell, he asked the owners what they would take for it. Whatever amount they said, no matter how large or small, Alan would hold out cash money and offer the owner exactly half. He never offered more, never less; he never bargained. Almost everyone took his cash offer.

He credited me for getting him off drugs. I asked what made him stop taking LSD, as he had quit that before he met me. He said he was tripping, alone, while sitting in a chair; suddenly he flew out of the chair and into the sky, flying faster and faster, farther and farther.

He neared a hole in the sky. To keep from going through it, he put out his hands and feet and braced himself on the outside of the hole against the force that was trying to pull him in and looked through it. He said what he saw was the most frightening moment in his life.

He knew if he went through the hole, he could never come back. He increased his efforts not to be pulled through. As suddenly as the episode had begun, he began to fall back toward his chair, faster and faster. Suddenly, he was in his chair and all was as it had been. He swore off LSD, never engaged again, and never wanted to.

I looked at him with an inquisitive expression silently asking, “What did you see?” He understood my expression and shook his head. I never inquired again; he never told me.

I tried to persuade him I had nothing to do with getting him off drugs, and his own story proves he got himself off drugs. He said I helped him stay off all drugs and cut down on pot.

At Murray State University I puffed a little pot. It was remarkably easy to procure, and I was curious; I had long before decided that I wanted to experience everything in my world as long as it is not harmful or dangerous. I believed then, as I believe now, wisdom is the paramount virtue and one cannot be both wise and inexperienced. I did not want to live a life that was ten yards wide and thousand yards long.

I have never seen or heard of someone high on pot wanting to fight, curse, argue, talk loud, throw things or throw up. People are attracted to what makes us laugh; weed is *the* social drug. No one ever, anywhere, has overdosed on pot.

Tommy Robinson is Aunt Artie’s son, therefore my first cousin. I spent a few days in Houston where Tommy was a bartender and knew that scene. While there, driven by the same curiosity with which I had smoked pot, I snorted some cocaine. This experience frightened me so much I have not touched it since.

It scared me because it provided me the greatest euphoria, rapture, ecstasy, bliss, pleasure, and happiness I ever imagined. I realized it could too easily become a powerful habit, one expensive to maintain. I could imagine my becoming like vampires who are too weak to resist human blood once they taste it. The experience ends badly for all involved.

(Cousin Tommy died decades ago; I liked him a lot. He was natural.)

I think my limited drug experience helped me relate to Alan.

A few years ago, a portion of Alan's work was put on permanent display at the Museum of Art in Vienna, Austria, where he also taught classes.

With the Museum's Director, Alan was touring the Schatzkammer, where Austria's treasures are housed, including the Holy Lance that, according to the Book of John, was used to pierce the side of the Christ while he was on the cross. A myth grew that who ever possessed the lance was invincible. Hitler demanded it.

Alan wanted to go out on Hitler's balcony where the German leader had addressed the Austrian people after Germany annexed Austria. The balcony was closed and guarded. Alan tried to persuade the Director to allow him to go on to the balcony.

Alan said the director told him, "I can show you something you will like more than the Hitler balcony."

He led Alan into a tiny, windowless, padlocked room, <u>below</u> the basement of the museum secured by an armed guard. The Director unlocked the door, which opened to narrow, wooden stairs down into a small single room lit by a single naked bulb hanging from a wire, turned on by a string. The only item in the tiny room was enclosed in a glass case on the wall. In the case was what the Austrians believe is the real Holy Lance.

When Hitler demanded the Holy Lance, the Austrians gave him the one displayed in the Schatzkammer. After the war, they claimed the spear they gave Hitler was a fake. The real one was where it is today. Whether it is authentic is unimportant to Alan, nor was how it looked. The existence of the idea of such thing was sufficient to get his creative juices going.

The fourth piece he gave me was in 2009; it is his interpretation of the Holy Lance. It is a twenty-eight-inch dark bronze spear tip, with liquid gold dripped on it to represent the blood of Christ. It is fastened into a six-by-six-by-four-inch, solid block of exquisite, pure, Chinese jade. The piece weighs twenty pounds. It is beautiful.

It sits in the encased opening between my kitchen and living room. The piece from his Masters of Fine Arts I have on an antique cherry table in my entry hall. Another thing he gave me a few years ago is a five-inch tooth from a forty-foot shark that lived in South Carolina twenty-five million years ago. It sits on a shelf in my library.

Alan evolved from a three-dimensional artist to a paleontologist, by which he has been financially successful. I am talking multi-millionaire successful. In North Dakota, he found and dug the most complete T-rex ever discovered. The head is unblemished, totally complete. He constructed the skeleton and sold it for more than eight million dollars to a Japanese businessman.

He also dug and constructed the largest fish fossil found in Kansas. At the annual paleontology action in Las Vegas, it sold for $475,000, the most paid ever for a Kansas fossil.

In 2009, he gave me a piece of 165,000,000-year-old coprolite (fossilized dung), an exact identical replica molded from the tooth of a 65,000,000-year-old tyrannosaurs, and a vertebra. These items I have displayed among my important stuff.

Alan Detrich with his Tyrannosaur.

At the end of April last year, he sent me another coprolite with fossilized fish in it.

Alan was selected by the *People* magazine in 2001 as one of the fifty most eligible bachelors in America. The magazine's layout included pictures of each of the men selected. Alan's picture was taken through the eye socket of skull of a dinosaur he had recently dug.

Among other *People* magazine's fifty most eligible bachelors in 2001 were Matt Damon, Ben Affleck, Benicio del Toro, Bill Hemmer, Russell Crowe and Tiger Woods.

The article's journalist wrote in caps, "HE IS HARD TO MISS." She then added, "'When I moved to Great Bend, I didn't know anyone,' says pal Holly Friend, 45, a homemaker. 'It didn't take long to figure out that Alan was the funnest guy in town.'"

Alan is a true friend of forty-one years. Except for high school acquaintances, he is the oldest friend I have.

Alan being in my Friday afternoon class almost did not happen. If it had not, the rest of my life would have been significantly differently—significantly less.

Boys behind house in Hays, Kansas.

* During the Christmas holiday of 1970, Mary Ann, the boys, and I spent some time in Prairie Grove to visit friends. This occasion allowed me to visit with Don Miller. He insisted on taking Mary Ann and me to dinner. After I took her back to Prairie Grove, I returned to the Fayetteville campus and visited with Don until day was breaking, though we did not know that in his office without windows.

As I was pulling away from the parking lot, Don came out of the building, wearing his familiar raincoat and carrying a bumbershoot, which is what he, without the slightest affectation, called an umbrella. He was smoking his ever-present cigar; took it out of his mouth; smiled that warm, special smile he had; and waved me good-bye.

In Hays, on Wednesday night, March 17, 1971, I dreamed in brilliant, startling color of Don Miller. He was leaving the University of Arkansas education building and waved me good-bye exactly as he had that morning three months before—exactly: raincoat, bumbershoot, cigar, smile, and waving goodbye. I even saw his shoes in my dream.

The next morning, I went to the campus and taught my scheduled class but could not suppress the urge to call Don. I felt I absolutely had to do it, as if a spiritual force had taken my brain and animated my body. I left the campus to drive home, absenting myself during my office hours, something I had never before done.

When I arrived home, Mary Ann was surprised; she looked at my face and asked, "What is wrong?"

"I have to call Dr. Miller," I responded.

He answered immediately, happily exclaiming, "James, my boy!"

Before either of us could say another word, it sounded as if he had dropped his phone. After a few moments, someone said, "I'm sorry. We have trouble here." I heard a dial tone.

I waited a couple of minutes and telephoned him again; no answer. I called the dean's office; a secretary whom I knew well answered. I told her of my experience while talking to Don and asked her what had happened.

Instead of telling me what happened, she excitedly asked, “Was that you talking to Dr. Miller? Was that you talking to him?”

“Yes,” I responded.

“He died while talking to you,” she exclaimed!

While still holding the phone, she began repeatedly to yell, “Dr. Miller was talking to James Willis when he died.” She knew those who heard would appreciate the irony; the faculty and students knew that Don and I had a special relationship.

Don had suffered a heart attack. He was forty-five. He was telling me goodbye in my dream that morning; the dream that caused—compelled—me to call him the instant he died. His dying, last words to me had been his first to me when he was alive: “James, my boy!”

The funeral was at three o’clock on a beautiful Sunday afternoon of the 1971 spring equinox, in Osceola, Missouri, with a population of 900. I and five other graduate students, each my colleague and friend, were pallbearers. The father of Don’s wife Mary Lou owned the mortuary that provided the ceremony.

He granted to his son-in-law a solid copper casket that was so heavy we six grown, healthy men staggered under its weight.

Afterward, we swapped Miller stories well into the evening. Thinking about Don, we realized we had never heard him ask anyone why. He did not judge nor ask others to explain or justify themselves.

Dr. Donald Ray Miller was the man I most wanted to emulate in the university classroom. Sometimes when I was teaching, I would see in my mind’s eye Don doing it the same way. His picture hangs near me at eye level when I am in my chair. He often asked me to call him Don. I never did. He finally gave up. I’m glad I did not.

Professor Donald Miller in his office where he died while talking on the phone to author

* A few days after returning to Hays, we received a card from Mary Lou. It read in part, “My Dears, How very pleased Don would have been for your show of devotion to him—your long trip, leaving the boys, traveling old Highway Thirteen, staying at the Commercial Hotel, your lovely flowers, and taking part in the service.”

Osceola is one of those iconic southern towns that time has forgotten. Mary Ann and I stayed at the Commercial Hotel, a two-story stone building, more than 100 years old in 1971; the brothers James and Younger stayed there on occasions. Harry and Bess Truman ate at the restaurant, while passing through when he was president.

The Commercial Hotel had thirty guest rooms. The fire escape of those on the second story, where we had a room, was a large knotted rope coiled by the window and fastened to a rung bolted to the floor below the window.

On a cold rainy Sunday in May 2009, I passed through Osceola on my way to Lawrence, Kansas, to visit Alan. I looked for a while for Don's grave but did not find it. The hotel is closed now, with a for sale sign on the locked door.

* My best friend at Fort Hays State University was Dick Baker, a colleague. He had played quarterback for Kearny State College, a D-2 college in Nebraska, and had been a public school teacher and high school principal. He was a tall, intelligent, handsome, charming easy-going man.

He and I sought each other's company and visited schools together to supervise student teachers. He always drove to the school. I drove back, being sure to stop at the first place that sold cold beer. Dick would buy enough beer he thought he needed to get back to campus. He measured the length of our trips by number of beers it would take him to return. "This will be a three-beer trip," he might say, which translated as about 60 miles.

A student teacher whom I was supervising was not progressing well. I was doing all I could to help her, but she did not improve. I told Dick about her behavior and her seeming inability to follow any of my suggestions and asked him what he thought I was doing wrong.

He asked, "If she had not graduated from college and was unable to follow your directions, what would you think is her problem?"

"She would have to be pretty stupid," I responded.

He smiled, enjoying watching me begin to understand what I had said, and asked, "What makes you think she isn't?"

I thought about that conversation years afterwards when someone asked me, "What do you call a person who graduated last in his class from the worst medical school in the world?"

"I don't know," I answered

"Doctor," the man said.

Dick was a quail hunter and trained bird-dogs. Men brought their dogs to him. He trained them so that they responded to hand signals only. He never spoke to the dog while hunting. He never punished his dogs or raised his voice. His dog was a Weimaraner.

For several years, I had quit wanting to kill anything and had not enjoyed hunting. Albeit, I went with Dick occasionally to watch his dogs and be out on the Kansas or Nebraska prairies early on a frosty morning. I understood why someone could be a fan.

Perhaps the funniest thing I have ever seen occurred while I was with Dick. We were on the way to the student union for morning coffee and stopped at the second-floor restroom in our building. I was at a urinal, Dick was in a booth. Suddenly he yelled and began cursing and bumping against the booth's walls. He began to struggle to get the door open. When he did, he fell outside on the floor, pants down, and began scooting along the floor, pointing back at the commode yelling and cursing incoherently.

Running out into the room was the strangest-looking creature I had ever seen. After a moment, I realized it was a soaking-wet squirrel. The nearly drowned rodent had crawled up the sewer pipe and emerged on the second floor into the commode between Dick's legs.

Trust me. This was funny. I said it was the funniest thing I have ever seen, not the funniest story I have ever heard._One had to be there to experience the full effect.

Mary Ann and I visited with him and his pleasant wife Mary in each other's homes, sometimes for dinner. They had a beautiful daughter. In spring 1972, in her senior year of high school, a stranger took her to an isolated place at a nearby lake, where he tortured, raped and killed her.

Several days passed before her body was found. When the man was caught, Dick recognized him as one he had seen a few times, before his daughter was killed, riding by their house on a bicycle.

After his daughter's death, Dick became tormented by the thought what if he had questioned the man or called the police. The death of his and Mary's daughter and its circumstances drove them apart; they divorced.

When he walked, melancholy dripped from him. Dick took a year's sabbatical, much of it in Wyoming, a lot of that time alone in a tent in the mountains. He returned to Fort Hays State University and continued teaching.

I passed through Hays in the early nineties with my third wife Marilyn. I called Dick; he met us at a restaurant, and we had a nice visit. After fifteen years, depression and melancholy were still upon him, though sitting more lightly.

Besides my undergraduate courses in teacher preparation, I taught graduate classes at night, one History of US Education, the other was named The Junior College.

When writing this story of my life, I ran across a forty year-old letter of a student in a class titled the Junior College from which I learned I taught my second semester at night at Cloud Community College in Concordia, Kansas. It was written after the class was over, addressed to Ralph Huffman, Director of Field Services. I recall nothing about the college, the class or the student named August M. Bohm. A part of his letter follows.

As a part of personal philosophy I have subscribed to the wisdom of an old sage who maintained that the mind could not absorb any more than the seat could endure. Now it appears that I must modify my philosophy.

At the beginning of our extension class in the Junior College under Dr. James Willis we agreed, somewhat reluctantly, to take it in a solid two and one half hour stretch with no rest period whatsoever. Since I find that chairs get pretty hard after one hour, I entertained misgivings regarding the two and a half hour bit, but then a funny thing happened.

After our first class session my apprehension disappeared because I re-discovered that when the mind is challenged and put to work the rest of the anatomy adjust accordingly. It is fun to think and all of us were challenged to thought provoking tasks. As a matter of fact, this course has been one of the most enjoyable I have ever taken. Furthermore, my sentiment expresses those of the class. Dr. Willis is an interesting, well informed, creative instructor who is not afraid to search for meaning.

Mr. Bohm asked that Fort Hays bring the second course Junior College Curriculum the following spring, ending with, "We request Dr. Willis as the instructor." I have no memory of teaching that class, but I probably did.

* During the first semester of my second year, I was in Dick's office when he took a call from the Kansas State Department of Education asking him to be a member of the North Central Association visiting team for a two-day visit to Phillipsburg, Kansas, to evaluate the high school.

He did not want to go but felt he should. He put his hand over the receiver and asked me if I wanted to go. I said yes. (While principal at Prairie Grove, I served on the North Central Association team visiting Harrison High School and attended the national meeting in Chicago, where ironically I served on the national committee to approve Kansas schools.) My agreeing to go satisfied Dick's obligation to the man on the phone.

Chair of the visiting team was Dr. Richard Mosier, president of Colby Community College, one hundred miles west of Fort Hays. During our meeting with the school board at the end of the first day, I asked them about several incongruities I had discovered. Some of the members became upset.

After our team meeting with the board, we returned to our meeting room, where a member of the visiting team, a superintendent of another school, took me strenuously to task in front of the team for embarrassing the school board.

I replied, "I did not embarrass the board. They were not embarrassed because of my questions. They were embarrassed because they could not answer them."

After I responded, the rest of the team spoke in agreement with me. The superintendent member agreed also. He, the team and I had no more problems among ourselves.

The superintendent came to Fort Hays State University the next week to tell my department chairman of the incident and what a great professor he thought I was. He said, "It just had never occurred to me the real reason the board was embarrassed. If they could have answered Professor Willis's questions, they would have been pleased."

* The visit to Phillipsburg was in fall 1971. In spring 1972, Richard Mosier called me from Colby to say he had been named president of Claremore Junior College in Claremore, Oklahoma, and wanted to talk to me about going with him as dean of instruction. He asked me if I would agree to drive to Colby and talk with him.

Claremore Junior College was originally the Oklahoma Military Academy. Founded in 1919, the Oklahoma Military Academy was a school with a long and proud history with several prominent graduates, who were officers in the army, some of them general officers.

Dick called me solely on his impression of my performance on the visiting team he chaired. Before that visit, he and I had never met or knew of each other. I drove to Colby. Richard offered me the job. I accepted. I called Dad and Mother that night in Little Rock to tell them that I was going to be dean of instruction at Claremore Junior College.

As with Lovington, University of Arkansas at Fayetteville, Prairie Grove, Arkansas State University, and Fort Hays State University, I knew not one person in Claremore and had never been there—another road I had never traveled.

My being in Dick Baker's office when he received the call from the Kansas Department of Education to go to Phillipsburg as part of the North Central Association team almost did not happen. If either had not, my life would have unfolded significantly differently.

DEAN OF INSTRUCTION, CLAREMORE JUNIOR COLLEGE, OKLAHOMA

(1972-1975)

I've never been to Heaven
But I've been to Oklahoma.
—Lines of a 1972 C&W song

##

Days before our move, Wes and Robb went about their day frequently singing the song above. We had acquired enough stuff that this move required a U-Haul truck, albeit a small one.

Oklahoma was not heavenly, but Claremore, about thirty miles northeast of Tulsa, was pretty, and especially the college campus was beautiful. It set among trees on a hill overlooking the town to the east, the full length of Main Street.

We moved into one of the houses for officers when it was Oklahoma Military Academy. Our backyard had, honest to God, real trees, unlike Kansas, and overlooked the college lake. I put in a small garden. Claremore is the hometown of Will Rogers. His memorial and museum were across the highway from our house on campus. Maybe we were in heaven.

We thought we had possibly made our last move.

* Albeit, at Claremore Junior College, right away I was in trouble. In 1971, when the legislature changed Oklahoma Military Academy to Claremore Junior College, it formed a new board that reasonably believed to change the goals of the institution from a military academy to a community college, faculty changes had to be made. The board told President Mosier to get rid of several of the instructors who were holdovers from the school's military period.

As often happens in these kinds of personnel situations, when Richard acted as the board directed, faculty became angry and hired lawyers, which caused the board to believe the new president did not do what they had told him. The board believed they had told him to fire longtime faculty without making any of them or their friends in the least upset. Our problem was exacerbated by Mosier bringing some faculty to Claremore from Colby Community College.

I was academic dean of the college and responsible for faculty; therefore, I had problems originating from above and below. I put in place a faculty evaluation procedure as required by the board and president. Junior college teachers consider themselves as college professors and did not take kindly to being evaluated. Some good teachers were on the faculty, and we made it through it all, but it was difficult and, therefore, a learning experience.

In the meantime, I had discovered at Claremore several Junior College faculty were immune to my charms.

(Claremore Junior College evolved into Rogers State College, a four year school. It is today Rogers State University.)

* The most interesting and fun experience I had in Claremore was with the community theater. The play was *The Death and Life of Sneaky Fitch*. It is set in the Wild West, about a no-account, cowardly bum who thinks he has died, as do the townspeople.

Just before they laid him to rest, he "woke up" in his coffin to the surprise of all.

Sneaky and the townspeople believe he has returned from the dead and is, therefore, immortal. His immortality makes him fearless, and he becomes a town-taming gunfighter, killing bad men in the streets and loving dance hall floozies and assorted other fallen women. It's a story that lends itself to broad humor. I played Sneaky Fitch.

Author as Sneaky Fitch with saloon girl.

It was a dinner theater that ran much of the summer of 1974. Wes had a part in it. Fun was had by all.

* Mary Ann and I bought a new home on the same street as the high school. We were able to pick colors and materials for the house. I had the contractor put in an all-black, three-quarter bathtub in the master bathroom. Everything had the same color of shiny black.

People who visited described it as "interesting," "different," and "just like you." If I had been listening, I would have known they were telling me that when we sold the house, an all-black bathroom would be a drawback. All I was interested in at the time was I wanted an all-black bathroom. Being only interested in what I wanted has been a reoccurring theme in my life that has rarely been helpful to me, especially when I got what I wanted.

* My next door neighbor wrote a gun-and-rod column for the *Tulsa World*. During dove season, he went with a hunting party for a weekend to Nebraska to hunt these birds, an adventure about which he planned to write in his column.

During his absence, Robert and the man's son of like age killed five doves in a field behind our house with 22 rifles. Robert killed one on the wing with his .22. The columnist did not kill a single bird; he decided the boys killing five doves in their backyard and Robert's wing shot was the better hunting story. He wrote his column about their exploits.

When I was about Robert's age, I killed a dragonfly on the wing with my BB gun. My feat did not mean anything except I had a great story I could not tell because no one would believe me and I could never duplicate it. Robert may not have been able to repeat his shot, but he had a witness and made the paper.

* Mary Ann and I divorced in summer 1974. I loaded a larger U-Haul truck with all our stuff and drove it to Little Rock, where my parents lived and where she and the boys would live.

As I pulled away from our house, the song playing on the truck's radio was "Mary Ann," sung in its original calypso style:

All day, all night, Miss Mary Ann,
Down by the seaside, she sifting sand.

Author, Dean of Claremore Junior College, 1973]

Author, Dean of CJC with members of Student Council.

Perhaps thinking optimism triumphs over experience, or more probably not thinking at all, I have been married five times to five different women. With the exception of Mary Ann, my other four wives had previous husbands before I married them, nine previous husbands in all. One had married the same man twice. Since our divorces, four ex-wives have added six husbands for a total of fifteen among my ex-wives.

Marriages of couples who lived happily ever after were not normal among people with whom I lived after I had left Monticello in 1962; divorce was.

Albeit, I have paid little heed to societal convention in my life. Therefore, I cannot say my marital history was influenced by the populace among which I resided.

Each wife and marriage was different and each union contained its own unique tension and contentment. I have succeeded in never speaking a discouraging word about any of my ex-wives, which has been easy, as each had many excellent qualities.

As a child, I believed the biblical account of a woman being made from Adam's rib. Feeling my rib cage, I thought one side had one less rib, confirming God had taken it to make *the* woman for me. Psychology tells us as many as forty thousand people have the qualities that would allow a specific individual to fall in love with them. A man and women made only for each other is a myth.

I have found it unhelpful and unhealthy to revisit causes for a divorce or to place blame. Placing blame for a divorce is like continuing to scratch the scab off a healing wound; it never heals. Certainly, a grudge has no healing power. Holding a grudge is like drinking poison alone while waiting for the object of your grudge to die.

If one wishes to analyze the cause of things, one begins with their common variable. Among my marriages, I am the common variable.

Repeating behavior and expecting a different outcome is a mild form of insanity. I did exactly that. I repeated a pattern without knowing what the flaw was or wherein it lay. I knew grounds for self-destruction can be found on the path that makes the same series of false moves that invariably lead to the same disaster. I did it anyway.

Often in relationships, we perceive within ourselves a cycle of repetitive activity, which is certain to end in paralysis of the will, or we continue loving those who have ceased to love us, those who have lost all resemblance to the beings whom we once loved!

I obviously missed the bit of wisdom that observes, "If first you do not succeed, try, try something different."

Each time I married, I was as surely in love with my wife as has been any man who marries and lives with his wife until death parts them. If my life were a character in a Shakespearean tragedy, I would have played the fool, sometimes the naïve; never the villain.

I am sure some perceived me a twit, defined as "an offensive term that deliberately insults somebody's commonsense or consideration of others."

One may argue what a man does, his behavior, is who he really is. I can say, without any equivocation, I have never behaved with malice in my heart toward anyone.

The great Italian poet Dante Alighieri (1265-1321), who knew something about hell, believed eternal justice weighs the sins of the hot-blooded and sins of the cold-blooded on different scales. None of my transgressions were cold-blooded. To be alone with my conscience is my judgment.

Our memories have only the life we give them. When I think about my ex-wives, each and every one, it is *always* with a smile. The Buddha said, "You, yourself, as much as anybody in the entire universe, deserve your love and affection." So it is with each of them.

I have given up hope for a better past.

"Old men miss many dogs"—Steve Allen.

* Single for the first time since I was nineteen, I moved into a one-bedroom apartment on the same street as the high school. Sometime afterward, President Mosier called me into his office, told me to shut the door, and asked me if I was a homosexual! I told him I was not. Without pause or change in expression, he asked if I was bisexual. I told him, "No part of me is the least possible part a homosexual."

Simply stated in the plainest terms, I have never had a sexual thought about a man and no amount of money or other incentive can persuade me to have one. It is a physical impossibility. From my countenance and tone, President Mosier saw how absurd his questions were. I asked him, "Where is this coming from?"

He said, "The publisher of the local daily paper told me. He said he had *proof* you are gay." It turned out his proof were two women who said they had observed me leaving a local motel in the company of two men.

I later learned one of the women had been a secretary for Dr. Moiser, who had made an unequivocal pass at me which I had unequivocally rejected. The other woman was her sister, whom I had never seen.

I think when he heard his own words, he realized how feeble the publisher's accusation was and how absurd our conversation. Neither of us ever mentioned it again. I told no one.

My total support for homosexuals to participate *fully* in all liberties of American life originates from the fact that my heterosexuality was not a choice. It is totally natural. How can I not believe homosexuals' sexuality is as natural for them as mine is for me?

Demanding people change who or what they were born is a sin against nature. If they changed to become what others want them to be, they would lose their very selves, their souls, and gain nothing, not even the world.

Author's sons and parents.

For my third one-year contract, Richard did not give me a raise. He believed I had not provided the leadership for the faculty he needed. He reasoned what the board had asked him would have been possible if I had provided effective help. I figured I was reading the handwriting on the wall.

* Alan Detrich met a woman in his last year at Wichita State University, the first one he really cared for. He called her, "My home-baked cookie." Previously, he had told me Mary Ann was my home-baked cookie.

Early one Saturday evening, out of the blue, Alan showed up at my apartment with a young woman whose image and deportment projected no confidence she was anyone's home-baked cookie.

I was surprised, pleased and excited to see Alan. I gave his companion my bedroom; Alan and I went out into the beautiful night until dawn. As always, he was smiling; though I could see, behind his facade, he was greatly burdened.

He told me his home-baked cookie had been killed in an automobile wreck the weekend before, about an hour after she left him, driving alone to her home.

Alan said about an hour after his sweetheart left that fateful afternoon, about the time of the wreck, a squirrel ran out on a wire that went from a pole to their apartment, as it often did to get across to the other side of the yard. This time, inexplicably, the squirrel stopped, looked directly into Alan's eyes for a moment and turned around and went back.

When her sister called Alan to tell him about his home-baked cookie dying, before she could tell him, Alan thanked her and said he knew already what she wanted to tell him.

Alan told me that when the squirrel looked into his eyes, without speaking, the staring squirrel communicated to him, "Your home-baked cookie is dead." Alan did not explain to the sister how he knew she was dead. He was as certain he understood the squirrel's message as he was sure he had been in his stomach where he saw a synapse on roller skates.

He said, "James, you are probably the only person who would understand." I considered his expression a serious, sincere compliment and thanked him.

He had met the girl he brought with him to visit me the previous night in a bar in Wichita. As their evening in the bar progressed, she kept asking him, "What do you want me to do?"

He finally told her, "Drive me to see James Willis in Claremore, Oklahoma."

* After Mary Ann and the boys left, President Mosier and I hired a new journalism teacher, Carol Colclasure. Her grandmother was a full-blooded Comanche, who had married a Caucasian of Spanish descent. Carol looked more Indian than her quarter heritage would indicate and was beautiful in the exotic manner of women of a Native American and Caucasian heritage.

Author dean at CJC conducting a faculty "Slave for a Day" auction. The "slave" in chains is Carol, author's second wife.

Carol said her Comanche grandmother had pictures of her father (Carol's great-grandfather) as a young man in front of his tepee with scalps of white men hanging on the entrance.

While Carol was in college in Tahlequah, the Comanche tribe of Oklahoma elected her Comanche Princess of Oklahoma, something like an Indian Miss Oklahoma. She reigned for a year. We married in June 1975.

I knew it was time to leave Claremore Junior College, but I had not focused on a job or location. Previous to our marriage, while Carol and I were visiting my parents and boys in Little Rock, I saw an advertisement in the *Arkansas Gazette* for superintendent's job in Mountain Home, Arkansas.

I had passed through this town each time in summer 1970, when I traveled between Arkansas State University at Jonesboro and Prairie Grove. I knew it was a beautiful town. With almost no further thought beyond the attractiveness of the town, I applied for the job. The board interviewed, and hired me.

My being at my parents' house to see the advertisement in the *Gazette* about the job at Mountain Home almost did not happen. If it had not, everything else in my life would have unfolded significantly differently.

SUPERINTENDENT OF SCHOOLS, MOUNTAIN HOME, ARKANSAS (1975-1977)

A perfection of means, and confusion of aims,
seems to be our main problem.
—Albert Einstein

* * *

Confusion now hath made his masterpiece.
—William Shakespeare.

* * *

I'd rather have a bottle in front of me than a frontal lobotomy.
—Dorothy Parker

* * *

Hell is truth found out too late.
—Sign on United States Highway 1, Miami to Key West

###

As with every previous place I had been, before my interview, I knew not one person in Mountain Home; nor anything about the town beyond what superficial impressions I gained passing through it.

When I was traveling through it, I had no thought of it as a future place to live. My impressions were general and vague, but still were more than with any other place I lived or worked. I had at least been there

Carol and I made trips to Mountain Home before we married to find a place to live. We found our perfect place about three miles from town on two and a half acres in a wooded area on a seldom-used gravel road. The exterior was of stone and redwood; it had a large fireplace in the sunken den. It was a great place for the life we both so much wanted to live—one of peace and tranquility, a quiet, private one, with dogs, cats and maybe a garden.

* Peace and tranquility for us were not to be. My introduction to being superintendent of Mountain Home Schools was a jingling telephone next to my ear at five o'clock on July 1, 1975, my first morning on the job.

I awoke to a man's voice asking if his church could use the high school gym on Saturday morning. I told him I would be in my office at seven thirty that day and would check on the school policy for the use of its facilities. He said he did not know where he would be then and wanted me to give him my answer. Still sleepy, I began to become disgruntled. I had no idea what I was doing, and the man clearly implied his request was routine; I told him his church could use the gym.

On Sunday, after the man's church used the gym on Saturday, a board member whom I had met once called and asked what I thought I was doing letting this man's church use the high school gym.

He explained the source of his anger. I learned in Mountain Home was disharmony between the Church of Christ and other protestant churches, mostly Baptist, as it was the largest denomination in town. All members of the board were Baptist or Methodist. They were taking sides. They believed that members of the Church of Christ believed only they would be accepted into haven.

Until that day, the only Church of Christ of which I had heard of was a very small one in Bowser that had played a humorous episode in my youth Involving Bill Linn, my best friend when I was a senior in high school. Bill was a kinsman of the Chambers family residing in Rock Springs, a placid, prosperous community northwest of Monticello. He was a tall, well portioned and handsome. He became the first male cheerleader at Drew Central and probably the first anyone had seen at the schools we visited to play. Playing on the girls' basketball team was Beverly Burton, tall, well proportioned, black haired and beautiful.

They fell in real love and married in the Bowser Church of Christ the summer after high school graduation; I was Bill's best man. After the ceremony, several of us were conversing in front of the church. The preacher approached me and in a soft voice and grave tone said, "James, we have made a terrible mistake. You and Bill were standing in the wrong places and I married you to Beverly, not Bill."

I was seventeen. The depth of my naivety was bottomless. I had not imagined a preacher joking about anything, much less something like this one had just said. He asked me, "Would you wait for the people to leave and we can go back into the church and perform the wedding correctly?" Shaken, ashen and wide eyed, I solemnly nodded agreement. All of us enjoyed the preacher's good joke on me, which is always more important to me than my ego.

Bill was living in beautiful mountains of Idaho when he came to Rock Springs. He and Beverly eventually moved back there and have raised a fine family. Bill is ageing well, a handsome man still. Beverly has aged mind bogglingly well. If she dyed her hair black, one could swear she has not aged a year since high school.

Author's high school senior best friend Bill Linn
as a junior

I read the official literature of the Church of Christ, which does not state plainly that only its members will be allowed into heaven, but strongly implies it. Though some of its members with whom I have talked dispute it is a principle of the Church's faith; others are confused about its meaning. Regardless, from the implications and inferences, one can see the possible cause for friction with other denominations.

At the next board meeting, I explained to the members that educational law is clear: they could have a policy keeping all church groups out of the school facilities or letting them all in. But they could not favor some churches over others.

They did not care what was legal. They believed they were the school board elected by the people of the district and would decide as they wished for their district.

A couple of weeks later, Carol and I were in a local eatery on Saturday morning enjoying an especially fine breakfast when the owner came to our table, pulled up a chair next to my ear, and began to complain for twenty minutes that the football coach was not playing his son enough.

* I either had no idea about what the superintendent's job was or, more likely, what the people at that place thought the job was. I soon came to realize I did not want to be superintendent of Mountain Home Schools. The problem was I was in the second month of a two-year contract.

Since 1962, I had moved about in my work, but always a step up and always for two years minimum. I could not afford to remain superintendent one year, much less a few months, without my next employer being legitimately suspicious of my qualifications.

My lack of success at Mountain Home was entirely my fault and I had to tough it out. I could not leave until my two-year contract expired.

The board tried without success to persuade me to leave after one year. They could not fire me in contract; they had no cause. The problem was I probably wanted to leave as much as most of them wanted me to. When they asked me to resign, I responded I had a contract to finish. They quickly backed off.

During my second year, an anonymous call was received at the high school reporting a bomb hidden in the building. Fred Dawson, the principal, a dependable man, called me. I told him to call the police and ring the fire bell to get the kids out in an orderly fashion.

After searching an hour, the police declared the school safe. The kids went back into the building, and school continued. The following week, Fred got another call and phoned me. I told him to ignore it and to tell no one. School continued uninterrupted. I guess Fred told no one, because I never heard about it. We received no more calls.

The second year with the board went smoother than the first. There was no tension; everyone knew how it was going to end.

Author superintendent at Mountain Home, Arkansas, conferring with a teacher.

* The two years at Mountain Home were enjoyable, having nothing to do with being school superintendent but with two friends we met, Leo and Opel Davis.

Leo T.C. Davis was my sixty-seven-year-young assistant superintendent. He had been in Mountain Home since birth, except for his World War II time in the Pacific. His wife, Opal, worked in the office. They were a couple much in love and a joy to be around. It was sometimes embarrassing to walk in on them in his office, but they just laughed and never seemed to mind.

They were native to the region and loved to show it off. The two of them, Carol, and I took frequent day trips in the area, including southern Missouri.

My life is fuller for knowing Leo and Opal.

Author, 1976.

Carol had given me a black Labrador retriever puppy as a wedding present. I named him Beau, an affectionate name by which my father called me when I was a boy. A starving Irish setter showed up and adopted us. Soon after a small, pretty, collie-type dog show up. Carol named her AddOn. They and Carol's three cats kept the place just the way we wanted it.

I had a red Jeep CJ-7 and loved to drive it in the snow and along the Buffalo River. Robb spent some time with us in Mountain

Home. One day, he and I "Jeeped the Buffalo," as was called by persons who explored the Buffalo River in their Jeeps. That was an especially fun day.

On another day, I was alone at the Buffalo River and became stuck. My Jeep would not budge. I began walking; after four hours, I met two men in overalls without shirts, plow shoes without socks, and hats advertising a feed-and-seed store. The most important thing I noticed was they were in an empty log truck, with log chains and hooks hanging neatly on the back of its cab.

These friendly gentlemen pulled me out after an additional two hours of trial and error. They absolutely refused any compensation and seemed on the verge of accusing me of rudeness if I kept insisting.

I told a longtime Jeep owner friend in Mountain Home about my experience and said I was going to buy a winch so I would not get stuck again. He said I would get stuck again and next time I would walk eight hours instead of four and it would require four hours for the men in the log truck to get me out instead of two.

Instead of a winch, I bought a pop-up camper and pulled it behind my Jeep. Carol's brother, sister-in-law, and her niece, a cute smart little girl named Guy, came for a visit. We camped on the river for three nights and saw not one other person. A beautiful place is Arkansas' Buffalo River.

* The handwriting on the wall was plain to see; I began to look for another job. The next one would be on the faculty of a university. This is the only thing I knew absolutely for sure, and I absolutely for sure do not say *absolutely for sure* often.

In spring 1977, I used the *Directory of Higher Education* to find salient information about public and private colleges and universities. Among the twenty-five hundred entries in all, I found about three dozen that were suitable to me. I sent these institutions letters of application, with résumés and letters of recommendation. I waited. Except for routine responses, I heard nothing.

My dad asked me what I was going to do, if I heard from no one. I told him I would get a "job-job."

He was puzzled by that term. "What is a job-job?"

"I'll drive a Frito Lay truck." He laughed heartily with relief to learn that my university education had not completely ruined his Drew County raised son.

* I had a couple of weeks of vacation coming and checked out of the office in the middle of June. Robb was visiting. I hooked the camper to the Jeep and loaded up for a trip to Florida.

On the day we left, Robb and Carol were sitting in the Jeep in the driveway with the motor running. I was standing in the front door, with my hand literally on its knob, checking the house for one last time. The very moment I was pulling the door shut, the phone rang!

My first impulse, a strong one, was not to answer it; I did not want to talk to anyone in Mountain Home but thought perhaps it was Dad. I had not told him I was going to Florida. Calling was not Dad but Dr. Ben Humphrey, chairman of the Department of Professional Studies at Murray State University in Murray, Kentucky—one of the colleges I had sent an application to; though at that moment, I could recall nothing about it.

He said he and the Department Faculty Search Committee were impressed with my credentials and recommendations and wanted me to come for an interview. I told him I was going to Florida and it would be at least ten days before I could get to Murray. This was fine with him. I was the only one he and the department wanted to interview, and they would wait until I could visit the campus.

In 1977, omnipresent real estate and land development had not yet arrived in the Florida Panhandle. Destin was a few years past being a backwater town. Unlike today, no high-rises or condos were in sight. Campsites were on the beautiful Destin beach itself!

We pulled into one of these sites and camped on the white sands of Destin beach a few yards from the surf, with an unimpeded view. We had a great time. The three of us returned to Mountain Home, unhooked the trailer, and took off for Murray.

* As all the other places I had worked, I knew not one soul in Murray and had heard nothing about the university, except what I read in the directory. I knew unless Chairman Humphrey and the Department Faculty Search Committee discovered an eye in the middle of my forehead, I would be offered the job. Moreover, I knew I would take it.

My uninterrupted success that had begun in Lovington ceased in Mountain Home. Given enough time, no upward-sloping trend line is immune from collapse, sometimes a dramatic one. However, I could not rationalize away the fact the failure at Mountain Home was mine alone; I have no excuse.

If I had been honest to myself and the school board, I would have resigned from the job after the second month. I made the choice not to; I reaped its inevitable consequences. To have different consequences, I needed to make different choices.

I knew how to make people like me when I wanted them to, and I knew how to convince myself to like them when it was important to me. The whole *like* thing was not going to be a problem at Murray State. About three things I was determined: I would like my job at Murray State; I would like the people there; they would like me.

If Chairman Ben Humphries had called me half a heartbeat after he did, or if I had not answered his call, either of which almost did not happen, everything else in my life would have unfolded differently.

PROFESSOR AT MURRAY STATE UNIVERSITY (1977-2005)

And now for something completely different.
—*Monty Python's Flying Circus* spin-off

##

My salary at Mountain Home was twenty-two thousand dollars. The assistant professor position at Murray State had an advertised salary of nineteen thousand dollars. I was ready to take it and prepared not to negotiate.

I interviewed all day with department faculty and chair, including an hour alone with the president, Constantine "Dino" Curris, with whom I was impressed. I believed my impression of him was reciprocated.

President Curris spoke quietly, walked slowly, exuding smoothness and intelligence that portrayed an abundance of confidence. He was a brown-eyed, handsome man who managed to look and act as a leader without a whiff of physical fitness about him. However, he possessed a courage packed viscera and a mind as brilliant as a flawless multifaceted diamond.

That night Carol and I attended a department welcoming party at the chairman's home. The affair was entirely social. I had not indicated I wanted to take the job at Murray State, nor had I been asked. No one had yet said a word about salary.

The phone rang at seven o'clock the next morning in our motel room. It was Dean Donald Hunter of the College of Education. In a mildly exasperated tone he said, "Come to my office and let's get this thing settled." It had not yet dawned on me what was not settled. If they offered me the position, I was prepared to say yes. No one had made an offer.

In Dean Hunter's office, I learned his problem. The president, the chair, and the department faculty wanted me; the pressure was on the dean to get me on board. He assumed salary was the impediment.

He began by saying that the president had authorized an additional thousand dollars toward my salary and that teaching in summer school I would receive an additional fifteen percent for a total of twenty-three thousand dollars. If anyone at Murray State knew my Mountain Home salary was twenty-two thousand dollars, no one mentioned it.

I nodded my understanding and told him I had a question; I asked him, "What is the promotion process at Murray State, and what would it require of me to become associate professor." The advertised position was for *assistant* professor.

I was not considering professional rank a condition of my employment. I had asked out of curiosity; he understandably believed it was a condition. He excitedly asked, "Would you come for twenty-three thousand dollars, rank of associate professor and two years applied toward tenure?"

"Yes," I said. He smiled and stood. I smiled and stood. We shook.

* My teaching assignment was three graduate courses for a total of nine semester hours. I taught three among the following six courses: Seminar in Higher Education, History of Education in the United States, Educational Law, Methods of Educational Research, The Superintendent and Supervision of Instruction.

Ben told me I was the first professor to teach a class on Wednesday night. Theretofore, Murray State had avoided Wednesday because that was "church night."

The problem with our university not offering courses on Wednesday night was public schools held no extracurricular activities on church night either; sometimes Wednesday was the only night teachers and coaches were not busy, and these people were our graduate students. Without classes on Wednesday night, many of these people would have been limited to attending graduate school during summer sessions.

My first office at Murray State was a windowless, recently vacated supply closet in a building adjacent to the education building, where education faculty was housed. It contained a small desk against one wall and two small chairs, neither a desk chair. In the wall above the desk was a hole about the size of a man's fist. I was the new guy. No matter how much I was desired, I had dues to pay.

In Benton, seat of the next county north, was a Walmart, still an uncommon store in Kentucky. As I was familiar with this chain, Carol and I drove to Benton to see what was there we might need. Among our purchases was a thirty-six-inch-by-eighteen-inch bathroom rug of many colors, which I bought to nail over the hole in my office wall.

* People noticed Carol. My recently acquired colleagues would come to visit the new guy in his new office, where they would see the rug, and ask, "Your wife make that?"

I was surprised to discover that educated people can know so little about persons with whom they share their country. My professorial comrades' image of American Natives was they weaved rugs and danced prayers of thanksgiving for rain and victory, when not scalping pale faces.

It was not unlike people warning me to take immunization shots and avoid drinking the water when I went to New Mexico, except these people at Murray were my colleagues, PhDs talking about persons native to their country.

Carol and I bought a house out of town on a piece of land in the county with a relatively little used, paved road along its front. Once during my first fall semester, I came home for lunch and found Carol much distraught; our dog had been run over. I buried him and went that afternoon to a realtor and told her I wanted a house where my dog could sleep on the road. She said she would look for one.

Her problem looking for one was she assumed my statement was an exaggerated expression for wanting a house in the country, not my literal desire. It took a while for her to figure out I had described exactly what I wanted.

The realtor found the perfect place in Graves County, about twenty miles from campus. It was a house with five acres on a rarely used gravel road that connected two other roads. More relevant to its isolation, the bridge just past our house was out and had not been repaired for two years, and there were no plans to repair it. This meant no one would be passing in front of our house; beyond it was nowhere to go.

The farmhouse was built in 1914; it had a sound foundation and roof. It had beautiful, old, large oak and maple trees and a two-and-a-half-acre tobacco permit, which meant I could raise tobacco on it. In the back was a tobacco barn for curing it; on the land were large, farm machinery shed, a small pond,and an old, well-seasoned garden spot. It was a lovely place.

Our nearest neighbor was a farm family who had lived on the same piece of land for four generations. They lived across the road, about a half mile down, at the end of a long driveway, and were good neighbors. As were all my neighbors, almost all belonged to the Church of Christ.

As Dad did when he moved into the house with electricity and gas heat at Drew Central, I thought I was in heaven. Carol had three cats when we married, and we accumulated three dogs. Our heaven was getting dog and cat crowded, just as we liked it.

Carol's favorite cat Toby was a larger than usual gray tabby with five toes on each foot. But his most interesting feature was his attention to people and his intelligence. When Carol and I began seeing each other, he slept in her bed. He lay between us with his back next to Carol and his four big feet on me, and pushed.

One of our dogs pestered him. Toby tried to persuade the dog to leave him alone by hissing and showing his fangs, but his efforts were to no avail. One day, the dog was sleeping and Toby got a running start and jumped on the dog's back, dug in all twenty claws, and rode on his back with him yelping and trying to shake off the beast. Toby got off when he was good and ready; the dog never bothered him again.

Carol was not religious in the usual sense. I never heard her reference Jesus, God, Church, or Bible in any fashion. She was, however, one of the most soulful, spiritual people I have known. She believed all life, not only human, was part of a single whole and all life had one universal, shared soul. She could not hurt any living thing because she and it had the same soul. The national religion of Japan Shinto is the only one of which I am aware that is similar to her beliefs.

She did not believe in the supernatural. Indeed, her spiritual world was not something that existed outside nature, but was a deeper, fundamental part of nature that existed in its own reality. In this reality no spirit was evil. Evil was so far from her nature; she could not tolerate a reality that contained it

She had a unique take on the world with an interesting mind. I enjoyed watching her deal with her world. She is a rare human being. From her I learned reality is frequently inaccurate.

Carol heard music in the streets and found flowers in the gutters. She was intelligent, thoughtful, beautiful and pleasant; she never complained or whined. I believe she was an old soul.

* At Murray State, during a professor's sixth year, following his five years of probation, is his "tenure year." He is either awarded tenure that year or not. If he is not, he is given a one-year, terminal contract. Since I came in with two years experience, my tenure year was my fourth, following three years of probation.

My tenure decision year was 1980-1981, the same year I became department chair.

Ben resigned the chair; he and several colleagues asked me to apply; I agreed. Two other department faculty members applied also. The dean met with every faculty member in the department. I was selected with all but three of my faculty approving my being chosen. Besides the two candidates who opposed me, the third was a close friend of one of the two who applied.

I found out later, the two department secretaries went to the dean together and told him, if either of the other two professors was selected, they would transfer or quit. Their thought was not so much in support for me as it was nonsupport for the other two. Both were fine, intelligent men. Albeit, one was disorganized beyond imagination and his handwriting was impossible; the other was a serious chauvinist, if not a closet misogynist.

Our department's name was Department of Professional Studies. It had more faculty than any department on campus. Within it were five divisions: School Administration, Higher Education, School and Institutional Counseling, Social Work and Rehabilitation. Each of these divisions had a head. I was an associate professor with classes in the Higher Education and School Administration divisions.

The division head of Rehabilitation in conversation with me referred to me as a *TAB*. I asked him what that term was. He said, "TAB, temporarily able-bodied, is a name we in Rehab call people like you. You are able-bodied now but are a car wreck or a fall away from being handicapped." I have not driven a car or climbed a ladder since without thinking how quickly I could become crippled.

At the beginning of my second year, I moved into an office in the education building. It had four solid walls, a desk, a window, and three chairs, one of which was a desk chair. When I became chairman, I moved into the larger corner office; it had seven chairs, four windows, table and credenza.

As mentioned, my first year as chairman was also my tenure year. It was a busy year. I had to learn the responsibilities and duties of a department chair and prepare my tenure file, which had to contain everything about my professional life and experiences with supporting documentation and information.

I passed all requisite committee and administrative levels and was recommended by the president to the Murray State regents, who granted me tenure in the spring of 1981.

A tenure contract meant I am always in contract, rather than being hired annually. Since I was always in contract, I could not be dismissed anytime without cause that the university had to prove in court, if I challenged it.

Contrary to popular thought, having tenure at a university does not mean one cannot be fired. Having tenure means the university must be prepared to prove in court a *legal* cause for firing. Unpopular speech; antagonizing the administration, such as organizing a faculty union; and nonconventional behavior or dress is not legal cause.

Tenure is important for academic freedom for higher education faculty, more so than for elementary and secondary faculty, because faculty in higher education are more greatly involved in aspects of decision making concerning the direction and policies of the university. This faculty activity often brings them within the blurred lines of the area of administration and governing boards.

As chairman, I had a twelve-month contract, rather than a nine-month contract, plus summer teaching, and was given an additional $2,400. My teaching load was reduced to six hours.

* Shortly after I came to Murray State, Wes came to visit. When he and I were walking in the hall in the education building, we met Jody Jaeger, my graduate assistant, from Falls Church, Virginia, a suburb of Washington, DC. When we got into my office, Wes wanted to know who that woman was we met in the hall. Later that day, Jody asked who the man with me was when she passed us in the hall.

They got together that night and soon married.

Without the completely serendipitous happenstance of Wes and Jody passing in the hall, my life would have unfolded significantly differently, as would theirs. My first two grandchildren, Bethany and John, are children of their union.

* The first spring in our farmhouse, Carol and I had a large party. Everyone in my department and many of the school people in Graves County attended. We held it in the huge tall equipment shed, which was filled with straw. It was a potluck with a bonfire; people brought their own liquor and lawn chairs. "B.Y.O.L and B,Y.O.L.C.," the invitation read. The conversation was robust. More than one hundred people attended. In ensuing years, the number of attendees grew, it became known as the Willis Barn Party.

Carol became despondent. She felt her spirit, important to her well-being, was not in balance. During this time of general despondency, she fed Toby a piece of roast beef that still had the string on it. The string lodged in his intestines causing severe distress. We left him with his veterinarian in Mayfield and went on a planned trip to Monticello.

The veterinarian called me in Monticello two days later and said he could not save Toby. Carol wept every inch of the 364 miles back home.

When in college to obtain her degree in journalism, a requirement in her college biology class, which was itself a requirement for graduation, was to dissect a cat. Carol refused. The professor told her to dissect the cat or drop the class—easy choice for her. Carol's love for cats in general and Toby in particular was real

She enrolled in biology every semester and continued making the same choice until she completed biology and graduated without ever cutting up a dead cat. She never knew how she managed that, and she never inquired about it.

I buried Toby behind the garage, covered his grave with a large flat stone, and put up a wooden grave marker on which I carved the words Toby the Cat.

Carol said, "This place does not like me." I could not consider relocating.

Carol returned to Oklahoma in 1980. She worked for a while in Tulsa at Oral Roberts University; there she was assigned to the mail room. She, in a locked room with other women, opened letters to Reverend Roberts, put the enclosed money aside, read the letter, and selected one of five prepared *personal* responses and included a colored ribbon the reverend had "personally blessed for the individual."

She eventually enrolled in the School of Social Work at the University of Oklahoma, graduated with a master's degree, and became an institutional counselor.

Most of her professional life, Carol was a counselor on the Blackfeet Indian Reservation, located contiguous to and east of Glacier National Park—a beautiful spiritual place. After five years apart, we divorced in 1995. She remarried, keeping Willis as her name, and soon divorced.

She called me in summer 2006. She was not married and lived in Chickasaw, Oklahoma, where her mother lives. She was still Willis.

She was working on the Blackfeet Indian Reservation when my fourth wife Dawn and I visited Glacier National Park in 2003. We three had dinner and a nice visit at Glacier Park Lodge.

When we married, Carol had a huge collection of phonograph records. They were the large vinyl 78-rpm records. She loved music. It was an important part of her life. She even tried *seriously* to teach me to sing.

Watching her enjoying her music, I began to realize how big a hole was in my life without music. I do not recall ever purchasing a record, and for all practical purposes, I never paid to enter an auditorium to hear an artist play or sing.

Whatever the extent of musical talent my parents had (Mother sang *and* played the piano), I can confidently say I was born without any musical talent of any kind whatsoever, including appreciation for music or even knowledge enough to be disappointed that I did not have an appreciation for it.

Again unmarried, I began to enjoy the company of women. One of the more interesting ones was Pam, an extraordinarily beautiful woman, who came to my house about one weekend a month arriving on Friday night. Saturday evenings we would go to a supper-dance club on the Tennessee line, near Fulton, which billed itself, “the banana capital of the world.”

Our routine was we arrived at the club at eight o’clock, had a prime rib and lobster dinner, and were ready to dance when the band began playing at nine. We remained on the floor for every dance until the club closed at two o'clock. It was a great time and great fun, until my brain and mouth became disengaged.

Driving back to my house one Sunday morning, Pam announced she was going to take dance lessons. I did not imagine why she would want to, but I said, "OK; Great idea."

The next weekend that she came, she had taken dance lessons. We followed our routine until well into the evening on Saturday. After the band's break when Pam and I were on the floor, she said, "I can't dance to that," turned, and walked off. Flabbergasted, I followed her. I had never had a dance lesson in my life and could dance to that music. She had lessons and could not?

At our table, I insisted on talking with her about this new phenomenon I was witnessing.

In retrospect, I realize probably the reason I could dance to this tune was because when dancing, all I heard was the beat and it sounded to me like others the band had played that evening. A beat I could follow, I was well coordinated and had rhythm. I never had a problem finding dancing partners, but born in me was no physical ability to hear the nuances among notes. Perhaps, *graceful* describes what I am not on a dance floor.

I was so interested in hearing her explanation and discussing possible answers, I failed to see she was becoming angry. She believed I was accusing her of something, which I was not. I failed to understand what she was feeling. We drove home. The rest of the evening did not go well; she left earlier than usual the next morning and never returned.

Once again, I had failed to see the situation from the other's view and, without having an inkling of what was happening; I innocently, stupidly stumbled over the cliff and fell until I hit the bottom hard. I began to realize perhaps there was something about not understanding I did not understand.

I did not see or hear from her again for ten years, when we accidently met at a shopping mall in Paducah. We were friendly and glad to see each other; we spent an hour talking and laughing. She had a husband and three children; none were with her.

* After Carol left and I ran Pam off, I believed my ability to maintain relationships needed introspection. I decided I needed to fix myself. Without telling anyone, I suddenly, quietly withdrew from *all* social contact for six months to try to understand what living wit me was like. I marked my calendar for the six-month period and began my hermetic existence.

I went to work each day and interacted routinely with my students and colleagues and went into town to purchase groceries, always with a pleasant countenance and always alone. Otherwise, my entire life consisted of three dogs on an isolated five-acre tobacco farm in western Kentucky. I engaged in no friendly phone conversations, no parties, no visits, no movies, nada—except reading, watching television and visiting the dogs; these activities I enjoyed alone.

The only words inscribed in the temple at Delphi, dating about 400 B.C., is "Know Thyself." Socrates famously and boldly said, "The unexamined life is not worth living." Lao Tzu believed, "At the center of your being you have the answer; you know who you are and you know what you want."

With the certitude of these founts of wisdom, I figured how difficult can one's introspection be? To examine my life, I sat around watching myself sitting around watching myself sitting around watching myself. I discovered trying to fix myself, was going to be as difficult as chewing my own teeth.

At some level, we must take ourselves as the calibration point for normalcy. We must assume our own mind is not, cannot be, entirely opaque. Whatever our self-admitted eccentricities might be, we are not the villains of our own stories. In fact, it is quite the contrary: we play, and only play, the hero, and in the swirl of other people's stories, insofar as these stories concern us at all, we are never less than heroic.

When Adolf Hitler combed his mustache in the mirror, he did not think he was looking at one of the most evil men in history. He thought he was looking at the greatest German in a thousand years. When we look at ourselves, we see what we want to see, hero. If we do not see a hero, we quickly accept our excuses for not being one. Therefore, if we are not a hero, it is not our fault.

As the only child, I never had to compete for my parents' attention or love. I grew up without learning how to compete for anyone's love or attention. When I made an effort and it was not reciprocated, I quit trying. Whether another likes me has rarely been important to my happiness or sense of well-being.

Dad intended I not be pampered, but he could not effect the real spoiling of a single child. The real spoiling was everything was mine. I had a bedroom that was only mine, clothes that were only mine and parents who were only mine. When we went on vacation trips, the whole backseat was only mine. I was as the seagulls in *Finding Nemo*; *everything* was mine, mine, mine, mine and mine.

I never had to measure myself in relation to a sibling. If I compared myself to another, and I do not remember doing so, the other did not come home with me.

Traits and characteristics of my parents survived in me throughout my life, but transformed, softened and darkened with the certainty knocked out of them. I grew up constrained by their strictness and at the same time received almost unlimited freedom and independence of mind that inclined me to a certain detachment in relationships.

While examining my life, I seriously considered the possibility of my being a sociopath—not a far fetched thought. I concluded not so; all I am can be explained within normal behavior. I have strong characteristics of *the only child syndrome*, to which is added a mild case of weirdness introvertness, glibness and superficial charm. These characteristics sometimes rise to a noticeable amount of emotional vacancy and self-absorption. Empathy is not a common emotion for me.

I concluded a possible explanation for my behavior may be found within the normal five stages of a person's life: infant, child, adolescence, maturity and old age. My life's stages are infant, child, adolescence, adolescence and adolescence. As is the character of adolescents, my greatest charms are my greatest faults. Without intention or forethought I am perfectly capable of simultaneously being both vexing and charming.

As are adolescents, I have been weak, sinful, flawed and sometimes petulant, punctuated with rare moments of intuitive transcendentalism. I suffer from a form of shyness. While I comfortably speak in front of groups, I do not perform well in small talk conversations. This failure encourages me often to withdraw into an introverted state, which can be perceived be some observers as my being conceited; which may cause me to become more standoffish. This downward spiraling cycle creates strangled communications and isolation.

I agree with those who think one's behavior is who one really is. In my "heart of hearts, where all men know the secrets of the days and the nights," (Kahil Gibran, *The Prophet*) I know I have never behaved with malice in my heart toward anyone. When I have hurt others, it was because I was vacuously floating through life on a blanket of misdirected, benevolence. I irritate others when I think I could not possibly do so.

I have accepted I cannot get rid of my inanity and nonsense without getting rid of myself. Popeye wisely explained, "I yam what I yam and that's all that I yam."

About himself, Walt Whitman concluded, "Do I contradict myself? Very well then, I contradict my self. (I am large, I contain multitudes.)" Without intending to disagree with Mr Whitman statement about his being large and containing multitudes, my experience has been contradicting one's self is normal behavior.

The web of my life is of a mingled yarn, good and ill together. Often my contradictions pass into my thinking undetected and remain there undiscovered until some thoughtless act of mine brings them forth to my surprise. And to others, if any are near by. My contradictions are a feast.

* Someone mentioned my house may be haunted by the spirit of a young woman. Among psychologists is a popular theory that, of all illusions the most difficult to surrender is the belief that consciousness exists after death. I have my share of illusions, but consciousness existing after death is not among them.

Hyper rationalizing without considering less logical possibilities can leave the mind incurably crippled in a closed and ossified system. I agree with Hamlet when he said to Horatio: "There are more things in heaven and earth, Horatio, than are dreamt of in your philosophy," Regardless, I don't believe in what is commonly referred to as ghosts, albeit I have had unexplainable *ghost* experiences.

My house had two bathrooms; one was off the kitchen and adjacent to the back porch, which had a screen door. I was sitting in this bathroom one warm afternoon when there came a forceful banging and knocking on the back door on the other side of the bathroom wall, and someone called my name demandingly, loudly and urgently, "James! James!"

I arose and began to get my clothes together and yell, "I'm coming. I'm coming." When I got to the back door, no one was there, but I saw my trash fire had gotten out of control and was near Toby's grave, next to my garage. I rushed to the garage and got a rake and a shovel, one for me and one for the person who had warned me.

I began to put out the flames. Thinking the person who called me had gone to the front of the house to rouse me, I continued loudly to yell several times, "I'm back here!"

No one came. When I had the fire under control, I hurried to the front of the house. No one was there, no car, no truck, no tracks, no one in sight. I thought about the voice and what was strange about it. It sounded as if it were disembodied, neither male nor female, perhaps not even human. I wondered if it was Toby's spirit calling me.

As was Spot, Toby was a special animal. When we looked in each other's eyes and he let me see into his soul, I often thought it was an old one. He had many lives.

Toby was beautiful and special, and he knew it.

I do not believe this experience was from the spiritual world, because I believe the dead, including cats, do not have experiences. I did satisfy myself, if I were living with some unknown spiritual entity, it liked me and I had nothing to fear.

Another unexplainable occurrence happened after I became social again. I was preparing to go out for the evening. As was my habit in that house, I had placed everything I would carry in my pockets—wallet, keys, bills in a 1964 President Kennedy silver half-dollar money clip, and change—in plain sight on the middle of my clean, freshly made king-size bed and went to the bathroom to brush my teeth.

When I returned to my bedroom, what I had so carefully placed in plain sight on the middle of my bed had vanished.

After several minutes of searching everywhere I knew my things could not be, because I distinctly remembered putting them on my bed, I returned to my bedroom and there everything was in plain sight, exactly as I had so carefully placed it.

I related this story to someone who explained my ghost was a female and a jealous one.

* In May 1980, while I was living my self-imposed hermitic existence, Dad called. He was the most distraught I ever knew him. With a trembling voice, he gravely struggled to say, "Son, I have bad news about Robert!"

I could not imagine. Steeling myself for the blow, I quietly asked "What?"

After great effort to gain the composure to speak, he said in a trembling voice, "He is marrying a black woman."

I laughed with relief and said, "Is that all? He is getting married! I thought he was on drugs or in jail or badly hurt."

Taken aback by my response, he said, "Son, I think you are being naive."

Naive is the word a person uses to define others he considers on the fringe, those on the margins of his cultural thought. Racially mixed marriage was on the fringe of Dad's understanding of what the world was about. Therefore, if I thought racially mixed marriages were within the realm of normal, I was naive. The conversation did not continue long. Before we hung up, he said Robert was marrying the next day.

Without telling Dad or calling Robb, I drove that night to his apartment in Little Rock. I arrived at ten thirty; he was not home. I parked where I could see the front of his place and waited; he arrived with his fiancée an hour later.

After a few minutes, I rang the doorbell. Robb thought I had arrived to stop his marriage and was angry. When I told him I had come to go to his wedding, he became fine. I met Linda, the girl he was to marry. We sat and talked. I asked them not a word about their plans, except time and place of the wedding and if I were welcome to attend.

The next day, I rented a tuxedo, Robb wore his marine dress blues, and we went to his wedding. Among the approximately seventy-five persons attending, my son and I were the only white people. Besides his grandparents, Robb's brother and mother also did not approve of his bride's race and did not attend his wedding.

The wedding dinner was a large informal buffet of various home-cooked dishes, mostly vegetables seasoned with fatback. It looked like the table at a Willis reunion, but much larger.

Dad had retired from the Arkansas Education Department; he and Mother had returned to Monticello and were living in Grandma McKinstry's house on Jefferson Street. Grandma had passed; Aunt Mary Lynn was living in an attached apartment. I figured Dad and I should talk. Without calling him, I drove to Monticello and arrived at about six o'clock in the evening.

We talked. I understood it was not going to be helpful to tell Dad that Robb's marrying a black woman was not a problem for anyone he knew but Mother. I successfully struggled with my desire to explain to him why he was the naive one.

After more words between us, Dad declared, "Well, Robert is just out of the family; that is all there is to it."

"I am not going to be part of a family my son is not a part of," I responded.

Neither of us saw my declaration coming. Dad was shocked by my comment; then he became crestfallen. Not just his face, but his whole body slumped into profound, silent sadness.

It was obvious, we both were determined in what we said. Nothing was left to say. I thought it best I not stay the night. I pulled into a motel on the way home.

While I was in Monticello, Mother did not come out of her and Dad's bedroom and I did not enter it. We would have had the infamous eight-hundred-pound gorilla in the room, which neither of us could have successfully ignored.

After a couple of days, I called Robb to tell him of my and Dad's exchange. He asked me to reconsider. I told him I was not going to change my mind. I did not tell him how easy my choice was.

My and Dad's standoff was between two intractable Willis men. I knew the future was on my side, and I knew Dad would eventually know it was too. What he needed was time and space to come around. Until he did, he ought not be challenged or put in a corner. Fortunately for everyone, neither of these happened.

Dad and I never again spoke about the incident.

The reunion of John Willis decedents that year was July 6, the Sunday nearest to July 4, the time we held it for several years. It began as a celebration of Grandpa's birthday, July 15. As the family spread into several states and became older, the time was changed many years ago to Memorial Day Sunday, providing a day to get there, a day there, and a day to return. Another advantage is the weather is more pleasant at the end of May.

Previous to my and Dad's unpleasantness, he had sent letters inviting everyone with particulars of the reunion. Robb and I had already replied we were going. Without any discussions with Dad or Robb, I attended, as did Robb, but without his wife.

If any of the rest of the family knew Robb had married, none mentioned it. I believe Robert has not missed a Willis *family* reunion since. I have missed no reunions since I was born, except the three summers I was in the army, 1957 to 1959.

Another reason I used not to miss a Willis reunion is it was an opportunity to buy a lug of Bradley tomatoes, a variety developed in the early sixties by the University of Arkansas Division of

Agriculture. This lug I took back to Kentucky and Tennessee. When the Reunion was moved to Memorial Day weekend, I continued never missing one.

I intend never to miss one. My life has been a journey with many changes. This reunion is my unchanging touch with John Willis and his descendants, blood and married, in one place, at one time.

With the reunion moved to the last weekend in May, I began to make a special trip to Monticello in July for the sole purpose of buying a lug of Bradley tomatoes.

* After four years, Robert and Linda divorced without children. Robert's second and current wife Rachel is black. By the time Robert and Rachel married, Mother had passed. Of my parents, Mother was the more racially prejudiced.

By 1989, Rachel had still not come to a reunion or met Dad. He had not called Robert at home; he told me, "She might answer the phone. I don't know what I would say to her."

Dad told his close friend, Monteene, "I drove a few times to Little Rock and parked outside Robb and Rachel's home, but could not make myself go to the door." He was struggling.

In 1989, Dad married Myrtis Davis, a widow whom he had known for `many years, in the country club home of Becky, Myrtis's daughter. She invited Robert and his family without running her idea by Dad.

Robert's family attended, and Dad discovered that the people of Monticello, or anyone in his family, cared not one whit about the race of the wife of one of his grandsons.

Robert and Rachel's first child, Richard, was nearly two years old when Dad married Myrtis and very eye-catching. He took notice of his great-grandpa. It took Dad a while to get all right, but with the help of Myrtis and Richard, their wedding was the beginning of the end of Dad's problem about Robert marrying Rachel, who, Dad decided, wasn't black at all. She was the mother of his great-grandson.

Some weeks later, Richard became ill and was in a Little Rock hospital. Dad drove up and spelled Rachel staying with his great-grandson. Rachel began coming to Willis reunions, and Dad was one hundred percent natural. It took Dad a decade to come to peace with his troubled mind. As was his nature, once he became all right with it, he was completely alright.

Rachel tells the story of when she and her family were returning to Little Rock from a Florida vacation, they stopped in Monticello to visit Dad. While there, he remarked, "Rachel, you are the only one who came back from Florida with a tan."

In 1994, alums of Drew Central had an "Earl Willis Day" for classes from 1936 to 1964 to honor my Dad for his service. Over Nine-hundred of Dad's students attended. Earl Willis Day began an annual Drew Central All Class Reunion held the first Saturday in May that I have never missed.

* During my first month on campus at Murray State, President Curris called a university-wide faculty meeting, an unusual thing. Its purpose was to tell us we could not hire any more professors from the universities of Mississippi, Kentucky, or Tennessee.

The reason we could not was we had too many professors from these three institutions; consequently, our faculty was becoming ethnocentric—a culture of persons who think alike, the opposite of diversity, what a university is about.

Author's Dad and wife Myrtis at the Earl Willis Day, 1991

A story the faculty told about Curris' first year as president was of an art student who created a piece that won a prize among the art department faculty and was put on display. The student's art was a commode with its top up. Thrusting up, out of the commode, was a sculptured penis. It was fastened to a contraption with a crank outside the commode. When the crank was turned, the sculptured penis moved up and down.

A group of townspeople met with the new president in his office to demand the offensive object d'art be removed. "This vulgar offense is not art, and Murray objects to it," they patiently explained.

President Curris patiently replied, "At universities, art departments decide what art is."

His leadership was of the caliber that can make a good university a great one. I was impressed and confident I had chosen the right place to work.

When Dino Curris came to the university, he was the youngest president of a major university in the United States. Murray State had a university high school where many towns' people had for decades sent their children. One of the new president's first actions was to close it.

Its teachers became faculty in the College of Education. Most did not have tenure and were put on the university tenure and promotion track, which means they had six years to become tenured or had to leave after the following year. Before one could be considered for tenure, one had to have a terminal degree, which almost all high school teachers did not have.

University high school faculty was supported by many persons in town, and university faculty, who were friends, supported them.

The history of the school's early development justified their thinking; but times were changing. History was on their side; the future was not—a conflict no one has ever won. Homer Simpson, a leading American intellect and observer of the passing scene, noted in his 2010 season, "The war is over and the future won. Past never even had a chance."

The governor appointed the regents, and pressure began to be put on successive governors to appoint regents who would fire President Curris.

On the afternoon of Monday, March 30, 1981, I was attending a meeting of the regents, sitting nearest the east door. This was the 1981 meeting in which they awarded tenure; they wanted to meet and congratulate everyone being tenured. One was I.

A few minutes after one thirty, the east door opened and a student, whom I recognized as working in the president's office, stepped in, said nothing and handed me a note. I began to read it.

I quickly realized it was not intended for me and I gave it to the chairman conducting the meeting. He read silently for a moment and then aloud. President Reagan had been shot and rushed alive to a hospital. After a brief discussion among them, the regents continued their meeting.

As far as my interest in the events of that day, the president being shot took second place to my being tenured. I quickly discovered my having this distinction occurred just in time, as the water I was in was about to become boiling hot.

* President Curris, whom I admired and supported, was summarily fired by the regents at a meeting the following year, at which I was in attendance, for what reason I was there I do not recall. He was in contract and refused to accept the causes for dismissal, which the board refused to make public. He was removed from office with pay and sued the regents for breach of contract.

The regents' action was statewide news. Television and print media were clamoring for information and interviews. The faculty took sides, though, as one may expect, the vast majority was silent. Most professors in my department were friends with those in the university high school; whether for that reason or another, they favored the regents' action.

Henry Kissinger said, "Academic politics are so vicious because stakes are so low." He was at least half right; academic politics are vicious. In ideal situations, politics would be like a theatrical company in which actors are cast in different parts depending on the play and issues at hand. An actor plays one part today and another tomorrow. The actor is serious; the roles he plays are not.

Academic politics are personal; consequently, they are nastier than politics in Chicago and Louisiana put together. They are tribal; they are about personal slights, a disrespecting of another's reputation. Metaphorically, before one's scalp is publicly displayed, one's horses are taken; one is stripped and slowly strangled into immobility, silence and impotence.

I saw the regents' action as being against everything in academia I was for. It was a fight between close-minded, exclusive thinking and open-minded, inclusive thinking.

I was in the public schools often and was known by or known of by all the superintendents in western Kentucky. I visited with Curris and asked him to show me the charges the regents had against him, which he did. He could if we did not discuss them, and I did not make notes or copies.

He showed them to me; they were so silly I do not recall them. I could not tell anyone what the charges were, but after I saw them, I could confidently say what they were not.

The charges were not about sex, money, malfeasance or misfeasance, which was being spread by gossip, and, because of lack of information, were believed. I personally saw or talked by phone to almost every superintendent in west Kentucky in three days.

Superintendents are sensitive to school boards firing school administrators without legal cause, and they had connections throughout the state. Much of the talking stopped. I also talked to my faculty in small groups and individually.

One of my faculty, an outspoken opponent of President Curris, and consequently me, said, "The causes are immaterial; regents fire a president when they have the votes." He found out more was required to fire a president in contract than regents having the votes.

At the next regents meeting, the press was in attendance. Shortly after the regents began, they went into executive session, and visitors left the room; several went into the hall. An attractive young woman, recently arrived at WPSD-TV in Paducah, with whom I had a passing acquaintance, was in the hall. We sat together, leaning against the wall, legs stretched out, and began talking.

We went to lunch. She took out her note book and asked me to tell her about the regents' action against Curris. I told her I would tell her all I knew but it must be off the record and I must never be quoted. She agreed and had an off-the-record conversation. I told her everything I knew, except what the charges were. After that day, all WPSD reports were favorable to President Curris, which was important because it provided a positive *official* view of local opinion to counter what was being gossiped around.

(The reporter's name I have forgotten; she moved on to a station with a larger audience. She had been the first television reporter with her camera man on the scene at the eruption of Mount St. Helens in May, 1980. Her reporting was picked up by national broadcasting, and her career was on its way up. WPSD-TV was her first stop.)

When President Curris sued the regents, the whole sordid affair was made public. I attended the trial every hour I did not have a class. By happenstance, I was seen on the local television evening news exiting a room with the president and his lawyer. It seemed to me everyone I knew at Murray State was watching television that day or talked with someone who had.

My friends had several realities; my enemies had a common purpose. Poison tongues were behind closed doors; knives were out and under the table. My being paranoid did not mean people were not out to get me.

The judge decided in favor of President Curris. The regents' causes for dismissal were declared invalid. The regents did not appeal the decision.

That spring, President Curris and his wife Jo came to my barn party.

* A graduate student earned what I thought was a generous C in my graduate class that she did not think she deserved. She came to my office to see me about it. She had missed six hours of class without an excuse and her test scores were low B at best. Occasionally, a student received a D or F in my graduate classes; I was a little surprised at her attitude.

I listened politely, if not sympathetically, and told her she would keep the grade she earned. She said, "I have brought your name and what you are doing to me before our Wiccan priestess. She asked to visit with you and is waiting in the department reception area." I went into the reception area and invited her into my office. Witches had come a long way since the *Wizard of Oz*. She was beautiful.

After some conversation that mostly repeated what I had said to the C student, the priestess said, "Dr. Willis, you have an evil aura about you, and your influence must be removed. My coven will make a Willis doll tonight and burn it."

It took a moment for me to realize these two women really thought they were witches. I said to the student, "You should have gotten the C for crazy." They huffed out.

They lived with several others in a large farmhouse I passed each day to and from work. Several days after our meeting in my office, the police raided their house and hauled them to jail for pot and cocaine possession, which explained a lot I had been wondering about.

* A Graves County elementary principal was Carol Higdon, whom I had in several classes. Her husband, Greg, and I and some other Graves County teachers and their spouses began to hang out together, had pool parties, took float trips and so forth. Greg and I became close friends. He decided to run for state senator from the First District, which included Graves County and Calloway County, where Murray State University was located.

I asked him if he would like a private meeting with President Curris, and I asked Curris if he would like to meet the man who is likely to be the next state senator from our district. Both enthusiastically agreed.

We three met in the president's office for more than an hour of uninterrupted talk between the president and the candidate. After the introductions, I remained with them as a silent observer.

On election night, only four people were at Greg's house to receive the election returns: Greg's brother, who was his finance manager; Greg; President Curris; and I. With victory won, we went to the Fancy Farm School cafeteria, a school in Graves County and in Greg's home town, for a victory celebration with three hundred family members and close friends.

Greg became a devoted supporter of President Curris and refused to listen to talk of nominating regent members who would fire him, and worked in Frankfort, Kentucky's capital, to thwart those opposed to him.

Another close friend of mine was Jeff Green, a man in his late twenties and an assistant to Dr. Curris when I had first met him. He also had political ambitions. He replaced Greg in the Kentucky Senate. Marilyn, my wife then, and I were often in Jeff and Sharon's home, most of the time only the four of us, often around their pool for beer and grilled steaks.

They were a wonderful couple; Jeff was a most deserving young man. Before he could file for lieutenant governor in 1998, he died suddenly of a heart attack while resting on his couch, leaving his beautiful wife and two sons.

Not unexpectedly, when President Curris' contract expired, the regents did not rehire him. He went to the University of Northern Iowa as president for twelve years and later to Clemson University. Currently he is a member of the Regents of Murray State University!

His term does not expire until 2015, proving once again the old maxim, "The best revenge is living well." I like to think of him picnicking beside a beautiful river, watching the bloated corpses of his enemies floating by.

A Murray State regent colleague of Constantine Curris is Sharon Green, Jeff's widow. She also serves on the board of Mayfield & Graves County Chamber of Commerce. She is referenced as *Ms.* Sharon Green, which in today's vernacular indicates nothing about her marital status.

If I did not have tenure when I publicly, strongly supported President Curris against the regents, the rest of my life *may* have unfolded differently, because I am confident I would have taken the same action without tenure. My choice was existential.

* I received highest student evaluations for my classes, in some of which were more than ninety students. Some classes had to be held in the nursing building auditorium, as no regular classroom was large enough. I served effectively on several university committees and visited schools to present workshops, for which I received almost universally excellent evaluations from the participants.

In my twenty-seven years at Murray State, I missed not one class because of illness. On the few occasions that I felt ill, I drove one hundred miles to teach a night graduate class, and as I began teaching, I began to feel better, not worse. By the time I drove home I was completely refreshed. Teaching was an elixir for me that cured about anything.

For some reason, which I am sure I did not know at the time, I answered a student's question, saying, "Exactly," but pronouncing it as Willie Wonka in *Charlie and Chocolate Factory*: "Ex-aca-laca-ly." Many of my students related to this silliness and began to use it in their classes. Occasionally, when I visited them in their schools, they would introduce me to their students, "This is Dr. Ex-aca-laca-ly."

An irregular undergraduate female of whom I have no other memory, came to my desk after a class one day and presented me with a sketch she had drawn of me teaching.

Author teaching at Murray State University, from sketch made by student.

Wesley in high school.

Robert in high school.

I loved my job and was good at it; albeit, my point is an important byproduct of my involvement and competence was I provided the regents no legal cause to fire me.

Dad knew I was a strong public supporter of President Curris; when I told him the regents had fired Curris, he was concerned about me. He had the vaguest notion about the importance or meaning of tenure at a university. I am not sure he ever got his mind all the way around it. While Dad was superintendent, Arkansas did not have tenure for teachers.

I assured him I was safe and was going to the bottom of the academic ocean, free of any storms on the surface, and not come up until no one could remember my name. As the Rye Whisky duck, I was going to "dive to the bottom and never come up."

I soon had a chance to practice my bottom of the academic ocean theory. In searching for Curris' replacement, many faculty meetings were held to discuss what kind of experience and characteristics we wanted in the new president. I attended none and was conspicuous by my absence.

The regents wanted to meet with faculty to be sure of picking the next president with our approval; I absented myself from those meetings. My absence was obvious enough to cause some faculty and regents to ask me why I was not there. I told them I was retired from academic politics.

The regents selected Kala Stroup, Academic Vice President at Emporia State University, Kansas and more importantly, according to the regents, she was the faculty's choice.

* By now it is 1984, and I was married to Marilyn Crawford, the third marriage for each of us. She was the eldest of five accomplished children of Jean and Bettye Crawford of Mayfield in Graves County.

Marilyn was a special education major and had taught eight years in public schools of Chicago, where she had gone after college. She lived there by herself and was married there twice. She was extraordinarily smart, tough-minded and one of the most independent and competent persons I have known. She was tall and slim and had deep dimples and blue-green eyes.

She had a most admirable quality for a woman. She could wake from a sound sleep and be out of the house in less than five minutes, face washed, hair and teeth brushed, dressed, smiling, ready to go, and looking good all day without makeup.

I met Marilyn during the first week I came out of my self-imposed isolation. She called my secretary and said she wanted to talk with me about an idea she had to build a school for a certain classification of special education students. My secretary gave her a four o'clock appointment.

During my residency for my doctorate, I had begun to smoke a pipe. I enjoyed sitting in the smoking room of the University of Arkansas' new library, smoking my pipe and reading. At work, I often smoked in my office. Just before my four o'clock appointment arrived, I filled and lit my bowl, and assumed a professorial pose of sincere interest.

After chatting a while, Marilyn began to talk about her idea; I realized I had not the vaguest notion of how to accomplish what she was talking about. I wrote for her the name and office number of the Special Education Department chairman and told her she really needed to talk with him.

She took a deep breath, smiled, seemed to become relieved of a burden and said, "I can't keep doing this; you are too nice a guy. Here's the thing: I am recently divorced and am looking for someone to meet. A friend of mine at Tilghman [Paducah's high school] had you in class and told me, 'Boy! Do I have a man for you!'"

She wrote her name, address, and phone number on a piece of paper, pushed it across my desk, and said, "If the idea of our getting together appeals to you, you can call me at this number." She left me nonplused, sitting shrouded in a cloud of pipe smoke.

As I was leaving the building thinking what an interesting woman she was, I saw her driving away in a four-wheel-drive pickup with raised suspension, fog lights on the top of the cab and mud all over. She became more interesting.

When I arrived at her house to pick her up, I met one of the smartest, prettiest, most fetching children I have known. She was Marilyn's daughter Molly Kate. When we were leaving, Molly was at her open upstairs bedroom window watching us leave, yelling as loudly and clearly as she possibly could, "Do-do balls! Do-do balls!"

Hearing but not understanding, I asked Marilyn what she was saying. Marilyn replied, "She is saying do-do balls. It is the only curse word she knows. She is mad because she thought you had come to see her."

Marilyn and her daughter Molly Kate about the time author and Marilyn married.

Reunion of John Willis descendents at City Park in Monticello, 1985. Author in first row center in redshirt; to his left is his wife Marilyn, then Robert and Wesley; Molly Kate is in Wesley's lap, then Wesley's wife Rhonda. Author's parents are third and forth from right in second row.

Marilyn, Author, Wesley and Robert standing, Author's parents seated, Molly Kate in author's dad's lap—taken at City Park same day as reunion.

Marilyn and I married in May 1984. A few days later, when Paducah Tilghman's school year ended, we spent three days in Edwards, Mississippi, near where there was a reenactment of the Civil War Battle of Champion Hill.

This battle was the only one in which my paternal great-great-grandfather probably fought. His unit, the Ninth Regiment, Arkansas Infantry, fought at Champion Hill, and the military record of William Jessie Willis shows him as "present" on the date of this battle.

Edwards had only one motel; it was a single-story concrete-block building with eight rooms. The faded sign baring its name was painted on a four-by-eight-foot piece of raw plywood on the ground, leaning against the motel. The sign read "The Motel."

When I checked in, the manager handed me a flyswatter. Marilyn and I went to our room. Shortly, I returned to get another one.

The only public place to eat closer than Vicksburg, which was twenty miles away, was the 7-Eleven across the street.

Marilyn had recently built a house of authentic saltbox architecture. I had only seen a few of them and never been inside one. It was in a newer housing division in Mayfield, consisting of a circle of half a mile. Our common practice was to walk the circle for exercise.

In 1984, I put in a fescue yard at the house, my first one since Hays; it was impressive. We began to landscape. I was partial to blue hydrangeas.

* Mother had congestive heart and diabetes, and her health capacity began to decrease. I went to see her in April, 1985. The morning I left, Dad told me Mother wanted to see me. I went into their bedroom; she was on her back and propped up on pillows.

She motioned me to her, kissed me on the lips and whispered in my ear, "Sweetest Wad," her pet name for me that she had never spoken except when we were alone and not since I was a small child.

Author's mother

On the evening of April 30, Mother was in bed in a hospital room in Monticello. With her were Dad and Wesley and Monteene McCoy, my parents friends. Monteene went home at eleven o'clock; Dad asked Wes to stay with him.

Mother expired on Wednesday, May 1, 1985. Dad told Wes, "Call James William and tell him it is time to come home." The phone rang by my and Marilyn's bed at three o'clock in the morning. It was Wesley McCoy. He said, "James William, it is time to come home."

My family left Dad's house in the funeral home's family car to go to Mother's funeral. Dad sat in the front seat with the driver. He was slumped over with sadness; he said in a tense, trembling voice, "I love everybody in this car."

The day after Mother was buried, Marilyn, the boys, and I were sitting around the breakfast table with Dad. I told Dad we would all be there or another day or two and asked him if he had something he wanted done.

His expression became determined; in a deliberate voice he pointed behind us into the backyard and said, "See that magnolia tree?" We turned to look and agreed we did. Dad continued, "I want it cut to the ground, cut up in small pieces, and hauled off or burned; and I want it done *today*."

The magnolia tree had become an issue between Dad and Mother. It had never been trimmed, and the limbs reached to the ground, which made it difficult to mow around it. He wanted to trim it, she did not; it was not trimmed.

Marilyn and I began to use this solution to solve our disagreements, as in "I guess this is something we can decide when one of us dies."

* In summer 1985, I began to get a discomfort in my chest while I was mowing. The discomfort stopped when I stopped. I was forty-six and had never been to a hospital. Except for the intestinal flu when I was a sophomore in high school, I had not seen a doctor in thirty years. I convinced myself my indigestion had become worse and laid in a larger supply of antacids. By July 1, my regimen of Rolaids was not working.

Marilyn kept encouraging me to visit her doctor. I kept refusing. On a Saturday, she and I went to a health fair held on Mayfield's town square. There, I had my blood pressure checked. It was so far above normal; the nurse manning the blood pressure area was alarmed. He strongly encouraged me to see a physician for an electrocardiogram.

Wesley as a young man.

Robert as a young man.

I went to Marilyn's doctor; he performed a resting cardiogram that showed irregularities. He recommended I see a cardiologist. One of Marilyn's brothers-in-law was Joe Slaughter, a good doctor and good man. He referred me to David Hall, Paducah native and one of the better cardiologists in Nashville.

Dr. Hall performed an arteriogram and found 90 percent blockage in my left descending artery. He and the surgeon he selected, named Lee, sat by my bed and showed me the pictures of the arteriogram and explained I needed a triple heart bypass and I needed it *immediately*.

I went from thinking I was in perfect health to suddenly having a serious affliction. I was slow to get my mind around the situation.

Whatever they said made me no difference. I could not do it on their schedule; I absolutely had to go home. "My hydrangeas need me," I patiently explained.

They told me, "You could very well die on the way home."

I had a triple heart bypass the next morning. Wes drove from Texas and walked into my room while I was in recovery. I was sure glad to see him.

AIDS was rampant in 1985, and my surgeon feared the hospital blood supply was tainted. If he had given me a transfusion, I may have become infected. The operation went well, but my recovery was slow because I went home needing a blood transfusion. For about six weeks, my recovery was slow-going. I returned to work full-time that fall but was not yet at full speed.

I recovered and resumed full activity, which continued until 1991, when the discomfort returned. Another arteriogram revealed another blockage, and I had another bypass. This one was a double bypass, done by the same surgeon.

Robert with his young family.

Wes with K.C. and Jessie.

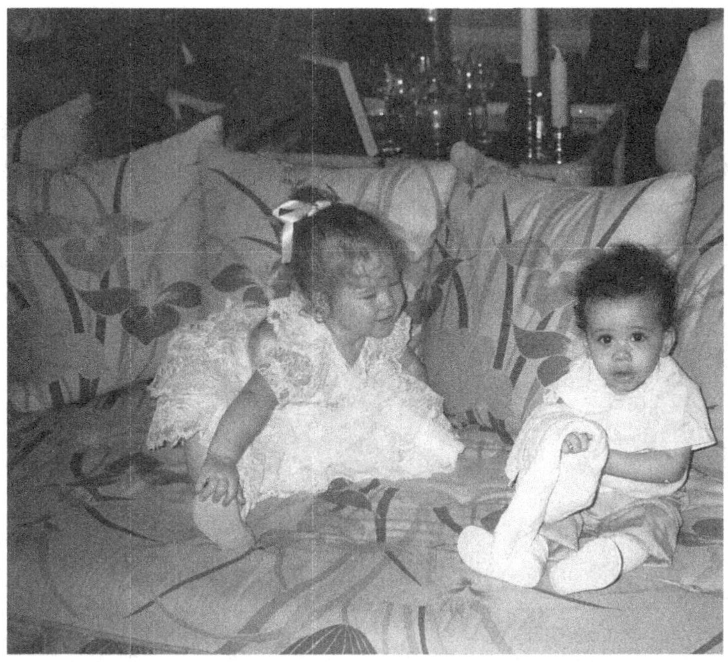

Author's grandchildren K.C. and Richard at their great grandpa's wedding to Myrtis.

Author's grandchildren Bethany and John.

Author's grandchildren Richard and Robyn.

Author's grandchildren Bethany and John with author's father, whom they called Pipa.

Author's granddaughter K.C., age 7years.

Author's granddaughter Jessie, age 5 years.

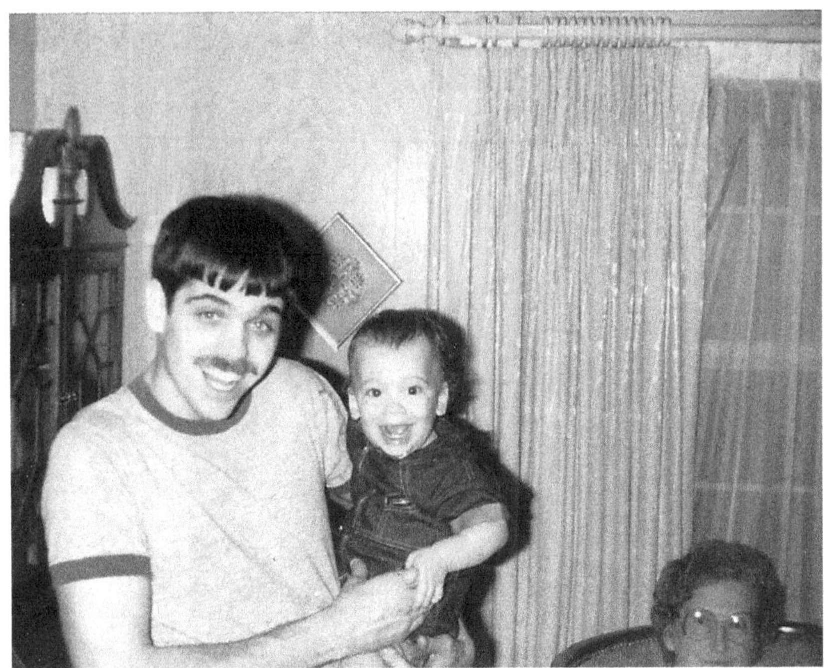

Robert and John; Uncle and Nephew. Clara at right.

Not wanting to experience failing to receive a blood transfusion again, I contacted several of my Church of Christ friends in Murray, who I figured were the least likely to be infected with HIV, and asked them to donate blood marked for James Willis at Saint Thomas Hospital in Nashville.

My second bypass went as smoothly as the first, but this time I was given a full blood transfusion, recovered, and was released in three days, at that time, the soonest one could be released from Saint Thomas after a heart bypass.

I returned in 1992 for an angioplasty. The physician, not Dr. Hall, failed to perform it correctly, and my artery began to close while I was on a gurney recovering and being monitored. I found out later I had a sudden cardiac arrest. If I had not been literally in the cardiology emergency section of the hospital, I would have died within minutes.

I was given a hypodermic injection to prepare me for the procedure. The last thing I remember Dr. Hall was pushing me on the gurney, running. He recognized a nurse in the hall, whom I had never seen and whom he respected. He excitedly asked her to help. Suddenly she was running beside me. I felt fine.

Hours later, I awoke; no one mentioned I had a heart attack. I was awake, but heavily medicated and my having a heart attack was last thing on my mind. Marilyn had called Dad about my condition; he came for a visit. His visit seemed strange to me but my laudanum-laden mind would not allow me to become aware enough to concentrate on it.

Instead of dying, I recovered after nine days, including Christmas Eve and Christmas Day alone in my room. I returned home with forty percent of my left front ventricle muscle, the largest in the heart, dead. My pumping action was reduced from normal to about fifteen percent. I had congestive heart disease.

Dr. Hall had an intern who came daily. After several days, he mentioned in passing my heart attack. I refuted his statement. He exclaimed, “No one has told you that you had a heart attack!” and fled the room in panic.

Shortly, Dr. Hall came in and updated me on all that had happened.

Since the experience with Dr. Hall and the nurse, I have lived with level one congestive heart, a level I work to maintain. After one is a heart patient, one is always a heart patient. Though stem cell research shows promise for regenerative heart muscle. Some of the most promising is at the heart hospital at the University of Houston of which my cardiologist is an alum.

Dr. Minton as said he could probably get me into a clinical trial. Problem is such studies are double-blind. I could be in the control group as the experimental one. Though there would be no medical cost to me, the other cost and inconvenience would be considerable. My current thinking is to wait.

If I had not gone to see Marilyn's doctor, which almost did not happen, the rest of my life would have unfolded significantly differently, including probably not being alive the past twenty seven years. When I returned for the arteriogram in 1992 and had a heart attack, I would have died if I had not been *literally* on gurney in a hospital cardiac emergency room, which almost did not happen.

* Mayfield had a great old theater that had been closed for several years; a group took it over, cleaned it up, and started a community theater. Marilyn encouraged me to participate.

I read for a minor, non-singing part in *The Music Man*. The director and Casting Committee insisted I read for the lead Professor Harold Hill, which required my singing solo "Seventy-six Trombones," among other songs.

After I read for the part, the director insisted I sing. As Marilyn and I knew, I was a total disaster, exacerbated by the director insisting I sing with gusto. He had never associated with someone who could literally not sing anything at all. He got up close in my face with painful expressions trying to pull the tune out of me.

Marilyn and I figured that was that, thanked everyone, and went home laughing all the way. Two days later, the director showed up at my house and said the Casting Committee and he had decided I was the man to play Professor Harold Hill, the lead in the musical! They had figured out how to make it work; I would sing "Trouble Right Here in River City," which is more a chanting rhythm than a song. The cast would sing the other songs, including "Seventy-six Trombones"; "Marion the Librarian" would be omitted.

I agreed. *The Music Man* played to nearly a full house for nine performances over three weekends. I have a video tape of the play. It was a great fun time.

I had the major non-singing part in *Annie Get Your Gun*. Our group also put on a farce titled, *Love Rides the Rails or Will the Mail Train Run Tonight?* I played the lead Simon Darkway, the villain. I had oil on my hair and oil on my tongue. The Darkway role was similar to Sneaky Fitch I played in Claremore years previously.

Dad and Myrtis came up to see all three plays in Mayfield. Dad and Mother had also seen me in the farce in Claremore. Mayfield was more than twenty-five years ago. Sneaky Fitch in Claremore was over thirty. When one experiences the roar of grease paint and smell of the crowd, it lingers in one's blood.

* Sometime in my youth, I developed ambition to be a trial lawyer or a stage actor. I never told anybody, because I thought these ambitions were not realistic. When I was five, I told Dad and Mother I wanted to cut wood in Bowser for a living when I was grown, which they thought was cute and told everyone.

My heroes are stand-up comedians. They walk onto a stage completely alone before an audience without a script, sidekick, or music. Their courage is admirable, which is more than I have been able to summon. Therefore, my admiration for them never morphed into an occupational ambition

When I returned from the army and took the double major of English and history at Arkansas A&M, which is an undergraduate preparation for law, I had a partial thought of checking out the possibilities of attending law school.

Law school was not within my reach, and I became a history teacher, which was my third choice. It turned out to be perfect; I was a natural at it, and a byproduct of teaching was I had to use the skills of a trial lawyer, an actor, and a standup.

* Two years after Marilyn and I married, she became principal of the Murray vocational high school and we built a house in a development just west of the city of Murray. We built no ordinary house.

Without any professional house plans, we drew our own for a Federal-style house, popular in the late eighteenth and early nineteenth centuries. We set about *painstakingly* creating one that looked as much like it was built in that style as we could make it.

Until early Twentieth Century, brick houses and buildings were built with double-brick construction, because the walls were load-bearing, unlike the modern brick-facade walls. Every fifth row, sometimes every seventh, the bricks in the load-bearing walls were turned sideways for strength, similar to stacks of hay bales. We told the masons what we wanted. They turned bricks that had been broken in half on the outer walls every five rows to appear as if the walls were double thick.

In the era we were attempting to replicate, exterior bricks did not rest on the ground but on foundation blocks of stone. This required lime stones for the foundation; we found them in an Indiana quarry. Our bricks were new, made in brick molds of colonial Virginia. We put down five-to-seven-inch-wide tongue-and-groove walnut and cherry wood floors; window sills were a full inch thick. In this era, wood was cut as advertised, in other words, a one-by-four-inch sill was literally one inch by four inches. We had to special order them and the bricks.

To facilitate efficient heating and cooling, we built the house with eight-foot ceilings, but added space between the floors and the attic for the house to appear from the outside to have two full stories with ten-foot ceilings. We made the interior walls six inches wide so we could offset the two-by-four studs. This arrangement meant the wall on one side would not touch the wall of the adjacent room, considerably deadening the noise between rooms.

Above the windows, common in the Federalist period, were "soldiers," bricks on turned long ways with both ends that were clearly seen. The windows had small panes and were taller than today's. The stairs were constructed in the Federal style. At an antique store in Louisville, we found the same newel posts as in the Dodge City boardinghouse in *Gunsmoke*.

Under the house was a thick plastic layer, covered with four inches of pea gravel. Beneath the house were wires for fluorescent lights, with a switch at the opening. The floor was not insulated, which helped the underneath remain dry. A few years later, the space was so dry I could smell the cement dust. I was very proud of that house.

* Sometime in the late 1980s, Marilyn, Molly, and I drove to San Antonio to visit Wes, who was stationed there. On that trip, the four of us drove to Monterrey, Mexico, where we found a Mexico quite different from the area along the United States border. We stayed in a Holiday Inn.

Then, in Mexico, poverty was more hopeless, miserable, wretched, and pervasive than today. At the motel was an upscale restaurant. Its excellent food was inexpensive; its service great. Most guests were upper class natives.

Our first night, I tipped the waiter a ten-dollar bill. He bowed, kissed the money, and thanked me, with what I thought was sneering exaggeration. Going about the next day, I understood how deep the poverty was; he was not exaggerating. He was that thankful for ten dollars.

We drove to a small town west of Monterrey, maybe Artega, up into the mountains; there we rented horses and rode them farther up into the Sierra Madre Oriental to a site off the tourist path, where there was a large, beautiful waterfall. It was a spiritual place; to guard it, ancient Mayas had carved two huge stone heads and placed them there hundreds of years ago.

We asked our guide about the stone heads. He knew nothing and had no curiosity about them. He had no idea who the Mayas were, much less that they were his probable ancestors.

We four were the only gringos. The men with the horses went out of their way to take care of Marilyn and Molly to insure their safety. It was an enjoyable, exciting afternoon. I compared it to what a night out, with a fine dinner and the theater might cost me, which was much more than the cost of this adventure; in this expansive mood, I began to tip the men.

They refused it. They thought I was trying to buy the horses. When they understood they could keep the money and I had no interest in the horses, they were surprised and extremely grateful.

Many Americans visiting Mexico took advantage of the cheap goods in their economy and also paid less for service than they would in the U.S. for worse service.

Author and sons.

* The longtime girl friend of a colleague and a friend of mine at Murray State University was the wife of the silent partner owner of the Cincinnati Bengals football team. Her husband, who knew all about her and my friend's relationship, invited him, another colleague of mine, Marilyn, Molly, and me to Cincinnati to be the guests in their home and attend a game, sitting in the owners' suite—a room midway up in the stadium, on the fifty-yard line with a private bath, kitchen, and cook. He sent his private plane on a Friday to Murray to pick us up.

The husband John, a great fellow, insisted I call Dad and Marilyn's father to invite them to the game. Dad drove to Mayfield on Saturday and spent the night with Jean and Bettye; Dad and Jean flew to Cincinnati on Jean's plane. (He was a C-47 pilot in World War II and dropped United States airborne troops behind the lines on D-day and had his own plane.) Dad and Jean sat in the owners' suite also with us.

In the owners' suite, we met and talked with Neil Armstrong, the first man to walk on the moon. Dad's highlight, however, was meeting Paul Brown, one of the original founders of the NFL and the founder and first owner of the Cleveland Browns. He had been pushed out of the ownership of the Browns and became an owner of the Bengals, with the help of my colleague's girl friend's husband as a silent partner.

The first man to walk on the moon spent most of his time at the game talking quietly and privately to Molly.

If the Bengals won, we were invited into their dressing room after the game. They won that day, and Dad and Jean joined us in the team dressing room. It seemed their eyes and smiles were larger than their faces. All seven of us flew back in Jean's plane.

It was a great day for all. Dad had stories to tell the Union Bank coffee bunch in Monticello that he visited almost every morning.

* A major form of entertainment in Murray was sit-down dinners at the home of friends of two to six other couples. I imagine Marilyn

and I averaged attending one every two or three weekends. These were fun because drink was available, but never to excess, and witty, humorous table conversations. No one turned on a television or any form of artificial entertainment.

Dinner conversation was Dad's long suit; as I mentioned, he was a talented raconteur with impeccable timing. I do not know if I inherited some of his talent or some just rubbed off on me from proximity, but I could usually hold up my end of the entertainment in these environments.

People visiting from out of town or newcomers to Murray marveled at the extent and spontaneity of the diners and wondered about the origin of this tradition. People in Murray agreed it was unlike anywhere else we had lived, and none knew how it began.

Author dressed as Santa Clause for a Christmas Fair in Mayfield, trying to get Molly to understand she does not know me.

* Almost all my graduate classes were in the evening. One was on campus; the other two were often one hundred miles off campus and were composed of in-service teachers scattered around west Kentucky with a few in southern Illinois.

At Murray State University, my teaching goal was to comfort the afflicted and afflict the comfortable. People do not like to feel uncomfortable with what they think or believe.

To learn is to change: to respond differently to the same stimuli.

I wanted my students to change their concepts. One of the major concepts I developed in my graduate classes, and to a lesser extent in my senior classes, was the danger of ethnocentricity, the dangerous belief within each culture that it is superior to all others.

A group does not have within itself the power to change; consequently, people cannot change, learn, without an outside influence.

No people can be completely, totally isolated; however, it is an obvious fact that the more isolated a people the more they think alike and the less likely they are to change. From this fact, cultural anthropologists theorize if a people could be completely isolated, they would not change at all.

With this in mind, I would ask my graduate class, numbering thirty or so in-service teachers from west Kentucky, how many of them taught in a school district from which they did not graduate or their spouse did not graduate or in a district more than one district from where they or their spouse graduated. Often, none raised their hands. Rarely, if ever, did more than two or three of the class, raise their hands.

The more ethnocentric a community is, the more persons who are not a member of that community are looked upon with suspicion by persons who are. The more isolated a community, the stronger is the belief among its members they have *the* truth: anything they do not understand is by their definition *stupid*, *wrong*, and otherwise not worth their interest.

With this attitude, its members have a strong proclivity to see differences among people rather than similarities; it follows they consider whoever or whatever is *different* is by definition wrong.

The papers and class discussions about ethnocentricity were interesting. My attention to ethnocentric quality of teachers caused most of my students to question their delusions. However, some knew only they became uncomfortable with their beliefs and I had made them that way. These were angry with me.

I was in my familiar position among students of being either well liked or not liked at all. Over the years at Murray State University, students told me if they asked someone if they had Dr. Willis as a professor, they always unhesitatingly answered yes or no. It seemed everyone knew who I was or had heard about me; no one answered, "I don't know if I have had him or not."

As mentioned, Don Miller had helped me with my own ethnocentric trap by letting me see why I believed and thought as I did. If I had been born to different parents and raised in a different time and place in a different environment, I would be different. In fact, it is interesting to contemplate whether two different me could understand each other, or would like each other.

In 1992, Kentucky had a budget crisis; university's faculties took a two percent cut. I wrote a letter to the *Paduch Sun* and the *Murray Ledger and Times.* It received considerable attention.

March 25, 1992

FACULTY
Department of Elementary/Secondary Education
Murray State University
Murray, Kentucky

Dear Colleagues,

The following letter was published in the Ledger and Times Saturday, March 21. Several of you have commented favorably on it and asked for a copy. To this end I have made one for all.

August of 1990, eighteen months ago, during the annual luncheon at our university, those who govern us gave a talk: a fine talk too, all about excellence and greatness in academic pursuits. This was not a partly talk, glib and hollow, the sort one may expect at such an affair with such an audience. No. This talk was a complete one with heavy and important words about mighty and real deeds to be done: a call to academic arms—Murray State University was going to become one of the best regional universities in the nation. But to govern is to choose, not to talk, and those who govern us made choices at the regents meeting on St. Patrick's Day which spoke louder than their words.

At this meeting the call to academic arms was abandoned when the choice was made to take one half of the budget cut from the academic area. Cuts in athletics, our governors reasoned, could not be larger than ten percent because more would jeopardize our status as a Division I school and OVC and NCAA membership." This reasoning offers the right answer to the wrong question, which is: would these cuts jeopardize our membership in the NCAA? The correct question: among what membership do we wish to be listed—among the list of NCAA schools or among the list of academically best regional universities in the nation? The question is either/or because we cannot be both among the best NCAA schools and among the best regional universities.

Comparing the 1991 College Guide: America's Best Colleges with this year 64 team NCAA tournament one can determine that among the list of the nine best specialty schools in America, none are playing in this year's NCAA tournament; among the list of the 25 best liberal arts colleges in America, none are playing in this year's NCAA tournament; among the list of 50 best major universities in America, only 8 are playing in this year's NCAA tournament; among the list of 60 best regional universities, the list for which Murray State was to a part, only 3 are playing in this year's NCAA tournament. (None of which is seeded with expectation of getting of getting beyond the final 16.) In summary, among the 124 colleges and universities listed as the best of their kind in America, only 11 are playing in this year's NCAA tournament, about 9 percent. Among the regional universities, MSU's category, the 3 out of sixty numbers amount to 5 percent.

But the 9 or even 5 percent odds is not the important consideration in determining our choice of either quality academics or NCAA athletics. The important consideration is found in the characteristics of these 11 schools in the NCAA tournament that are also considered the best of their kind in the nation. These schools are: Duke, Georgetown, Michigan, North Carolina, Stanford, Princeton, UCLA and USC among the major universities, Four of these 11 schools were founded in the 18th Century, 6 in the 19 Century, and 1 in this Century, UCLA founded in 1919. Looking over this list one may notice more than half are in California and North Carolina, two states with an almost unbroken history of supporting excellence in all areas of education. Seven of these 11 schools are private, parochial or independent institutions, with huge endowments and long histories of academic excellence, and the remaining 4 of these schools are major state schools with wide and deep public support and long histories of academic excellence. One does not have to see the emperor has no clothes to see Murray State University and, for that matter, our sister schools in the OVC hardly fit any of these caratagories. The single, simple and inescapable fact is the important one to consider when determining our choice either quality academics or NCAA athletics.

The emperor-has-no-clothes observation that is difficult for some to see is that the basketball champion of the OVC conference, with automatic bid to the NCAA tournament is not even among the list of the 64 best basketball teams in America. This fact means the regents decision insures our university will not be on any list of the best in the nation. And who wants that?

(Copies sent to university President, Academic Vice-President, college Dean and Assistant Dean.)

* After ten years as department chairman, I resigned and returned to full-time teaching. I felt much relief. I was as Dad was when he took so long to learn to heat my milk and put it in a thermos. I wondered how intelligent I could be to have remained department chair so long.

When I returned to full-time teaching, my department elected me to represent them in the faculty senate. They reelected me for two more terms of two years each, during which the senate elected me faculty senate president. I found myself back in campus politics. As before, they had to do with the office of university president.

As mentioned, after the regents did not rehire President Curris at the end of his contract, they hired Kala Stroupe. They said she was "the faculty's choice." At the end of her second contract, with no faculty input, President Stroupe was not rehired,

With no faculty input by the regents than when she was not rehired, they replaced her with a retired four-star admiral whose previous position was president of the United States Coast Guard Academy. The faculty, including me, waited, expecting to be impressed.

Bless his heart, Admiral Ronald J. Kurth, Harvard PhD, was smart and worked hard, but he did not have as much business being president of a *public* as a college freshman. He had no understanding or respect of any sort for the way academicians view the world as a whole or view their place in it.

Each faculty member is an expert. University professors disagree among themselves. This is what experts do. In the military view of the world, the commander is the only expert; if he wants others' opinions, he will ask for them. What Murray State University faculty considered an honest exchange of views among colleagues, Admiral Kurth took as a personal affront to him.

Further, the admiral was clueless. The first time I met him was at his initial faculty reception. Making conversation, Marilyn asked him about his boat. With a line of people waiting to greet him and regents present, he stood there and lectured her on why he had never been on a boat but on a ship. He stiffly explained, "Madam, a man can stand in the middle of a boat and jump out of it in every direction. I was never on a boat."

On the way home, Marilyn and I discussed how long he would last. We agreed not past his four-year contract: "Unless he is an extraordinarily fast learner."

He was a fast learner. But not fast enough to stay ahead of the regents, who seemed to be gaining speed and confidence, but not knowledge, in getting rid of Murray State University chief executives.

I pointed out their lack of ability in another letter to the editor of the *Murray Ledger and Times* and the *Paducah Sun.* (August 24, 1993)

Dear Sir:

Admiral Ronald J. Kurth, PhD (Harvard) arrived to the office of president at Murray State University with less than noticeable skill in understanding the role of president at a public university, much less one found in rural west Kentucky. However, as one expects from an intelligent, well motivated person who cares about doing his best, President Kurth learned: the awkwardness so prevalent early in his administration ceased. But now, after he has learned how to be president of this place, several regents want not to renew his contract. All the public reasons given for this are too trivial to be believed, while the real reason can be compressed into one tired, old, retread of a hollow chestnut: he is not one of US ("WE the people" . . . of Murray) and unlike previous, recent presidents, he does not even feign a pretention he wishes he were.

As people have noticed about these regents, "There they go again:" contemplating with provincial views what is best for a state university. Believing that MSU is Murray's university, they wish to return it to local control—their own. An arrangement satisfactory to everyone who thinks the old days are good. An arrangement satisfactory to everyone who thinks ethnocentricity is the main determinant of, not detriment to quality education. Neither arrangement is one by which an institution of higher learning or a community can prosper.

The question that must be answered by the regents whose "only motive is to serve" [they say] is this: what has President Kurth done (or failed to do) that his being retained would be more ruinous to Murray State University than his not being?

* When the Regents did not rehire President Kurth, after they did not rehire President Stroupe, after they did not rehire President Curris, they finally realized they had not gotten much right in selecting presidents. They decided to hire a professional

presidential search team at a cost of one hundred thousand dollars to find a replacement for Admiral Kurth.

To lead the search team, they hired the president of Western Kentucky University, our sister university about one hundred miles east of us. His name was Kern Alexander, a brilliant, experienced man and national expert in educational finance and law. Dad, in his capacity as chief financial officer of the Arkansas Department of Education, had occasions to work with him and was much impressed; something I did not know for several months.

After fits and starts attempting to find a president, the regents and Search Committee were not successful. Murray State University had earned the reputation as a place a competent president would not want to serve.

No faculty meeting had been held to discuss anything with the regents about the hiring of Alexander and no faculty were part of the hiring process, except the faculty regent who had lost the faculty senate's confidence.

After the regents announced Alexander was their choice, faculty at Western Kentucky University began to contact faculty at Murray State University regarding his lack of fitness to be president, with newspaper articles and materials supporting their position.

Our faculty senate met and, after a clamorous discussion of our opinions and options, voted to oppose Alexander being hired and to ask for a meeting with the regents. Our vote was 27-0.

Unanimity among faculty on any issue is so rare many believe it is a myth. They believe, if all professors at a university were laid end to end, they would not reach a conclusion. The lines were drawn. I was about to experience déjà vu all over again.

The issue was professors *are* the university. Regents *govern* the university.

In the better universities, everyone recognizes this precarious balance of responsibility in division of labor works best in an atmosphere of mutual respect where no one ever feels the necessity to speak of it. When one attempts to define this balance, it often gets out of kilter.

I was the leader of a faculty, whose representatives to the Faculty Senate had voted 27-0 not to hire Dr. Kern Alexander to become president of Murray State University. I was required to go once more into the breach.

The senate leadership, five of us in all, met with the regents in their plush cherry-paneled room with kitchen and bathrooms. The first question was asked by a regent whose name I have easily forgotten. He said, "Before we talk with *these* people, I want them to tell me why we should listen to twenty-seven troublemakers when we have more than 300 people on our faculty. Why don't we hear what these other 300 professors have to say?"

After an embarrassing silence, the regents looked at me. I responded, "In 1941, our country with a population of 131,000,000 went to war against Japan after the nation's congress voted 434-1. [Montana's representative Jeannette Rankin voted not to declare war in both world wars] No one asked why we should go to war because a few trouble makers wanted us to."

I tried to keep the sarcasm out of my voice but probably not successfully. I think it was Aldous Huxley (1894-1963), author of *Brave New World* who observed, "Facts don't cease to exist because they are ignored."

All remained respectful and attentive for the rest of the meeting.

We knew something the regents did not know we knew; they had already told Alexander they were going to hire him that night, and he was on his way to sign the contract. While he was on route, the regent chairman told him they had to meet with the faculty before they could hire him and not to show up as planed. He stopped en route and checked into a motel.

The upshot of the meeting was we listed and discussed everything we knew, or thought we knew, that would cause the regents to have second thoughts to hire Alexander. They had not heard about most of our objections. Because I was faculty senate president, the regents directed most of their questions to me; I did most of the talking for the faculty.

After ninety minutes, the regents closed the meeting; a motion was made to hire Kern Alexander as president of Murray State University. The motion passed with two dissenting votes; both dissenting members said they had changed their minds after listening to the faculty.

The dissenters were safe; they could grandstand and not effect the hiring of Alexander, something probably some regents recognized.

The new president was hired. It was official and done and over with. The regent chairman told us that he had called Alexander to tell him he was hired and that Alexander had asked to meet with faculty senate leadership the next morning at nine o'clock.

We gathered at the appointed time and place. I expected the new president would do most of the talking and we would listen attentively.

I was impressed by how Kern began the meeting. He said, "I have spent most of my academic life as a professor and have been a member of faculty senates. With the vote 27-0, I know, if I had been at your meeting, I would have voted as you did. I want to hear your reasons."

My colleagues turned and looked at me. I began to tell him what we had heard and why we were concerned. He respectively listened and quietly answered everything we brought up. He did not try to gloss over his mistakes. He was disarmingly forthright.

As our discussion progressed, I decided he was the person for the job and worthy of faculty support and we had made a mistake opposing him. I realized much of our problem was with the regents, who had badly handled the whole process, and he was our focus of their mistakes. I told him that. He sympathized and said he would work to get them to learn how the best universities involve faculty in all decisions and honor faculty input.

Though our discussion he was startlingly, even breathtakingly frank. He never mentioned we must speak in confidence. He respected us enough to know confidentiality was a given among competent faculty. He definitely talked the talk, which, I think, is the first thing a person has to do to walk the walk.

One of the things that impressed me was our meeting lasted four hours without a break; he drank as much coffee as the rest of us and never left the room.

I became a strong supporter of him. He was the first real president Murray State University had since Constantine Curris. Under Alexander, the university got back on track and it continued to grow and become respected in the academic culture of universities.

President Alexander was a tall, lean man, who exuded alertness and physical fitness. He purportedly ran ten miles daily. He had a strong face with high cheekbones and piercing blue eyes. I imagined him as Shakespeare's Cassius, with "a lean and hungry look."

In October of Kern's first year, I took a call at home early on a Saturday morning. Calling was Angie Muhs, the respected education reporter of the *Lexington Herald-Leader*. She said she was calling me because I was faculty senate president and she had questions. She asked if I would agree to an interview.

She asked unequivocal and detailed questions about Kern's hiring and his administration thus far at Murray State University. I assumed she knew I had a part in the ruckus over his hiring, but she never let on. I answered her many questions directly and unequivocally.

Among other things, I told her I thought the regents were more at fault in the hiring of President Alexander than was he. She asked me to sum up my impression of the new president. I said, "You cannot beat him because you cannot outwork him, and you cannot outthink him."

More was said; her interview continued for twenty minutes, one question and answer after another. The article was most of a page in the next day's Sunday paper. Reading it, I discovered I was the only Murray State University faculty she mentioned that she had spoken with. She identified me as the Faculty Senate President quoted me verbatim at length in paragraphs, including my statement about the botched hiring of Alexander by the regents and why one cannot beat him.

Our interview caused a stir on campus and in the state.

After this article, the perception among state politicians and legislators was the squabble over Alexander was finished. He had been accepted by faculty at Murray State University, and the campus was moving forward. My enemies were quieter, but still there and more determined.

I was again vociferously supporting the university president, which raised suspicion about me with many of my colleagues, several of whom had not forgiven me for supporting Curris eight years before. Academic politics is unforgiving, because it is personal.

* Fortunately, my life as a professor consisted of more than teaching and fighting with the regents. I began research

that culminated in the publication of my first book, *Arkansas Confederates in the Western Theater*.

This book was my most important *professional* accomplishment. As many things in my life, I began without much thought or consideration as to what I was getting in to. It began with my wanting to research information of my eight great-great-grandfathers.

During the Civil War, six of my great-great-grandfathers lived in Arkansas, one in Kentucky, and one in Mississippi. Seven fought for the Confederacy. The eighth, Great-great grandfather Jordan, when conscripted, sent his sixteen-year-old son Mitt to go in his place. I began with my paternal ancestor William Jessie Willis and his Civil War experience. I began this research in spring 1984. The book was published in December 1998.

I quickly found his war record in the archives of the Arkansas Historical Commission. He served in the Ninth Arkansas Confederate Regiment of Volunteer Infantry. My next step was to find an account of that regiment's actions in the war, by which I would learn what Private William J. Willis did.

From the *Official Records*, I learned the Ninth Arkansas Regiment fought in the Western Theater. Except for three inadequate primary regimental histories, an account did not exist of any Arkansas Confederates fighting in the Western Theater.

I was dismayed to discover that, if one depended on Civil War secondary sources to learn about any Trans-Mississippi Confederates who fought in the Western Theater, he will have driven his ducks to a dry pond. As I expanded my research about the Ninth Arkansas Regiment, I took notes and began to put these notes into narrative form.

The Ninth Arkansas Regiment was one of the hardest-fighting units in the Confederacy. It fought alongside every Confederate infantry organization in the Western Theater. Whenever I found that it joined with another regiment, I would research that regiment, because where that regiment went, there would also be the Ninth.

My research and narrative grew until it became a history of Arkansas Confederates in the Western Theater, thus the name of my book. It was thoroughly researched and footnoted and tells their story for the first time. Researching and writing it was enlightening, exhausting and enjoyable.

Literally, I mean literally, a day did not pass in these fourteen years on which I did not do *something* with the book, except when I was unconscious in the hospital. I was days or weeks in the university, county and state libraries, the Library of Congress and National Archives in Washington, DC. Other days, I made a call, took a call, wrote a letter, received one, or took a note. But *every day* it was *something* for fourteen years.

What began without my thinking about it filled my professional thought and activity longer than anything ever had. Concerning the publishing of my book, my serendipitous luck held, as the following account will reveal.

In the fall of 1985,I drove to Atlanta to attend a three day conference on the Civil War battles in Georgia. The primary presenter at this conference was Edwin Bearss, Director of the U.S. National Military Parks and author of several Civil War books, including the three volume work on the Vicksburg Campaign, which remains the definitive work on that subject.

The conference began with a banquet where Bearss spoke, The next day our group boarded four buses to travel to Kennesaw Mountain, where we would be led over the battle by Ed Bearss. As the bus I was on was pulling out of the motel parking lot, it collided with a car. The bus driver stood and told his passengers we would be delayed until this situation could be taken care of.

I was sitting next to the window on the front seat opposite the driver. Sitting with me on the aisle was a man whom I had not yet met. He jumped off the bus and began running. I right behind him. "Where is your car?" I asked him. He pointed.

"Mine is closer" I responded. We both turned and continued running toward my car. We followed the Conference busses the rest of the first day of the battlefield visitations in my car.

The man was Robert Younger, owner of the largest Civil War publishing house in America (therefore, I assume in the world), Morningside Press in Dayton, Ohio. We became close acquaintances that day, and he asked me to send him what I had finished on my manuscript.

I had sent a few chapters of my manuscript to the University of Arkansas Press. They were not interested. I sent them to the University of Missouri Press. The Editor-in-Chief called me personally and said he liked the work and wanted to publish it but I would have to get it under 300 pages. He sent me a contract that required I make Missouri my exclusive publisher. I was confident the story of the Confederate Arkansans in the Western Theater could not be told in 300 pages. I held the contract and had not signed it when I met Bob. He told me to send it to him. If he liked it, he would publish as written

Bob Younger and Edwin Bearss were close friends; they with their wives visited and traveled together. Bob introduced me to Ed the first night. The three of us associated during the Conference. Ed heard Bob and I talking and asked me to send him the finished parts of my manuscript. I agreed.

A week later, I received my manuscript with edit comments, which were superficial. He added the following paragraph.

I found your manuscript interesting and well written. More important, it tells the story of men and units from Arkansas, whose role in the war has been too often ignored. Consequently, your manuscript, if published, will fill a gap in Civil War historiography.

Early in 1986, I sent Ed more chapters at his request. In his letter back to me he wrote, "Once again, I commend you for your research and writing skills. I believe you are well on your way to providing Civil War readers, be they scholars or buffs, with an outstanding regimental history."

The next year, Ed held a conference in Chicago about General Grant. I put in an application to the dean for expenses to attend a "Grant Conference in Chicago. I believe she thought the conference was about writing grants. But she did not wish to appear that she was mistaken and never mentioned it.

Ed wrote the fly leaf information about me and *Arkansas Confederates in the Western Theater.*

My book consists of two volumes published as a single book. It has 903 pages, of which 41 are bibliography of nearly 800 sources, including 600 primary ones, many never having been cited before.

As Ed's comment suggested, research in Arkansas Confederates fighting east of the river had never been done beyond the most rudimentary level before I entered the field.

The service record of every soldier in the Ninth Arkansas Regiment is in the Appendix of my book—over 1,470. In the 37 pages of Index are over 2,500 entries.

It sold out quickly. Used copies may be found on the Internet listed for more money than were the new ones. I once found two on sale in the United Kingdom.

The older my book becomes, the more expensive to purchase it becomes. When I was writing it, I envisioned my going into a book store in six months and seeing one of those signs saying, All Books in the Box Half Off and the box filled with my book. Instead, my book is considered the definitive work on its subject. People still ask me about it and desire a copy.

One person knowledgeable about the Civil War writes that my book is "thoroughly researched and meticulously footnoted." Another critic writes of *Arkansas Confederates in the Western Theater* theirs was "a spectacle of sacrifice, courage, and ultimately historical obscurity."

Not long ago, these two comments were found on the Internet. When published, My book was reviewed by more than a dozen critics; almost all of them university professors and Civil War authors and editors. Excerpts from ten critics follow.

1. "This is the best Civil War Book I have ever read"—**Harriett McGarth**, long time proof reader for Moringside House Publishers (Dayton,Ohio; October, 1998).

2. "This story . . . is told in a compelling and action-filled narrative by James Willis.

"Willis, an avid researcher, spent more than a decade ferreting from countless manuscripts and published sources the grist used in weaving Arkansas Confederates in the Western Theater. The book is a must reading for those who follow the western armies and will appeal to the larger audiences that appreciates the trials, tribulations and heart break that were a common experience of the Civil War in America"—**Edwin C. Bearss**, Historian Emeritus, National Park Service (Arlington, Virginia; December 1, 1998).

3. "Prof. Willis has crafted a wide-ranging and scholarly study that will stand for decades as the starting-point for any aspect of the Razorback State's activities in the nation's darkest hour"—**James I. Robertson**, Professor Emeritus of History, Virginia Pollytechnical University, winner of the Douglas Southall Freeman Award in 1997 before I won it in 1999 (Blacksburg, Virginia; December 8 1998).

4. "Thanks for the Willis book. A great piece of Work . . . . Man has really done his research"—**William C. Davis**,

founding editor of *Civil War times Illustrated* and editor of the five volume: *Images of War* (Mechanicsburg, Pennsylvania; December 14, 1998).

5. “I looked at this book for more than an hour this morning. I am REALLY IMPRESSED with it! From the slight reading, I find that he writes with good style, power, often light touch, very personal . . . many allusions to the classics in well put places . . . The introduction, From Quiet Homes and First Beginning, is just wonderful. My god what a TOME!

“I am not a CW buff . . . don’t believe ever read a CW book. But this man can WRITE and I mean write well”—**Rebecca DeArmond**, Arkansas author, historian and director of the Portland History Project (Ozment Bluff, Arkansas; December 21 & 22, 1998)

6. “He has mined all the research necessary to make this one comprehensive book the source book for generations to come. . . . Willis takes care in presenting the men as individuals. . . . He crosses the battlefields, using just the right touch of personal letters and recollections to make the journeys, trials and tribulations of these foot soldiers come alive. . . . Willis’ work is indeed a treasure for Arkansans, Civil War fans and history”—**Maylon T. Rice**, staff writer, *Northwest Arkansas Times* (Fayetteville, Arkansas; January 31, 1999).

7. “I am currently reading for the third time. It is that good “—**Tom Ezzel**, author of capsule histories of Union and Confederate regiments (Little Rock, Arkansas; February 2, 1999).

8. “Read a little more . . . last night—very, Very, VERY well put together. I particularly like the framing things in terms today’s person can understand/relate to—think , , , [Willis has] instituted a new way of teaching WBTS events/people in the 21st Century . . . !!! This book is BOTH well written and

well researched; an INSTANT classic indeed !!!!! (i.e.—buy it!!!!!)"—**Kenneth Byrd** (Indianapolis, Indiana; February 4, 1999).

9. "This book is at once the first to examine in depth the subject of Arkansas Confederates in the Western Theater and undoubtedly the definitive work on the subject. It is difficult to imagine how any other author could find material that James Willis missed, or could relate the material with more care and in plainer or more readable prose. . . .

"This information, in many cases, has never been published or obscurely so. As a consequence, the Willis book is a treasure of 'new' information on a variety of Civil War topics. . . .

"Anyone interested in Civil War history west of the Blue Ridge Mountains and south of Virginia will enjoy and learn from the comprehensive, wonderfully researched book"—**Jerry Russell**, National Chairman, Civil War Roundtable Associates (review written for *The Arkansas Librarian*, Little Rock; March 1, 1999 edition).

10. "The book is a sheer masterpiece. Well researched, well explained and well presented. . . . This comprises more than a remarkable feat when one considers that Willis is treating a subject seldom focused upon in the Civil War"—**Jack Koblas**, author of several Civil War magazine and newspaper articles; quoted in Northwest Arkansas Times article titled "UA grad wins prestigious writing award;" September 19, 1999.

While at MSU, I received a letter from London, England from a Patrick Rearam, who had read my book.

James Willis

April 23, 2001

Dear Professor Willis,

I trust you will forgive the imposition of an unexpected letter from somebody you have never met. However, having just finished reading your "Arkansas Confederates in the Western Theater," I simply felt I had to write to express my deep appreciation for your excellent work.

I enjoyed your book from beginning to end. It was a delight to read such masterful combination of the big picture united with the essential human details will bring such stories as you have told to life. I confess I found it impossible to remain unmoved by the account of the Arkansas woman and her veteran husband in the grand review of 1917. Composure took some time to return.

I have studied the War for most of my life; I find it absorbing indeed compelling beyond adequate description . . . . I did not have much insight into the wider Arkansas contribution. Now, thanks to your scholarship and expertiseI am a fervent admirer of General D. H. Reynolds and all the indomitable Arkansans who served east of the Mississippi. I will continue to develop this new found interest.

Again, forgive me for intruding upon your time. It was essential to me thank yoy for a book which has now an honorable place in my library . . .

During Christmas 1998, Dawn and I drove to Monticello, where the Drew County Historical Society had scheduled a book signing for me on the Sunday afternoon before Christmas in the Drew County Historical Museum. All profits for the sales went to the museum. The museum made more than $1,600 in two hours. While there, Dawn and I had a great visit with Dad and Myrtis.

#If I had not been sitting on the tour bus with publisher Bob Younger, when the bus hit the car, the rest of my life would have unfolded completely different

Advance MONTICELLONIAN

BOOK SIGNING -- James Willis, author of "Arkansas Confederates in the Western Theater" autographs one of his books at a recent book signing held at the Drew County Museum.

Author signing his first book *Arkansas Confederates in the Western Theater* for Drew County Historical Museum, December 19, 1999

* Monday, December 1, 1997, Michael Carneal, a freshman at rural Heath High School, fifteen miles west of Paducah, Kentucky, shot and killed or wounded several of his fellow students. It occurred during the spate of school shootings in the nation.

That afternoon, a Heath High School teacher, whom I had in class, came by my and Dawn's house to talk to us about what happened and to try to make sense of it. The next morning, I took a call from Mrs. Carneal, Michael's mother, whom I had in a graduate class spring semester of that year. We talked about an hour. Or rather I listened while she talked.

It was a tragic, sad time in a rural community in west Kentucky that had seemed safe from tragedies that were far away in big cities and other places crazies lived.

* On the Cumberland River adjacent to Fort Donelson Military National Park is a bed and breakfast that had delicious food. Dawn and I often ate there and had reservations for lunch on Valentine's Day 1999, a Sunday. We were looking forward to the day.

At home that Sunday, while I was still in bed but awake, Dawn was dressing in our bath; we were talking through the open door when we were interrupted by the phone ringing by our bed. It was Myrtis. She said, "James William, your daddy is dead." It was nine thirty.

Dawn, Hayley, Hope and I went to Monticello instead of the bed and breakfast. I called Robb, who came with his family, and I called my oldest grandchildren Bethany and John. They both came with their mother.

Wes was in Korea. I contacted the Tennessee headquarters of the Red Cross, gave them Wes's rank and unit, and asked them to find him in Korea and confirm with his commanding officer his grandfather had died. I gave them the number of Drew Memorial Hospital, so they could speak with the physician on duty to confirm Dad's passing. Wes came from Korea, via Texas, with his family.

The funeral was on Thursday to allow time for Wes to get to Monticello. Dad's funeral was well attended. He was eighty-four.

In his last years, Dad's foremost desire was to see all six of his great-grandchildren together before he died. He worked mightily to get that done but he could not make it happen. His six great-grandchildren saw each other together for the first time when they saw their great-grandpa in his casket.

He died when he was at Drew Memorial Hospital, diagnosed with a non-terminal, stomach ailment. I talked to him by phone the night before. He said he was recovering and feeling better. I told him we would be down next weekend. He said he may not be good company. I said, "You can sit there and I can look at you." We laughed.

The last time I saw Dad was when I was in Monticello for the book signing. My last words to him were the night before Valentine's Day 1999, when I called him in the hospital: "I love you, Dad."

"I love you, Son," Dad responded.

I find it ironical my father's last words to me were the exact ones he had such difficulty saying to me until he was in his seventies.

I thought an autopsy should be Myrtis' call. We did not have one. We still do not know of what he died. The cause was not what his death certificate said, which was a digestion ailment.

My grandpa John Willis and his son Earl Willis, both died at 84, both alone in a bathroom—Grandpa at Clara's; Dad at Drew Memorial Hospital.

* I was hired at Murray State University as associate professor. I gave little to no thought about promotion. Only faculty pay attention to rank. Students do not; all of them referred to me as Dr. Willis. My rank did not keep me from serving on important faculty committees; I was elected faculty senator and faculty senate president as an associate professor. Preparing a promotion document is a time-consuming, difficult undertaking. I decided a promotion application was unnecessary.

However, when my book was published in November 1998, it received favorable critical notice, including the S.A. Cunningham Award from Arkansas for best author of book about Arkansas in the Civil War and the prestigious Douglas Southall Freeman Award "for most outstanding work in Southern History from

Colonial Time to the Present," which included one thousand dollars.

"To select the book . . . nine judges from seven states considered effectiveness of research, originality of thought, accuracy of of statement and excellence of style"—*Northwest Arkansan Times,* Sunday, September 19, 1999; article "US grad wins prestigious . . . writing prize."

I began to think maybe I ought to apply for promotion. Also the salary difference between the two ranks had increased to $2,500. Promotion had become worth considerable bother.

I prepared my promotion application, which took several days, and submitted it September 11, 1999, the promotion deadline for spring of 2000.

A professorial promotion application follows a specific, rigorous process. It is submitted first to the Department Promotion Committee, which recommends to the department chair to promote or not to promote, with supporting reasons in writing attached. And so on it continues from the department chair, through the College Promotion Committee, to the dean of the college, to the University Promotion Committee, to the provost, to the president, and finally to the regents.

My application was favored by the Department Faculty Promotion Committee and the department chair. The College Promotion Committee turned me down, as I thought it might. A psychology professor in our department, who was strenuously opposed to me on the Curris and Alexander issues, managed to stop me by observing my book was not in my field, which was not a requirement for promotion. But it was a talking point to stop its progress; if someone needed a hook to hang one's hat on, here it was.

If trauma can cause memory loss, it follows a tiny bit of trauma can cause a tiny bit of memory loss, which may explain why I so easily forget names of people I do not appreciate. I recall the professor's first name was Charles; he liked to be called Chuck. He wore a badly fitting toupee. I remember nothing else.

The College Promotion Committee was composed of four professors, one from each of the four college departments. It required three votes to pass an applicant and two to stop him. Chuck found a friend. He was the representative from another department who did not support me in the presidential hiring politics.

If a faculty member' promotion is denied at some level, it is returned to him. He can keep his application going forward, but it will show rejection at the level that rejected it with reasons in writing. After the College Promotion Committee rejected my application, I kept it going forward.

Next, my application went to the college dean, who was the same man who as Calloway County school superintendent had transferred Marilyn rather than fire the incompetent teacher of his church, who Marilyn had recommended be fired. He passed it, with reasons in writing.

I had strongly supported Marilyn in her dispute with him. What tipped him was I had in class his oldest son, since graduated from Harvard Law School, who told his father I was one of the two or three best teachers on the campus. Next my application went to the University Promotion Committee.

Professor de Toupee represented the College of Education on the University Promotion Committee; he needed no friend to persuade that committee not to promote me. Its members, by their nature, were inclined not to.

Professors in liberal arts colleges have the proclivity to be easily persuaded that liberal arts faculty ought not to approve of a faculty in the college of education doing historical research and having a book published based on one's research. Such activity is their bailiwick, an area of specialized knowledge. A professor's bailiwick is jealously guarded from interlopers, as I was perceived by them.

My application went next to the provost who, as expected, followed the recommendation of the University Promotion Committee. A provost failing to follow the University Promotion Committee's recommendation is exceedingly rare.

It is absolutely unheard of or imagined for the president to reject the provost's recommendation if it agreed with the University's Promotion Committee. Therefore, it is unheard of for a rejected faculty member to take his promotion beyond the University Promotion Committee and provost levels. My enemies thought I was finished.

A few days after receiving the provost's letter, telling me he had turned me down and reasons why, I attended a small meeting called by President Alexander, having nothing to do with faculty promotion. When it was over, I took the opportunity to ask him if he was acquainted with Dr. James I. Robertson Jr., professor emeritus in history at Virginia Tech, where Alexander had been on faculty.

Professor Robertson won the Douglas Southall Freeman Award in 1997 for his book on Stonewall Jackson, as I did in 1999 for my book.

Kern said Robertson was a good friend of his and an outstanding professor in Civil War history. I showed him what Professor Robertson had written about my book: "Professor Willis has crafted a wide-ranging and scholarly study that will stand for decades as the starting point for any aspect of the Razorback State's activities in the nation's darkest hour."

President Alexander did not know I had written a book. I had taken a copy to the meeting and showed it to him. He took it and looked carefully through it, noticed the extensive bibliography, footnotes, and index, and was impressed by it. He smiled broadly and congratulated me on a job well-done.

I told him the University Promotion Committee had turned me down. He frowned and said, "The provost should help me on this."

I said, "The provost has also turned me down; but with your permission, I will forward it to your office."

Kern fully understood the implications of what I had asked. Momentarily taken aback, he said, "Give it to me." He took it from me. We did not communicate again about my promotion.

At the next regents' meeting, on President Alexander's recommendation, they unanimously promoted me to professor with a $2,500 raise over my normal annual increment. Chuck de Toupee rarely found occasions to speak to me again.

Each fall, Murray State University had a faculty and staff luncheon in a large hall at the Curris Center with about eight hundred in attendance. At the luncheon after my promotion in the spring, the president was recognizing a few of the faculty for special mention.

At the end of his remarks, he said he had attended a national meeting of university presidents, and shared, "The President of [I think Michigan State University; I don't know because I was not listening closely when he began his statement] commented to me about a professor at Murray State University who wrote the best Civil War book he had ever read. It was our own *Professor* James Willis."

Don Miller would have been proud; he would have loved my telling him the academic politics of it.

Dad had died before Kern made his public remarks, but he would have appreciated them. He was proud of my writing *Arkansas*

Confederates in the Western Theater. He told me with a twinge of awe, "I don't see how in the world you found all that stuff."

When I retired three years later, the regents unanimously recognized my work at Murray State University, awarding me *professor emeritus*, an honorary title of recognition and respect.

Some people who have never been taught by a good teacher or have never been themselves a good teacher believe, "Those who can, do; those who can't, teach." About such nonsense, Voltaire (1694-1778) observed, "A witty saying proves nothing."

My parents, two uncles, four aunts, three first cousins, and I are or have been teachers whose careers epitomize the observant quote of Henry Adams (1838-1918): "A teacher affects eternity; he can never tell where his influence stops."

While I was exercising several months ago, at the Southeast Arkansas Rehabilitation Center, I experienced an example of Mr. Adams' observation. A man approached and introduced himself to tell me how much he enjoyed my two books. After visiting awhile, he asked if I knew Don Fleming. "Don Fleming was the best teacher I ever had," he said.

The man was Richard Reinhart, father of Jeff Reinhart, my physician. Dr. Reinhart is one of the largest benefactors of the Drew County Historical Society and its museum.

The observation of Henry Adams is undeniable, as is the wisdom of Sir Thomas More, mentioned in the opening to the Lovington chapter.

I have successfully served in the world's most important profession—teaching. One may find it strange (to say the least) that a profession as ubiquitous as teaching is the most important. True: if one has a deadly disease, medicine is the most important profession to that person, and for one with serious legal trouble, law is the most important profession to that person. However, no less a personage than astrophysicist Neil deGrasse Tyson, PhD, observes, "Teaching locks in progress," and progress is consistently the most important activity for **all** cultures, **all** nations and **all** who therein reside. Physicians and attorneys could not exist without teachers.

Shakespeare writes of life, living and making a contribution.

Tomorrow, tomorrow and tomorrow,
Creeps in this petty pace from day to day,
To the last syllable of recorded time,
And all our yesterdays have lighted fools
The way to dusty death. Out, out brief candle!
Life is but a walking shadow, and a poor player,
That struts and frets his hour upon the stage,
And then is heard no more. It is a tale
Told by an idiot full of sound and furry,
Signifying nothing—McBeth Act V scene v

While in my life, I have made no contribution to mankind that warrants notice. My image will never be on a postage stamp. Beethoven, Sauk or Rosy Parks I am not. Albeit, as every good teachers can say: after I have strutted and fretted my hour upon the stage and am heard no more, the stage will be a better place than before I arrived upon it . . .

* In the late 1980s, my schedule changed. I began teaching two sections of Foundations of Education to seniors the semester before they student taught and graduate courses in Educational Law, Philosophy of Education and History of United States Education.

Foundation of Education was a two-hour course that I taught, Tuesdays and Thursdays from 8:30 to 9:20 a.m. and 9:30 to 10:20 a.m.

In 1998, when Dawn moved to Henry County High School from Paris City Middle School after her second year, we moved from

Murray, Kentucky, to Paris, Tennessee. I began to make the thirty-mile drive one way each day.

The day after my sixty-third birthday, I was driving into Murray to meet my Tuesday 8:30 class, listening, as always to Murray's National Public Radio. I pulled up to a stop sign behind a car driven by a woman driving children to school.

Her car had in its back window an exaggerated cartoon map of the United States divided into red and blue states. The larger area of red states was named United States of Americans; the smaller area of blue states was named United States of Liberals.

I was thinking what pathetic mind could have conjured such thought, much less be so proud of it to display it on a car, when Karl Kesselman of National Public Radio read a news bulletin saying that a plane had hit one of the Twin Towers.

I remembered news reports of a plane that had run into the Empire State Building in 1945. This crash was caused by fog and incompetent pilot. I assumed the plane that hit the Twin Towers was some similar story.

When I pulled into the parking lot, Kesselman was handed another bulletin. "The plane that hit one of the Twin Towers had two engines," he said. The plane that crashed into the empire building was a B-25, two engine bomber. I thought no more about it, same old same old; I turned the radio off and went into my office, where I did not turn my office radio on, as I had some last minute things to get together for class.

After I called the class role, I asked if they had heard about the twin-engine plane running into one of the Twin Towers. One of the students answered it was not a twin-engine plane; it was two planes and both towers. A few others nodded in agreement of what she said. I thanked her for her up-to-date news and asked if anyone had anything they wished to add, ask or talk about.

My class of thirty-five college seniors was unreservedly unperturbed. No one said a word or changed expression. I began teaching as if September 11, 2001, was as any other class day. The class proceeded normally. Students in my second class were equally unperturbed.

When my classes were over, I returned to my office, where I turned on NPR. I intellectually understood what I was hearing, while continuing oblivious to it. I remained in that non-conscious state on the drive home with the radio on NPR.

When I arrived, I made a sandwich, sat down in front of the television and turned it on. The Twin Towers were smoking ruins on the ground, a plane had been forced to crash in Pennsylvania and the Pentagon had been hit. The United States had been attacked not unlike Pearl Harbor; and I still just did not get it. To be more accurate: I did not *feel* it. I was lacking empathy

As I had been when teaching in Lovington in my twenties, forty years later at Murray State University in my sixties, I remained as the lost gods in Psalm 82; "I was walking about in the darkness."

I was planning to prepare rib-eye steaks, baked potatoes and salad for Dawn, the girls and myself. To buy steaks, I walked to a small nearby grocery, which was the oldest one in Paris, founded in 1874, in the building that had always been a grocery.

The owner was also the butcher, whom I had known for three years and who was unfailingly friendly, was profoundly preoccupied and hardly spoke to me. I ordered two one-and-a-quarter inch steaks, paid for them, and returned home.

When I got home, I discovered my friend the butcher had sold me four quarter-inch steaks. When I returned to make the exchange, he apologized and, with tear-filled eyes and trembling lips, explained, "I have just been too upset about what has happened to think clearly."

Author 2001

Thinking one of his family or friends had died, I literally had my mouth open to ask the cause of his profound grief and to offer my sincere sympathy when I mentally slapped my forehead.

Just in the nick of time, I checked my thought. I realized this nice gentle man, living in Paris, Tennessee, as I, was crying about the Twin Towers in New York City having been knocked down, killing thousands of people, mostly Americans. I thanked my friend and returned home.

Okay, I got it—finally. But I still did not *feel* it. It was as if the terrorists' attack was a tornado in Iowa or a fire in California or a flood in Indonesia. I did not feel angry; I did not feel horror, nor was I feeling heart-stricken. I felt sorrow, but only as a person watching the passing of a funeral procession of strangers.

Empathy I still did not feel. Perhaps more importantly, in relation to the eventual nation's response, I did not *feel* threatened; I did not *feel* fearful. I still do not. I am sure a freshman psychology major could explain how I was experiencing textbook disassociation.

I wonder if someone in America on December 7, 1941, had no excess of *feeling* about what had happened in relation to Japan bombing Pearl Harbor.

My thoughts returned to the woman in the car in front of me at the stop sign that morning and her red-and-blue-states cartoon map. I wondered if she was shedding tears over the death of the socialist, godless, liberal New Yorkers whom that very morning she believed were not Americans.

I wonder how much of my lack of feeling was caused by the initial reaction of my classes that day. Terrorists knocking down the Twin Towers and killing nearly 3,000 people, mostly Americans, had impacted the seventy people in my two classes, light years **less** than the assassination of President John F. Kennedy thirty-eight years previously!

Neither Husain nor Iraq was responsible for the attack on 9/11. Regardless, President Bush publically compared Husain to the Nazi Fuehrer, he announced America was going to war with Iraq and would do it without a smidgen of sacrifice. The war would be fought with a professional military, taxes would not be raised to pay for it and the President told Americans to go shopping and take vacations.

I wrote a letter published in the Murray and Paducah papers opposed to going to war against Iraq. Shortly after it was published, I was at the Murray Animal Shelter. When I was in my car to leave, a large, scraggly appearing man in overalls approached me; I smiled, stealthy locked the door and rolled down the window. The man asked, "Are you the one who wrote that letter to the paper?" I did not waste his time asking which letter.

Hayley and Hope.

"Yes," I told him, holding my breath to see what he would do next. I thought I could take him if our disagreement did not become physical.

The man smiled, stuck his large, unwashed hand into my car, shook mine and said, "Thank ya'll. I shore do agree with it." I thanked him with relief and drove away. He was the first of several who sought me out to express agreement and gratitude. I knew Mr. Bush's war was not going to be as popular as the media commentators and politicians would have us believe, unless it was short and cheap.

Dawn and I enjoyed several great vacations. We went twice to St. George Island, off the coast of Apalachicola, Florida (once with the girls), and stayed in a beach house in a gated community. The second vacation, we stayed there two weeks. Joining us for three days was our friend, Rick Kreisky, the superintendent of Henry County Schools, with his wife and daughter.

Dawn and I drove west, through South Dakota, visited friends in western Montana and went on to Glacier National Park (one of my longtime Meccas). We returned through Yellowstone and Grand Teton National Park.

We spent a night in two lodges at Glacier, one night in the Old Faithful Lodge at Yellowstone, and five nights in the Jenny Lake Lodge at Grand Teton, where President Clinton and his family spent one of his family vacations. This lodge is composed entirely of cabins in the wild part of the park at the very base of the Tetons.

On the return to Paris, we spent a night in Great Bend, Kansas, and visited Alan. Dawn was much impressed one of the fifty most eligible bachelors in America was my friend.

Two years later we flew to Calgary, Canada, and rented a car for a ten-day vacation in the Canadian Rockies, including five days and nights at a resort at Lake Louise, believed by many, and so advertised, to be the most beautiful place in the world.

We resided on the seventh floor in the Fairmont Inn in a 500 sq. foot lake view room. on the Gold Plan which included gourmet breakfast private elevator and sundry luxuries.

Food at these lodges in the States and Canada was beyond just excellent.

Over the two-week Christmas vacation in 2003, we flew to Cancun and spent several days on a newly built all-inclusive resort directly on the beach twenty miles south of Cancun. On this vacation, we spent an interesting day at Chechen Itza, an impressive Maya ruin.

Family dog William Shakespeare with Hayley and Hope.

Hayley.

Hope with the casual look.

Hope with the glamorous look.

Another day, we went to Playa del Carmen, a town an hour south of Cancun. It was a quaint fishing village just being discovered by tourists. Today, Google says, it "is the fastest-growing town in Mexico." Many newcomers are from Europe, who sold all they owned and moved to Playa to live; some began a business, more than a few of which are restaurants.

Author and Dawn on deck of house on St. George's Island, Florida.

Dawn and Alan in Great Bend, Kansas.

Dawn and I loved to dance. We were in Cancun at the resort for the New Year's Eve party, which featured food, drink and a mariachi band; one of the better parties I have attended. Many of the guests were from Chicago, Canada and Germany.

Though I have danced with other women, Dawn was my only wife with whom I danced. I played bridge with Mary Ann and canasta with Carol. Marilyn did not play cards or dance. She had won equestrian tournaments and had a small stable. We rode horses, which I much enjoyed, and attended and gave dinner parties.

One of my horses was a palomino, which I named Trigger, of course. My favorite to ride was a Tennessee walking horse. It had a fast, smooth gate, about which I had heard but never experienced.

Lake Louise and Fairmont Inn, Canada.

* I retired June 30, 2003, and began teaching two classes, rather than the usual four, during fall and spring semester. For my halftime work, I was paid 50 percent of my regular salary. My state retirement was 60 percent of my salary; which totals 110 percent of my salary. In addition, I received twenty-two thousand dollars annually in social security, totaling a hefty sum for a poor schoolteacher.

My employment was a halftime contract, but it was actually less than a half, because I was not serving on any committees or boards, which had been a large portion of my workload.

I had been a senior member of the Department Faculty Evaluation Committee; department representative on the College Academic Council; chair of the Department Program Evaluation Committee; chair of the College Research Committee; chair of the College Student Teacher Committee, the final arbiter of who is allowed into student teaching, and various ad hoc committees.

Such service is an important part of the best of academic life, and I enjoyed it, but did not miss it after the years I had been involved.

My situation after retirement was I was working less than halftime and making thirty-five percent *more* salary than during full-time employment. My halftime contract was for two years, after which I would receive annual mutual agreement contracts.

Forty-two years before, in Lovington, New Mexico, my beginning salary was $5,200, a comfortable one for a teacher in 1962. My income as a *retired* halftime professor at Murray State University was nearly twenty times more, not including Dawn's principal income.

I was living under no man's thumb and no man's dime.

All required of me was to teach, which I enjoyed after more than forty years. I was beyond the reach of academic revenge by colleague malcontents. My health was good. I had more free time than since I had been bored out of my gourd as a child; I had plenty of money to go anywhere and do anything, at least anywhere or anything my imagination could conjure up.

My personal life included an extraordinarily beautiful, intelligent, accomplished and caring wife, who was principal of Henry County High School, and two intelligent, pretty, talented charming, loving stepdaughters.

I began writing a column for the *Paris Post-Intelligencer,* averaging about one every month, which gave me a new audience that Dad astutely observed I needed.

The publisher Mr. Michael Williams titled my columns "A Second Opinion," drawing attention to the fact that I offered an opinion contrary to that of other columnists and to that of most of the authors of "Letters to the Editor."

Mr. Williams headlined my columns, which he usually composed to increase readership. Four of them were: "Ten Commandments, Ten Commandments," April 9, 2002; "God Will Bless America Again When We Accept Homosexuals," March 2, 2004; "Jesus Would be a Democrat," May 26, 2005; "Final Column Defends Evolution as Scientific Certainty," June 13, 2005. Another column favored *choice* in the abortion issue. Others were similar.

I never wanted it all; albeit I had it all. Each morning when I woke up, I looked forward to *everything* I was going to do. It was a good time to be me. Russell Harrison, one of my jackrabbit-hunting buddies from Lovington would have observed, "James, you've got a bird nest on the ground."

* In 2004 things transpired with Dawn that caused her love for me to lessen. Her job, which was primary for her, ran into a rough spell, as such jobs will. She was angry, confused and despondent.

I suggested I find for her an excellent psychologist out of town. She agreed. I talked with the counseling faculty in my department, without saying anything about Dawn being involved. Among them, a consensus name came up. Dawn called him for an appointment and began visiting him weekly in Clarksville.

I never asked her a word about her meetings with her psychologist. She never volunteered one.

Near the end of 2004, she came home from a visit, sat in my lap, hugged my neck and tearfully said, "James, if I keep seeing him, I am going to leave you."

I asked her, "Do you think he is helping you?"

"Yes," she replied without hesitation.

"Then, you need to keep seeing him. Help for you is what seeing him is about," I responded. She kept seeing him.

MONTICELLO
(2005-2010)

The joys of love, they last but a short time, the pain of love last all your life all of your life.
—*Song found in Paris* by Morris Townsendsung sung to Catherine Sloper;
The Heiress, Paramount (1949)

* * *

A relationship, I think, is like a shark . . . .
It has to constantly move forward or it dies.
—Alvy Singer, *Annie Hall*, 1977

* * *

Love is of all passions the strongest for it attacks simultaneously the head, the heart and the senses
Loa Tzu

* * *

Where does a man go when he is not wanted?
Back to his own people.
—Spotted Bull to Cheyenne Bodie, *Cheyenne*, "Cross Purpose"

##

I had a bird nest on the ground, until the morning of Valentine's Day 2005, a Monday, the sixth anniversary of Dad's death, when

I awoke and found Dawn already awake. When she discovered I was, she looked at me. I waited for her to speak.

Voice even, eyes dry, she said, “Goodbye.”

“Where are you going?” I asked.

“I am not the one leaving,” she replied.

Psychology is the study of attempting to get inside one’s head to answer that person’s question *what is wrong with me?* Often, even good psychologist settle for the answer to that question to be what ever the patient says it is. What ever its source, Dawn’s psychologist found inside her head I was the answer to what was wrong with her.

My life had become a loaded gun staring at my heart with a yellow eye.

When we married, a friend of Dawn observed to her, “James loves you so much he hardly has room to breathe.” Months before we parted, I knew Dawn did not care for me as she did in the beginning. I naively believed I loved her enough for both of us.

Dawn and I married in October 1996, after my and Marilyn’s divorce became final on August 28. We had been seeing each other before my divorce and were, or thought we were, much in love.

People actually in love feel, think, and behave exactly as people who only *believe* they are in love. The couple cannot tell the difference, nor can people with them. One may wonder if romantic love exists in reality, in mythology or at all.

* After Marilyn had been the successful Murray Vocational High School principal for a few years, she was asked to take the Calloway County Middle School principal job. She was superb in

both jobs and was nationally recognized by the *New York Times* as one of the better middle school principals in the nation. Yes, the nation. Yes, the *New York Times.*

She was interviewed by the female education reporter of the *New York Times,* who came to Murray for three days. She had dinner at our house with a few of our friends. Great conversation ensued.

In the course of her job at the middle school, Marilyn dismissed an incompetent teacher who badly needed to be dismissed. Maybe as many as one hundred people showed up for the board hearing in the high school gymnasium in support of the teacher. Almost all of them belonged to Church of Christ, as did the teacher *and* the superintendent.

The upshot was the teacher was not dismissed and Marilyn was transferred from principal of the middle school to director of a special school for unsuccessful students for the same salary. (Kentucky law allows a superintendent to transfer anyone without giving a reason as long as the new position carries the same salary as the previous one.)

Marilyn became dissatisfied with Murray, something like Carol's "This place doesn't like me," except with Marilyn the disliking was more palpable. Without discussion with me, she became determined we move to one of her father's five farms; the one between Mayfield and Paducah. It had a house on it that her parents had been renting to a family but was far from ready for Molly, Marilyn, and me to live.

As I have mentioned Marilyn and I and built a great, unique house, in which we were living. This work took us two years to complete and was a period of energy, fun and closeness between us. However, the extensive, lengthily remodeling for the farm house was being planned by Marilyn and her mother *exclusively*. I was clearly made to understand any thought of mine was absolutely positively not to be sought, and was deafeningly ignored if offered.

I asked her about this development. She replied, “Trust me. I will take care of my mother.” I took her response as an attitude of profound emotional separation from me. The only way the distance that had grown between us could be bridged was for her to push her mother away and pull me closer. Talking to her would not help us, as she had taken that possibility off the table for discussion.

I had worked at Murray State University for twenty-one years, was a member of the Rotary Club, shopped and banked there, attended games and movies and the theater there, lived there and had friends there. It was my home base. Almost every time I went out, I was recognized by my students, past students, and colleagues and friends. Not only was my reputation Murray-centered, it had become my hearth; I worked there, and I belonged there. My audience that my father said I needed was vanishing.

Jean’s farm, where Marilyn intended for us to live, was in another county, forty-five miles from the Murray State University campus. I was being placed out of sight, soon out of memory. Inch by inch, I was being erased; I was imperceptivity fading into oblivion as surely as the Arctic ice cap.

My and Marilyn’s relationship going south is not an excuse for my seeing Dawn while married to Marilyn, but if our marriage had been stronger, or, perhaps, if I had been stronger, I would not have become interested in anyone else. Many members among the saint hood have never been tempted to be human beings.

Dawn and I knew many people would not approve of what we were doing. However, as is the way of persons who think they have, with clear eyes and true hearts, found their lives’ soul mates, we just plain did not give a rip what the world thought.

We discovered, as is the case of the self-absorbed, the world was not the least interested in us.

* In June, I told Marilyn I had met someone else and was moving out. Our divorce process began politely, if not friendly. Early in the process, Marilyn discontinued any pretense of civility; neither of us tried to reconcile.

The June evening I moved out, I called Dawn, told her what I had done and that I was driving to see Dad in Monticello the next day to tell him what I was doing, and asked her if she wanted to go with me. She did.

We drove to Monticello and checked into a motel; I went alone to see Dad and Myrtis. They were surprised and glad to see me. I sat in the chair next to Dad. He smiled and said, "You have been on me mind a lot lately. I have been remembering you mostly when you were a young child." I felt a lot of love between us. I wondered if he remembered my preaching to the chickens.

I began by saying, "Dad, I've got something I need to talk to you about." I told him *everything* I had done.

I was taken aback by his response, "Well, I must say I am not surprised." Then, he said the most interesting thing I have ever heard Earl Willis say: "I can certainly understand how someone can be *powerfully* attracted to another while he is married." I wondered how many important experiences in my father's life I had never imagined.

I joined Dawn for the evening in the motel, and we joined Dad and Myrtis for breakfast.

Dawn and I married in October; a few weeks afterward, Dad and Myrtis came for an overnight visit. They were both taken by my step-daughters, Dawn's girls: Hayley and Hope.

During Christmas 1996, Dawn, the girls, and I visited her family in Benton, Kentucky, and Dad and Myrtis. Wes and his family were in Monticello while we were there. Wes liked Marilyn and Molly Kate and had a hard time dealing with my decision.

On Memorial Day Sunday 1997, the Willis Reunion was held at Dad 'and Myrtis's home. This was the first time the family met Dawn. Dad got the attention of all of us before we ate when he said, "Dawn will give us our instructions on how to proceed."

Everyone got the message; Dad and Dawn were fine.

* Jean and Dad had become good friends. After Dawn and I got married, they visited Dawn, the girls and me in Paris and he and Myrtis visited Jean and Bettye in Mayfield.

Later, Myrtis told Dad that visiting a child's ex-in-laws was not the proper way of doing things when one's child divorces. He called me to tell me what Myrtis had said and asked me what I thought. I told him, "Myrtis is right; what you did is not the *usual* way for a parent to act when a child divorces."

I reminded him, "I have never put much store in usual ways of doing anything; you are grown and can choose your own friends and should not be affected by my divorce in your selection." We never mentioned it again.

When Dad died in February 1999, Myrtis asked me to "please" let Jean and Bettye know, thinking they would surely want to acknowledge his passing with a card or call to her.

I called them, received no answer and left a message on their machine. I called Marilyn and left a message on hers, telling her I had tried to contact her parents. Myrtis never heard from them.

Myrtis told me that after Dad had called me about having a relationship with Jean, Marilyn, who I guess had missed the *blood is thicker than water* bit of folk wisdom, called Dad and began to tell him all the unforgivable stuff, real and imagined I had done.

After telling her twice he did not want to hear it, she continued anyway; he hung up while she was in midsentence. Dad's hang-up ended any contact between him and all Marilyn's family.

* When Churchill led the English people to victory in World War II, he was surprised they voted him out in 1945, the year the war ended. He said, "I received the order of the boot," and went into retirement. Sixty years later, I received the order of the boot from Dawn and decided to hang it up at Murray State University and get the hell out of Dodge.

We *are* born knowing how to hold on to what we have, but we must learn how to let go of what we have. It helps to learn one's heart is a very, very resilient little muscle; when broken it continues beating. When love is lost, its story ends in tears or in a journey.

Where am I going? Why am I in this hand basket?

I googled retirement places from Florida and Virginia to Tennessee and Texas and settled on beautiful Monticello, Arkansas, where were people the same as I, many of whom knew me when I was growing up.

After moving about for forty-three years, Monticello was the first place I had gone that I knew something about, including several people living there.

During my second trip to my hometown looking for housing and finding none, I picked up a copy of the *Advance Monticellonian* and went to Ray's for lunch. In the paper I read an advertisement for an apartment described to my satisfaction.

I called the number in the advertisement; a lady answered. After trying to tell me how to get to the apartments at the corner of

West Wood and North Hyatt Streets and having trouble with my not understanding, she asked where I was from without asking my name.

I told her, "I used to be from Monticello, but now I am from Paris, Tennessee."

"James William!" she exclaimed. My luck was holding.

She was Gladys Mitchell, one year behind me at Drew Central High School, and whom I knew well. She had married James Youngblood, who was with me in the National Guard. He had gone to Camp Chaffee when the guard was activated in 1961.

After James' successful years in Monticello as a mailman and co-owner with Gladys of the largest and most successful florist shop in town, James and Gladys had recently built an attractive apartment complex. I reintroduced myself to them both and checked it out. It was exactly what I needed. I gave James a check for the rent for the remainder of the month. This was the first time I had seen Gladys in fifty years and James in forty-four years.

I recalled lines of a Robert Louis Stevenson poem from Mother's senior English class:

> Here he lies where he longed to be;
> Home is the sailor, home from the sea,
> And the hunter home from the hill.

I attended the 2005 Willis Reunion in Little Rock on Memorial Day Sunday and drove to Monticello afterward. When I turned south on Highway 63 at Pine Bluff, it began to rain so hard I could not read the signs well enough to tell where I was on the unfamiliar road. I drove nearly to Warren before the rain slowed enough I could get myself found.

* When I returned to Monticello, most people introduced me to others as “James William, Earl’s son,” as if this introduction said everything about me anyone could possibly be interested in.

I was troubled by this development, until I realized these people who thought they knew me had not seen or heard of me for forty-nine years. They knew nothing I had done or where I had been since high school. To them, my adult life was a blank sheet.

I laughingly told my Willis cousin Max, whose father Hugh was superintendent of Crossett School for decades, “People in Monticello think I am Swedish.” He wanted to know what I meant. “They introduce me as James Willis Earlson,” I said. He chuckled, nodding his understanding.

Interestingly, over the years, some people who knew my parents have told me I resemble more my father in appearance, but in temperament and attitude I resemble more my mother. Dad knew each of us and concurred with this sentiment.

[I was recently in a grocery in Little Rock and approached by a man I thought a stranger who asked me, “Are you Hugh Willis?” I told him Hugh was my uncle. “Oh, you are James William. I knew you had to be a Willis of some sort because you look so much like Earl Willis.” About my age, the man had grown up in Drew]

Dawn and I had agreed to divide our property, but had gotten a legal separation, not a divorce. Soon, she wanted a divorce and arranged for a lawyer in Clarksville, Tennessee, so we could keep our personal business out of town, which is almost never worth the effort. People just plain don’t care, unless you are a celebrity and your divorce is on television. We divorced in October 2005 and split the lawyer’s cost.

In the four divorces and separation I have had, my wives and I settled everything before seeing a lawyer and used the same lawyer. This is called a *collaborative divorce*. I had considered this a worthy personal accomplishment, until I mentioned it to a lawyer in passing. "My! Aren't you the charmer," she replied with a tinge of sarcasm.

* I took my dog Booter to Monticello, after James Youngblood graciously agreed for him to live in my apartment, but it did not work out for him. Booter was used to the freedom outdoors.

Within a few weeks, I found the perfect place for him, the Jordon Hunting Camp. The camp is in a beautiful area with a pond of seven acres and houses for members. He enthusiastically greets me when I visit.

He is popular with the camp members to the extent he rides with them in their four-wheelers and some of the hunters put him in their deer stands.

Before I took Booter to the Camp, I walked him twice a day. One occasion, we were passing a house when we were accosted by quite an elderly woman on its porch, who yelled, "Is that your dog?"

"Yes'um," I answered.

She asked, "Do you want to sell him?"

As I told her no, I remembered that house as being the one Dad and I had passed years before while driving. Out of the blue, without any antecedents, he told me the name of the woman who lived in that house, adding, "She taught at Drew Central twenty years and suddenly moved away." When he told me that, I silently recalled her and remembered her as a pretty woman.

The woman on the porch asked, "Who are you anyway?

"James Willis," I answered

"What Willis are you kin to," she asked?

“I’m Earl Willis’ son,” I said.

“Earl Willis! I was in love with that man for twenty years! Finally I had to leave Drew County to get away from him.” Again, she asked me if Booter was my dog. I realized she was in an early stage of dementia. We continued talking for a while. After she asked me two times more if Booter was my dog, I bid her good day. Booter and I continued our stroll.

While talking to the women, I recalled Dad’s observation when we passed her house years before and I also recalled what he said when I told him I was leaving Marilyn and seeing Dawn: “I can certainly understand how someone can be *powerfully* attracted to another while he is married.”

Author and Booter at Jordan Hunting Camp

* Dawn married her school superintendent Rick Kreiskey, her boss, with whom she had worked closely for ten years, first as high school principal, then, after she told me good-bye, as his

assistant in his office. She e-mailed saying, "I love him so much." They have moved to North Carolina, where he is superintendent and she teaches English.

Dawn's two daughters and I were close and have remained so. They have visited me overnight in Monticello four times, including Christmas 2009 and 2010 and call me **every** Father's Day.

After I went to Monticello, I returned to Paris and watched Hope play high school tennis and soccer. When she played in the Memphis area as a junior and senior, I also watched her there.

In May 2007, I went to Hayley's graduation from North Carolina University School of the Arts in Winston-Salem. She is living in New York City and auditioning for acting jobs. In August 2009, her first part was on *Law & Order: Special Victims Unit* television series.

It was episode 237, which played originally on October 21. It was a guest part, albeit large enough that she had most of the lines in her scene and was paid union wages. The camera was close-up on her for a full two minutes; but the part was not big enough for her to quit her day job, which was waitressing in a Mexican community restaurant in which she and the bartender were the only Anglos.

The restaurant chef was arrested for rape at a bar, put into handcuffs in his own kitchen, and hauled away. *Hardwork* is Hayley's middle name, the way her mother and I raised her.

For a while, Hayley walked Tony Shalhoub's dog. Mr. Shalhoub played Adrian Monk for several years in the popular television show of the same name. She was a hostess for a upscale West Side restaurant; she continues to read for parts, from which she has received several callbacks. Her drama mentor since high school is Cherry Jones, the actress who played the United States president on the television show *24*.

Hayley career has begun to get started. She was selected for the female lead in Odon von Horvath's *Judgment Day,* a 1937 German play that was a thinly disguised criticism of the Nazis. The play was closed by that régime. Horvath moved to Paris, France, where he was killed by a falling limb, while standing under a tree in a storm. He was thirty six. The play has been re-discovered with rave reviews in London in 2009.

In 2010, It became part of the Summer Scape Festival of Bard's College, couple of hours from the New York City on the banks of the Hudson. The *Wall Street Journal* called it, "one of the most intellectually stimulating of all American festivals." Hayley was paid six hundred dollars a week, with room and board provided.

In early 2011, she played Leonora in "Shakespeare's lost play, *Double Falsehood"* as part of the New York City Classic Stage Company. She has been given the female lead of Becky Thatcher in the revised *Tom Sawyer* that will be on the road across the nation the last six months of 2011. Becky, in the play bill, is described as "beautiful and feisty." I will see her in it in St. Louis in December.

She has become established sufficiently in the acting scene in New York that she no longer requires a regular day-job to maintain herself. She contracts for an occasional private instruction position that allows her flexible time for auditions.

Hayley lives in an apartment in Manhattan, a half block from Central Park.

Hope is a senior on an academic scholarship at the University of Tennessee at Chattanooga. She is exploring graduate schools in the Pacific Northwest, where she will pursue a major in zoology. Her childhood affinity for animals has continued and she wants to become a zoologist, manage an animal refuge, perhaps, or become an entomologist, about which she is currently interested.

I have often said, "If the entire world were on one side and Hope on the other, I'd bet on Hope." Dawn's two girls are not only delightful, they are extraordinary bright and special. I am proud they love me as I do them and they want to remain my step-children.

Wes, my oldest son born in Monterey, California, when I was there studying Russian, has two grown children by his marriage to Jody, my graduate assistant whom he met at Murray State University.

Their oldest Bethany is a PhD candidate at the University of Delaware, majoring in Family Psychology. She gave birth to my great-grandson Jaeger on July 31, 2009, to whom this autobiography is dedicated. She and her husband, Robb, have two pleasant, intelligent children from his previous marriage.

In 2005, she called me shortly after I arrived in Monticello. She was worried about me and wanted to come to visit for a week. I was happy about her coming but wondered how in the world I would entertain a woman in her mid-twenties for nearly a week.

Our time together passed quickly. She has an amazing independence and maturity and did not need to be entertained.

Bethany has been hired as professor at Towson University near Baltimore in the fall, 2011.

My grandson John was a naval lieutenant; after two deployments at sea, he was stationed in Iraq on an extended tour for most of 2009, where he was on the ground with an army unit. When he returned, he came to Arkansas before Thanksgiving Day, where he visited me and joined his Uncle Robert in deer hunting. He was a successful hunter, as he had been the previous year, when he killed his first deer.

John is completing his master's degree in business at Gonzaga University, a Jesuit university in Washington State. He left the navy, lives in Virginia and worked in the Pentagon for a company that consults the navy on nuclear energy security. He applied to both the Drug Enforcement Agency and the Secret Service. Each accepted him. He selected the Secret Service. Hie is now in the Secret Service Academy, which will end in March, 2012; after which he will be stationed in Los Angles. He is continuing his commitment to the navel reserves.

John provided an opportunity for me to fly to his mother's for five days over Thanksgiving Day 2009. I visited with Jaeger; Jody; my friend since 1977; John and his fiancé Meryl; and Bethany and her family.

Twenty-eight people sat down at Jody's for *the* dinner. All were Jody's family and assorted in-laws, excluding Jaeger. He slept through it all on a couch.

For a previous Thanksgiving Day, Dawn and I visited Jody and her family when Bethany and John were living at home. Thanksgiving Day at Jody's is always a big fun deal.

Robert, his family and I attended John's and Meryl's wedding in Richmond, Virginia August 27,2011, same time Irene came ashore. Bethany obtained a Virginia Justice of the Peace license and married them.

Wes retired from the army as a major. He had been a member of the 101st Airborne Division and fought in the First Persian Gulf War. I was worried and wrote him a letter in all caps

28 JANUARY 1991—MONDAY
MURRAY, KENTUCKY

DEAR SON,

I HAVE NOT WRITTEN YOU SINCE THE WAR STARTED BECAUSE I DO NOT NOW WHAT TO WRITE. MARILYN SAID

I NEED TO WRITE YOU AND TELL YOU I DO NOT KNOW WHAT TO WRITE YOU. OF COURSE, AS (ALMOST) ALWAYS SHE IS CORRECT.

I THINK ABOUT YOU SEVERAL TIMES A DAY. I WATCH A LOT OF CNN (AND THE OTHER THREE), I READ THREE NEWS MAGAZINES A WEEK AND TWO NEWSPAPERS A DAY AND I TRY TO HEAR AND SEE WHAT THEY ARE TELLING US—NONE OF WHICH HELPS ME FEEL ABOUT ANYTHING, BUT I DECIDED A LONG TIME AGO IN MY LIFE THAT KNOWING IS ALWAYS BETTER THAN FEELING GOOD. EXCEPT FOR WATCHING CNN AND SO MUCH OTHER TV NEWS, MY HABIT HAVE NOT CHANGED SINCE AUGUST 4 WHEN BUSH DECIDED TO SEND TROOPS AND I FIGURED YOU WOULD GO.

[PARAGRAPH OMITTED WHERE I SPECULATED HOW TROOPS WOULD MOVE WHEN ATTACK BEGINS.]

MARILYN KEEPS SAYING YOU AREN'T A TRIGGER FINGER AND THE ARMY WILL WANT TO PROTECT ITS MEDICAL PEOPLE, WHICH MAKES SENSE, BUT WHAT MARILYN KNOWS (BUT IS TRYING TO MAKE ME FEEL BETTER) AND I KNOW SENSE IS NOT WHAT WAR MAKES. ALL OF WHICH MAKES ME WORRIED ABOUT YOU.

WAR MAKES DESTRUCTION AND DEATH. (IT ALSO MAKES SOME PEOPLE RICH, BUT DON'T GET ME STARTED ON THAT.) AND SADAHM KNOWS THAT DESTRUCTION AND DEATH CAUSED BY BOMBS OR OIL SLICKS, BULLETS OR GAS IS STILL DESTRUCTION AND DEATH. HE DOES NOT HAVE THE SMART BOMBS AND AIR SUPERIORITY TO BE SELECTIVE, WHICH DOES NOT MEAN HE WON'T KILL AND DESTROY. IT JUST MEANS HE CAN'T BE SELECTIVE. IN OTHER WORDS, I AM AFRAID THAT WHETHER ONE IS AT THE FRONT OR NEAR THE FRONT IN THIS WAR—WHEN THE REAL WAR STARTS (WHICH WILL BE SOONER THAN LATER)—IS NOT GOING TO MAKE A LOT DIFFERENCE ON

HOW SAFE ONE IS. ALL OF WHICH, AS YOU MAY GUESS, MAKES ME WORRIED ABOUT YOU.

YOU ARE IN DANGER AND I AM HELPLESS TO SAVE YOU. THE DECISION WAS MADE TO GO TO WAR, AND I WAS HELPLESS TO STOP IT. BEING HELPLESS IS NOT MY FAVORITE FEELING, AND IT PUTS ME INTO A DEPRESSION THAT AFFECTS MY THOUGHTS ABOUT EVERYTHING ELSE. THAT'S WHY I HAVE NOT WRITTEN.

BUT KNOW THIS AND KNOW IT WELL: I AM VERY PROUD OF YOU. I SUPPORT YOUR DECISION. MY FAILURE TO WRITE YOU IS NOT BECAUSE OF A LACK OF SUPPORT FOR YOU AND IS SURELY IS NOT FOR A LACK OF LOVE FOR YOU.

MOLLY AND MARILYN ARE WELL. RHONDA AND K.C. ARE FINE, AND DAD AND MYRTIS ARE OK TOO. ROBB, RACHAEL AND RICHARD ARE OK. DON'T WORRY ABOUT ANYONE HERE. DO YOUR JOB, DON'T BE A HERO, CONSIDER YOUR OWN SAFETY BEFORE OTHERS TAKE CARE OF YOURSRLF AND COME HOME TO YOUR FAMILY WHOLE AND HEALTHY.

I LOVE YOU.

DAD

With one olive out of the bottle, other letters came easily.

The night before the U.S. attack began, Wes' MASH unit was placed forward by helicopters to be nearer the action the next day. By mistake, it was placed nearer the enemy line than intended.

A sand storm kept the rest of his unit from being brought into that area or his team being moved back that night, and his unit was abandoned. Wes was senior officer present. He took command, directed the establishment of a parameter and organized a defense. For his leadership and action he received a Bronze Star.

Wes' children by his second marriage to Rhonda are two girls, Kimberly Claire (KC) and Jessie. KC is a junior in college, majoring in nursing. Jessie graduated from high school this past May and now attends college with her sister. Wes and his wonderful family live in Yorktown, Texas, northwest of Victoria, on a small ranch. Wes continues to work part-time as an anesthetist.

Robert, born in Monticello and the sixth generation Willis in Drew County, has two children, a son, Richard, and a daughter, Robyn. They live in Little Rock, where Robert runs an Aaron's; his wife Rachel is co-owner with her mother of a successful beauty college. Robert, a devoted deer hunter, has joined the Jordon Hunting Camp, where Booter lives.

Sometimes in my life, an occurrence I thought was a tragedy or at least a setback, turned out to be beneficial to me. Dawn getting me out of her way is one of these. I enjoy being in Arkansas and nearer association with Robert and his beautiful family.

I have two sons, two stepdaughters, six grandchildren, and one great-grandchild.

The missing stepchild is Molly. Her mother Marilyn and I used the same lawyer in our divorce, which was not as amicable as my others. Our attorney was a mutual friend, Jeff Green, mentioned previously. Since our divorce, Marilyn has obtianed her PhD from Vanderbilt University and is a nationally recognized expert on curriculum and school organization, with books published. She has been more successful without me.

Molly graduated with honors on an academic scholarship from the University of Kentucky. In 1997, she applied for a position in a United States Attorney office, which required an FBI security check.

A FBI agent visited with me at my home in Murray for about forty-five minutes, asking me questions about her background, as forty years before the FBI had come to Monticello and asked about me. The agent volunteered Molly was living unmarried in Chevy Chase, Maryland.

I have heard nothing about her since. With her good looks, fetching personality and 4.00-GPA brain, she can do and be whatever she can imagine.

A famished feral cat showed up at my house in Monticello. She would not let anyone touch her. By my controlling her food intake, within a week, she was eating out of my hand, sleeping in my lap and joining me when I went to bed. Sometimes she curled up next to my head on my pillow.

She is black and white, pretty, and well mannered, which means she uses her box and does not leap on kitchen cabinets, the dining table, or onto people's laps unless invited. The vet says she has quite a bit of age. Her front claws had been removed. Since she began eating at my house, she has gained three pounds, and her fur is indeed soft and warm. Recalling the name for one of my students' floats in Lovington, "I Love My Little Pussy; Her Fur Is So Warm," I named her Pussy Cat.

* When I retired to Monticello, I became come acquainted with new friends and reacquainted with old ones.

One with which I became reacquainted was Shirley Bridges whom I knew from Drew Central High School. We think we possibly had a couple of dates in high school. Years before, Dad had mentioned to me, "Shirley Bridges is one of the best-looking, older women in Drew County." In May 2003, I was in Monticello and invited to her class reunion. Shirley was there. Dad was correct.

After I returned to Drew, I looked her up. She mentioned that when she was younger, men told her she resembled Rachel

Welch. I could understand that. We married the last day of March 2006. It was the fifth marriage for us both.

Author and Shirley at Union Bank Christmas party, 2005, before marrying March 31, 2006. Shirley's jewelry is made from a 50 thousand year old Mastodon tusks given to her by author

While we were dating, Shirley had regaled me with stories of her dancing into the night. To prepare for a relationship with the dancing woman of Monticello, I drove weekly to North Little Rock for several weeks and took dancing lessons at the Arthur Murray Dance Studio for hundred dollars an hour.

I discovered Shirley's dancing is what some folks affectionately and accurately call *boot scooting*, which is two-stepping in a circle to country music. That and her proclivity to lead ended my lessons and any dancing we might have done.

When she was out of town a couple of times, I went to the Friday night dance at the American Legion in Monticello. It was all country music all the time. I was frequently invited back, but kept making excuses until they gave up.

Unless I regain leg strength and coordination, my dancing opportunities have ended. But I enjoyed them while I could.

My favorite new friend is Buddy Carson, an active ninety-year-old, golf-playing,World War II bomber pilot, who is one of the most pleasant persons to be around I have known and has a great sense of humor. His politics are liberal, and his opinions inclusive. He listens regularly to NPR, allowing us to share agreeable comments on latest world events. He also watches *The Daily Show with Jon Stewart*, which gives us more to discuss.

Buddy lives in the Youngblood apartments. We usually have coffee or breakfast in his apartment on Wednesdays, during which James Youngblood, another favorite, often joins us. On Saturday mornings, Buddy and I go to breakfast at Lena's, a meat-and-three café, where my cousin Hardy often eats breakfast.

One of Buddy's most interesting experiences was a being member of the fabled *Wandering Weevils*, a unique football team representing A&M College from 1939 to 1941. The team was an ad hoc bunch that traveled throughout America in a green school bus, with Wandering Weevils painted on the sides. The bus went into thirty-eight states and Canada, taking these Weevils to play other college football teams.

A story about the Wondering Weevils is they are the only college football team in America to practice on Notre Dame's playing field.

I commented to Buddy one does not find many among persons in pastoral Drew County with his liberal, inclusive social view. He said it was not college or World War II that broadened his perspective; it was being a member of the *Wandering Weevils*.

Ira Lafayette "Doc" Jones, Drew Central High School principal and enemy of Spot in their faux bone battle, was Buddy's teammate on this only-one-of-its-kind football team.

Buddy and I love football and are strong supporters of the Arkansas-Monticello Weevils, Arkansas Razorbacks and Dallas Cowboys, pretty much in this order. We have both recently become fans of girls' softball and attend University of Arkansas at Monticello's Cotton Blossoms games, which have a winning tradition.

In football season, much of our conversations are about this subject. When it is not football season, much of our conversations lament about how long it will be before the next one begins.

Buddy played golf with Dad, albeit I did not meet him until I moved into James Youngblood's apartments in May 2005.

Buddy invited me to join the Monticello Rotary Club, my fourth club membership in three states. This is the club of which my father was a member and president.

I see Myrtis occasionally, always a good thing. Dad was fortunate to have her as a wife. Her beauty, love of family and culinary skills are exceeded only by her agreeable nature.

Reuniting with Wes and Monteene McCoy has been a delight. As I have mentioned, they lived next door when I was growing up. They love me in a manner not unlike my parents.

Fay Chandler, a retired high school math teacher, whom I did not know until I came to Monticello, is an attractive, intelligent, humorous woman, and bridge player of the first rank who has helped me become reacquainted with this game. I play with various groups in town from time to time.

Fay has moved to Virginia to be near her children and grandchildren. Gone is another friend.

Faye Chandler visiting College of William and Mary in Williamsburg, Virginia, 2009

I was asked to begin a canasta group. The group that began as one table consists now of four tables that meets Thursday afternoon at First Assembly of God.

Mary Ann Jones, a retired nurse, heads up the canasta bunch. She is a pleasant and attractive woman who handles everything with ease and a smile. She is another favorite friend.

Buddy and Monteene are in the canasta group; Monteene also plays bridge.

Kay (Groce) Grant, a student from my student teaching days at Drew Central High School, has an interesting view on life and living. She is a member of the canasta group.

Author and friends playing canasta, summer 2010. Left to right are: Monteene McCoy, Buddy Carson, Mary Ann Jones and author

W.J. McKiever, druggist; Eddie Eubanks; tomato farmer, and Billy Lansdale, retired merchant are friends of fifty years or more from Drew Central High School days, whom I gladly bump into from time to time.

* On a particular day in June 2006, I returned from a walk of about two miles from Buddy's apartment, where I previously lived, and sat in the court yard with him and James Youngblood drinking coffee. I had to get back home to drive Shirley to her dental appointment in Little Rock.

For the first time that year, I had worn my Birkenstock sandals that I had for a few years. Each year when I wore them the first time, they rubbed a blister where the strap crossed my feet. I had to hurry home to drive Shirley to her dentist in Little Rock.

I arrived home, quickly procured a Band-Aid and put it over the blister. While I was doing that, Shirley came into the room, stuck her face down to within a couple of inches from my foot with the blister, and asked, "Whatcha doing?"

Her putting her nose within inches of what ever I was doing, including my plate from which was eating was not unusual; I paid no attention. Therefore, I answered with no particular tone, "Putting my shoe on."

As we were leaving out the side door to the car to go to her dental appointment, she asked, looking at the front door, "Is that door locked?"

I said, "Yes." I knew because I came in that way when I returned from Buddy's.

Acting as if she believed me, she walked to it and looked out its window, while sneakily attempting to feel around for the key in the door to see if it was locked. She fount it was and made a remark about the flowers in the front yard being pretty. When she turned around, she saw by my expression I had seen her trying to conceal from me she had checked the lock.

We did not exchange another significant word, until as we passed the Methodist church about 400 yards away, she yelled, and I mean yelled, in my ear, "I hope your feet rot off!" I was so startled, I did not respond. She remained sullen all day.

On the way to Pine Bluff, I mentioned I wished to stop at the produce stand in Pine Bluff on our return home. She said, "There is not such thing in Pine Bluff."

I replied, "There has been one for several of the years I have been passing through Pine Bluff driving to Monticello."

When I stopped on the way back to Monticello at the produce stand in Pine Bluff, she asked why I was stopping. Then she saw it was the produce stand. That was the last straw for her. In the store, she introduced me to a man, ten years my junior, who had been in the third grade at Drew Central when I graduated, as "Earl Willis' little boy."

Her mad was still on. The man seemed puzzled and replied, "I did not know Mr. Willis had any children." I appreciated his attitude. Shirley's not so much

After she remained sullen and distant for nearly a month, I decided to talk to her. I reminded her of her remark about hoping my feet rot off and asked, "Do you still feel that way?"

After laughing derisively, she screamed again, "What is wrong with you?"

I am not sure what made Shirley tick. After the second night of marriage, she began a contest between us: who knows the most and/or who is correct had to be understood between us, before anything else can go forward. Instead of marrying a life's soul mate, I had married a life's adversary mate. And if she is not right or does not know the most, she feels she is disrespected by me and takes it personal. The door being locked and the produce stand being in Pine Bluff struck her naked *I'm right* nerve.

Shirley may have a different perspective. I respect her for that. I am not sure perspective is reality; but reality cannot exist without perspective.

Or maybe I had slipped again into my state of obliviousness and angered someone without any intention whatsoever.

Regardless of who was who and what was what, I began to have a visceral awareness of a new perception, a new reality—a powerful epiphany. I needed to find friendly persons with whom to associate.

The next Sunday, July 25, 2006, I walked to the nearby Methodist church, a religion that has as its creed "Open hands, open hearts, and open doors"—a philosophy of inclusivity that appeals to me. I went there to visit the senior Sunday school class, to which I had been frequently invited by Buddy Carson, and James Jordan, owner of the Jordan Camp.

When I arrived at the church I saw many people I knew besides Buddy and James. They were Clyde Ross, the Monticello superintendent who was going to get me fifty dollars a year more for my starting salary in 1962; Claude Babin, who was one of my favorite professors at A&M and later as president offered me Don Fleming's position; James Jordan and his wife Bonnie; and others who graduated from Drew Central High School. Wes and Monteene are members of the Sunday school class.

The class members greeted me warmly in friendship and pressed on me their strong desire I teach their class one Sunday a month. I told them I was a Secular Humanist. They continued to insist. I finally told them, if they really understood I was not in the least orthodox and wanted me to teach a class, I would. To my surprise, It worked to everyone's satisfaction for more than four delightful years, during which I almost never missed a class, never one when I was teaching. I was the youngest member. A couple in their nineties had doubled-dated with my parents before they married.

After each class, several members came forward; each shook my hand and said nice things about my teaching. Once Claude Babin came up, shook my hand and said, "James William, you are a "Smarty Pants."

Einstein's comment on his belief came to mind: "I am a deeply religious nonbeliever. This is a somewhat new kind of religion." It is a loss for humanity he did not say more about this "somewhat new kind of religion."

Friedrich Nietzsche, German existential philosopher and author (1844-1900), said, "What is sacred to a people is what they do not laugh at."

Mark Twain, a deist, considered organized faith ridiculous and enjoyed laughing at it in general and Christians in particular.

His *Letters from the Earth*, the last writing of arguably America's greatest literary genius, was finished a month before he died. In his previous works, he had chided religion with wit and sarcasm. In *Letters from the Earth*, he wrote plainly and unmistakably critical of organized faith.

Letters from the Earth was not published until 1962, because his daughter, who controlled her father's letters and manuscripts, worried about his reputation. Her father probably knew, as Rhett told Scarlet, "With enough courage, you can do without a reputation."

Atheism is a benefit to mankind because no connection can exist between this belief and killing people who do not believe in the correct deity. The world would be a far safer place of habitation today if it contained more atheists. John Adams, second president of the United States, wrote in his last letter to Thomas Jefferson April 1826 before he died July 4, "This would be the best of all possible worlds if there were no religions in it".

President Adams added, however, that if he expressed this thought publically, he would be considered too radical. He believed religion was helpful in keeping the masses in line. "Without religion, the world would be something not fit to be mentioned in public company—I mean hell."

Adams' friend, the more radical Jefferson, was less ambiguous. He wrote Adams April 11, 1823, "And the day will come when the mystical generation of Jesus, by the Supreme Being as His Father, in the womb of a virgin, will be classed with the fable of the generation of Minerva in the brain of Jupiter."

Dad and I exchanged letters every few months or so. I kept many of his letters and found one the other day, in which Dad told me he understood my questioning religion. I don't remember what I had written him to which he was responding. He was a deacon in every Baptist church he was a member in White Hall, Little Rock and Monticello. I was, therefore, surprised when he wrote, "I am 59 and still have trouble believing many of the Baptist creed.

I would never expect another to adopt my world view and am not trying to persuade anyone to. In this view, I agree with Brad Pitt.

He was born and raised a Baptist and became a skeptic. In an interview in *Entertainment Weekly*, September 2011: "I see the comfort it [religion] brings to people and I don't want to deny anyone that. I just don't like the separatism that comes from religion, and, without fail, the need to put your beliefs on someone else. When you start telling someone else how to live, you should check yourself, man. It drives me f—king crazy. I'm serious,"

Mike McGinnis has returned to Monticello after a successful life as an international chemical engineer. Following his first wife's death, he married his beautiful high school sweetheart Mildred, also a school mate of mine. For awhile, they were in my Sunday school class. It is always a pleasure to associate with them.

* In mid-March 2006, before I married Shirley, my breathing became difficult on a Saturday evening in bed and was worse on Sunday. I went to see Dr. Reinhart on Monday, who listened to my heart, took an x-ray of my lungs, found them filled with fluid and placed me in Drew Memorial Hospital. There I was intravenously fed a powerful diuretic. Within nine hours, I lost five liters of fluid and went home the next morning.

Shirley came to visit me in the hospital room, set close by my bed in a caring manner.

Unknown to me, Robert had called Dr. Reinhart at his office at about six o'clock in the evening and asked him what was wrong. Robert's calling him impressed Dr. Reinhart; he has often mentioned it with a chuckle.

Author's four youngest grandchildren—Jessie, Richard, Robyn, K.C. Christmas, 2010

Author's two oldest grandchildren—Bethany and John

Neither Jeff Reinhart nor my cardiologist Randal Minton could explain why on that particular day fluid built up in my lungs, beyond my heart's ability to get rid of it.

* In spring 2007, I went to New Orleans for a vacation. While there I contracted a severe stomach ailment. Shirley had this same ailment before I left. I called her to tell her I had caught it.

While I was recovering in New Orleans, Robert began to call me. I kept assuring him I was fine. He said he would call back in an hour to check. However, I was weak and had a hard time staying awake. Every time he called me, I had gone back to sleep. At ten thirty the night of the day I woke up sick, a medical emergency team in their vehicle showed up at my door with lights flashing and said, "Your son Robert has called us to check on you."

They gave me a resting cardiogram, took my blood pressure and pulse, and interviewed me. They were satisfied and left.

I called Robert and asked him what the heck he thought he was doing. He said Rachel told him, "If you do not do something, I will drive to New Orleans to take care of him myself."

* On a Friday in July 2009, I went into the local hospital not feeling well. Dr. Reinhart sent me to Baptist Health Medical Center in Little Rock by ambulance. My cardiologist was on duty that weekend. I had called Robert to meet me there. Just as I was being wheeled into my room at 8:30, I began to get worse, a lot worse. My breathing became so labored; my last thought before I passed out was I was dying. I was completely lucid, not under the influence of medication of any sort.

While I was passing into oblivion, I was suddenly, boldly aware I did not fear my own nonexistence; my life and I were about to part company with neither regrets nor formal farewells, like two, best old friends at a wonderful feast leaving too dazed with drink to say good-bye. I was no longer looking forward to seeing the spring, hearing birds, enjoying the pleasure of loved ones or finish writing a book. Everything so important while living was suddenly of no interest at all.

When I began to come around, I had absolutely no idea where I was. I saw a bright light, in which I indistinctly saw two, glowing human figures whom I heard talking quietly about me with tones of concern.

As I became more conscious, I found I was in the critical care ward; later; when I regained more of my senses, I saw the bright light I had seen was the one in the ward; the two men talking were Dr. Randal Minton in his white smock and Robert standing at the foot of my bed. It was two o'clock in the morning.

Dying changes everything. Almost dying can change what one thinks about dying. From my experience, I learned if one does not know how to die, he need not worry. Nature will tell a person what to do on the spot, fully and adequately. Death will do the job perfectly for us. We need not bother our head about it.

I secretly hope, as do we all, that my family and friends are, at least, a little affected by my death. But they will mourn alone. For me, my death will be nothing about which I will be bothered. The dead do not mourn.

Shirley drove to Little Rock in my car and boarded with my cousin, Rose, with whom Shirley had played basketball in high school. She visited me twice, an hour each time, and drove me home in my car when I was released. She charged me $132 for her expenses.

What had happened at Drew Memorial Hospital in March 2006 had occurred again, but much worse. I recovered in a few days and returned home still so weakened I could make it upstairs to my bed *only* by sitting on each step and pushing myself up to the next step. Shirley had retired for evening.

That experience was the beginning of my viscerally understanding what I had long known and long ignored. Not anywhere in Shirley's DNA is an iota of caring for the lame and ill, at least none for me. I realized that some day I would be obliged to obtain a legal separation, if not divorce, to get her out of my life.

The next morning, I called Robb and told him how I got myself upstairs.

Robert called some Drew Central High School graduates, men he knew from the deer camp. They came over and succeeded, with help, in moving my upstairs bedroom down stairs to what was the den. They moved the den La-Z-Boy recliner and large easy couch into the living room. The two couches in the living room I gave to the Methodist church.

One they put in the youth center. The youth in the church sent me a great card, which was a picture of all of them on and around their new couch, thanking me. The smaller one they put in the secretary's office. She sent me a card of thanks.

Weakness developed in my legs in fall 2007. When I came to Monticello in 2005, I had for several years routinely walked two miles in thirty-five minutes, which my cardiologist considered healthy. After a couple of years, I began to weaken. Reinhart and Minton scratched their heads and began to try various tests based on whatever theory they had at the time.

In the meantime, I was getting worse by the month. During my stay in Baptist Medical, my weakness had become worse.

* Reinhart sent me to a neurologist in Little Rock. Under his care, I took extensive tests and gave the most blood I have ever given at one time. The blood was sent to major diagnostic laboratory centers across the United States.

By August, no negative results came back on my blood tests; the neurologist ordered a myelogram. The image found that my spinal cord was being squeezed by my spine between the third and fourth cervical nerves. I had spinal stenosis. My neurologist referred me to a surgeon.

My surgeon described my condition as analogous to the ceiling of a room dropping down. An operation was necessary. I had it on October 16, 2009.

I told Shirley not to come to Little Rock. She did not ask why; she did not come.

The surgeon removed the top of these two vertebrae, freeing the spinal cord, and performed a spinal fusion of surgical steel over the wound.

As the joke goes, the operation was a success but the patient died. Well, no; after the operation, I had stopped breathing and was scarily, slowly waking up. When I did awaken, I found myself back in critical care, hooked up to the same stuff I was hooked up to last time, plus a ventilator. I remained there and in rehab for a total of sixteen days.

The rehab was two worthless thirty-minute sessions a day. I placed square pegs in square holes and round pegs in round holes and played solitaire. I did get to walk some with the staff holding me with a belt to keep me from falling down.

Robb and Robyn did not miss a night visiting. They would go into the rehab room to get a belt and fasten me up, and we would take off, I in my hospital gown. I would walk as far and as long as I could and was making daily progress. Counting the floor tiles, we decided I walked two hundred yards during the latter stages. Robb and Robyn's rehab is what got me ready to go home, not the hospital's rehab.

Over the years, my PCPs and cardiologists had worked out a regimen of medications that was carefully balanced. In rehab, I was assigned a physician who did not understand my congestive heart condition and especially my need for the eighty milligrams of diuretic. He took me off it because he thought my blood pressure was too low.

I told every nurse I saw that my normal blood pressure is usually about ninety-five over sixty and the readings they were getting were normal for me. I told each one of them I wanted to talk to the doctor myself. All assured me they would tell him.

I learned the next day, he had visited my room in the night and wrote on my chart at the nurses' station, "I tried to see patient at 11:15; he was asleep." DUH. Well, I realized no one was going to help me. I was about to get panicky when my first wife Mary Ann came to my rescue.

She had been prescribed the same diuretic as I, and during her visits, she smuggled in enough from her supply of what I needed. Without her intervention on my behalf, things could have become much serious.

Robert and his family brought me home.

When I returned to Monticello, I told Dr. Jeff Reinhart what had happened. He said, if Robert had called him about what was going on, he would have driven up there. I expressed surprise he would do this; he said, "I have done it before."

* Before my operation, my surgeon had told me the operation *may* not make me better but will surely keep me from getting worse. When I went in for a follow-up, he told me, "Your spinal cord was more damaged than I thought." He said, "You *may* come all the way back, but it will require eighteen months." Eighteen months after my operation was April 2011. I am improved but not all the way back.

My improvement after the operation slowed and soon stopped altogether. I became as ill as before. My surgeon suspected my spinal cord was being squeezed in my Lumbar. I had another myelogram in May.

I changed surgeons. The new one read my myelogram, and I did not have spinal stenois in my Lumbar. He did not know what was causing weakness in my legs and sent me back to my original neurologist. I am back to zero and getting worse and older. Saying, "He is on his last legs" took on a new meaning for me.

I have thought about what my director of the rehabilitation division at MSU told me about being aTAB.

In a myth of the mighty Norse god, Thor, from whom the day of the week Thursday (Thor's day) is derived, Thor was obliged to fight an old woman. She defeated him every time until Thor gave up fighting her. Divulged in the myth the aged woman is Thor's old age. Even mighty Thor could not defeat his own old age.

Old age is so powerful, James Bond probably died of it and alone.

I have believed one is as old as one feels. Because age curtails options and truncates wonder and experimentation, I put it off as long as possible. In spring 2008, I could postpone old age no longer.

That year began my physical affliction—illness, pain, disability and aging, As Shakespeare had Hamlet say, "The heart-ache and the thousand natural shocks the flesh is heir to." (Until that spring I walked two miles in thirty-five minutes.)

In the opening scene of Shakespeare's *King Lear*, the king is an old man. Out of his hearing, his daughters are talking about him. The first daughter Goneril observes, "You see how full of changes his age is . . ."

His second daughter Regan responds, "'Tis the infirmity of his age: yet he hath ever but slenderly known himself."

My age is full of changes, and I have ever but slenderly known myself. When a man's body appears as a stranger to him, his interest in its temptations lessen.

One may wonder what I have learned in my old age about all the wisdom in the world. I think not asking questions one does not want to know the answer to is wise. I think understanding a new concept before arguing against it is wise. I think understanding the concept, whoever discovered water, it was not a fish, is wise. I think it is wise to understand the concept: a person's behavior is caused by how he perceives the world; by what soup is he swimming in. It is wise to know the world is divided into two kinds of people: those who divide the world and those who do not. None of these wisdoms is all the wisdom in the world.

One need not look for the meaning of life; he will not find it. One may find the meaning of a life in living his own.

Carol Willis wisely wrote me 27 years ago, "Nothing changes but changes."

I believe *all the wisdom in the world* is any question profound enough to *force* me to contemplate it in all its various facets and complications. Among such questions, my favorite is *why is there something instead of nothing?*

This question will come into my mind, sometimes uninvited, and occupy it as might an old friend whose company never tires. While thinking on this question, I have realized how infinitely insignificant everything is that I *think* I know, until I eventually doubt my own existence.

Professor Miller said, "The greatest wisdom is that which finds similarities among things, not differences." I think he is right. I believe when we know all there is to know about everything, it will be the same thing.

I vividly recall as a small child, I often lay in bed waiting to fall asleep wondering where God came from: I seriously wondered if God made everything, who made God? I asked Dad. He said, "God made himself; he has always been here."

French philosopher and mathematician René Descartes (1596-1650) concluded that his existence was proven by his being unable to doubt that he was sitting there, doubting his existence. ("I think, therefore I am," he observed.) With apology to Descartes, I believe some knowledge is beyond human experience, perhaps all important knowledge is.

Within limits of human experience, I think all the wisdom in the world is found somewhere within the mystery of becoming old. Old age is a mystery because it is the only stage of life we can never grow out of, and can never look back on. I am glad I have lived to experience mine.

Part of the answer to what is all the wisdom in the world may be found in a story told by Mother about an experience in 1928, when she was fourteen, that she told me shortly before she died.

One of Mother's favorite family members was her Grandma McKinstry. In 1928, while wearing a yellow low-cut sundress with string straps, she visited her grandma. A neighbor woman was also there. When she saw how Mother was dressed, she exclaimed disapprovingly, "What are children of today coming to!"

Mom's grandma removed her sweet gum twig from her mouth and answered, "Old age."

All the wisdom in the world is children come to old age.

Circumstances cannot change this wisdom. Many important parts of my life have happened haphazardly; albeit regardless what I experienced in my life or failed to experience, or if I had been a completely different person with altogether different experiences, all the wisdom in the world would have been the same—children come to old age.

For instance, I never stood "on the corner in Winslow, Arizona, with such a fine sight to see . . . a pretty girl, my Lord, in a flatbed Ford slowing down to take a look at me," albeit if ever I had this experience, all the wisdom in the world would be unchanged—children come to old age.

Without drama from his momma, Alan arrived at the same conclusion. When he called in 2009 to wish me Christmas and New Year's Greetings, he told me, "James, if you live long enough, you will become old."

In a 1932 W.C. Fields movie *If I Had a Million*, a character in a rest home says, "There ain't any jail of steel or stone that can hold a body prisoner as tight as one built of old age . . ."

The only escape for a body held tightly in the prison of old age is sufficient money. Worse than being old is being old and sick. Worse than being old and sick is being old, sick and broke.

The Oracle of Delphi declared Socrates the smartest man in Greece because he said, "All I know is that I know nothing."

Pyrrho is credited with founding the skeptic philosophy. He begins with Socrates' point that all he knows is he knows nothing, but then adds in effect, "And I am not even sure about that."

Sarah Bakewell is author of the outstanding, if not the best, intellectual biography of Michel de Montaigne (1533-1592), recognized by many as the greatest thinker of the Renaissance. About Pyrrho's notion, she wrote, "Having stated its one philosophical principle, it turns in a circle and gobbles itself up, leaving only a puff of absurdity."

One seriously seeking all the wisdom in the world can find himself ending in a puff of absurdity. It may be such thought Abraham

Lincoln had when he wrote, "I pondered the meaning of life with such intensity until I wore the ideas threadbare"—*Abraham and Mary Lincoln*, part three of six part series, AETV, (2011).

Well, okay, if you really want the answer to life's greatest question, I refer you to my choice, expressed by Douglas Adams, British humorist and author (1952-2001): "The answer to the great question of life, the universe and everything else is forty-two."

Another thing one may wonder is, if I could live my life again, would I change anything. Would I do anything differently? No, I would not. Contingency haunts us all; no one knows the role of chance in our lives. Every choice has a ripple effect. One cannot know, when one makes a choice, how much one's future will be changed. Every choice I have made, no matter how non-consciously or tiny, has made me who I am today and I like who I am.

If I did *anything* differently, I may not have the children, stepchildren and grandchildren I have. I may not have been where I have been or be where I am now or who I am now. I would not know what I know or whom I know. I would change nothing for the possibility everything would change.

Saying I would change nothing is not to say I regret nothing.

I have made mistakes. For some I apologized, for some I did not. Some apologizes were accepted; some were not. I expect I have made mistakes I know not of. Regardless, I continued my life unafraid. Decisions must be made.

Der Fuhrer explained 15 May 1942, "However one lives, what ever one does or undertakes, one is invariably exposed to the danger of making mistakes . . . And so what, indeed, would become of the individual . . . paralyzed by fear of a possible error and refused to take the decisions that were called for?"—*Hitler's Table Talk*, p. 483.

I have noticed people who never do anything never do anything wrong.

I regret I was not a better father to my sons. They are excellent men and fathers and I have often thought and sometime said, "If I had been a better father, it is no telling how great my sons could be." I love them and am proud of them.

George Orwell said, "At 50 a man has the face he deserves." Both my sons are in their fifties. Looking at their lives, no matter whose sons they are, I respect them for the men they are.

I regret not spending more time with Spot. I still miss him. I wish I could believe I was going to see him when I am dead, at least long enough to tell him of my love and say, "Thank you."

A computer word search program finds the word *dog* is mentioned 15 times in the Bible; the word *dogs* is mentioned 24 times. Though several times dog or dogs are mentioned, it is not in favorable terms, the word cat or cats not at all.

Some Christians believe the thought of dogs in Heaven a sacrilege; only souls go to Heaven, only human beings have souls. Reverend Billy Graham finessed the absence of dogs' soul when he said "I think God will have prepared everything for our perfect happiness. If it takes my dog being there [in Heaven], I believe he'll be there"—Dog Quotes. Com.

I also regret I simultaneously had a double hernia and a vasectomy operation; and went home the same day without pain medication.

* After I retired to Monticello, I wrote a Civil War novel, titled *The Other Side of Silence*, that was awarded *Publisher's Choice*. My novel is about a boy of seventeen years from Monticello who goes to war in 1862. This story is about his life as a Civil War soldier in the Ninth Arkansas Regiment and evolved from the research I did for my book *Arkansas Confederates in the Western Theater.*

It has been well received among family, friends, and neighbors, those for whom I wrote it. It is available to order from Amazon and Barns & Noble.

My book impressed Patrick Schmidt of Austin, Texas who wrote a review for Amazon Books more erudite than the subject of his review.

> *James Willis' The Other Side of Silence is a great read and one that touches on the key questions of life. This Civil War novel/factual memoir is in the voice of Billy Butler who looks back on his life and specifically on his years in the Civil War as a young Confederate enlistee who goes to war seeking glory but who learns of the hardships, horrors and losses of the war. The battle scenes are mesmerizing and engaging yet Willis an historian, who really knows the Civil War and its realities, also allows his protagonist to relate to the behind the lines movements, marches, experiences and frustrations that are so much a part of war.*
>
> *In addition Billy learns that glory is ephemeral and wonders if love might be as well. Will his new-found love Rebecca wait for him? Will his brother, his closest friends, his mentors survive the war? Will he? How will the war change him? And those around him?*
>
> *Another strength of the novel is in the detail of place. The reader envisions the woods, the marshes, the fields where battles are fought and where marches are forced, and where loved ones must be left behind. One sees the landscapes and scenes vividly: a dark woods where renegades torture a black women, surgeons tables with innumerable discarded limbs beneath them, a pastoral town where Billy's beloved teacher, Donald Miller, shares his wisdom with the young narrator. The sweeping scope of the novel takes the reader through Tennessee, Arkansas, Mississippi, Alabama, Georgia, the Carolinas*

in the Confederates' noble but doomed effort to stop irrepressible force under Generals Grant and Sherman.

The choice of the memoir genre is brilliant. It allows Billy to live in the moment but also wryly comment on his situation and to draw on literary quotations for a richer reflection on life's experiences and his coming of age. This novel brings those life's questions again or anew; it's a novel not to be missed and one that will remain on your mind for quite sometime.

I came to writing late in my life and enjoy it more than anything I have done, except teaching. Dad came to golf late in his life and loved it. About his enjoying golf, he said, "Contrary to what I have believed, one does not have to be good at a thing to enjoy it."

One's success in playing golf is expressed in measureable terms; one knows whether one is a good golfer. Whether one is a good writer is subjective and personal.

I think it was Franz Kafka who said, "Writing is the gift we give ourselves."

* Shirley frequently was absent from home for some reason or another. For ten days over the 2009 and 2010 Christmas and New Year's holidays, Shirley visited Norma, a sister who resides in Memphis, in a trailer on Lake Chicot in Lake Village. The casino boat is in Greenville, Mississippi, across the river, sometimes a destination of theirs.

In her absence, Drew County experienced single-digit temperatures for the first time in fifteen years. I went to the camp and brought Booter home to keep him warm. I read, wrote, caught a couple of movies, prepared and ate some Wiener schnitzel, kept the faucets dripping and sipped some good Scotch.

Booter jumped into my bed next to Pussy Cat. Cats have alpha brains; therefore, she thumped him on top of his head with her soft, harmless paw, satisfying her need to establish who the number one pet was. Booter knew already who it was.

These two kind and kindred souls went to sleep side by side.

I brought in the brass monkey and joined them.

Author's Father's last picture, October 1998, before Dawn and I visited him for the book signing in December. He died February 14, 1999, age 84 years, 3 months and 7 days.

WOODLAND HEIGHTS (2010-?)

I speak the truth not so much as I would, but as much as I dare, and I dare a little more as I grow older.
—Michel de Montaigne

* * *

I feel so good life is running around inside me like a squirrel—
Mr. Kolinkov, Dance Instructor, *You Can't Take It With You; Columbia (1938).*

##

The day that I knew would inevitably come, when I had to decide about Shirley in my life, was October 7, 2010. I told her I was selling my house, moving to Little Rock, and obtaining a legal separation from her. I handed her a generous property settlement I had prepared.

Leaving Monticello was emotionally difficult; I faced the inescapable fact that I must go for my sanity and health.

I was in a weakened physical condition and did not have a plan to facilitate moving, but the luck that had followed me through my life held.

Robert brought U-Haul boxes the next weekend on his way to his camp. Without knowing I was moving and needed their help,

Hayley and Hope arrived for a visit the next weekend from New York and Tennessee and gladly packed my stuff into the boxes Robert had provided.

He arrived the next Saturday afternoon with an Aaron's truck, his Hummer with a trailer, a coworker, Robyn, and her sister-in-law Bianca. They loaded everything and slept Saturday night at the camp, and we all arrived at Woodland Heights just before noon on Halloween.

Robert had prearranged with Comcast to meet us in my apartment at one thirty. My television, Internet, and phone were soon up and running. Robb's team moved my furniture and boxes in and set everything up, except contents of the boxes, but including, especially including, my bed.

A couple of days later, Robb and Robyn came by, emptied all the boxes, and took the empty containers to the trash.

Later that week, Bethany flew in from Delaware for a three-day visit. She helped me place pictures, books, and my *stuff* in my new home. She has a great eye for home decoration. I am proud of her work and much appreciative of her help.

As a child, Hayley did an imitation of me in which she pounded the table with both fists and demanded, "I want my stuff. I want my stuff." Hope, Dawn, and I laughed uproariously. We all recognized me; she captured my character perfectly.

Now, I am surrounded by all my *stuff* and am living alone doing what only I want to do, as much as it is possible for one to do what only he wants to do, if he knows what he wants. I began a comfortable, interesting, meaningless life that I intend to continue the remainder of my natural existence.

Save the Date

08.27.11

MERYL & JOHN ARE TYING THE KNOT!

MAYMONT PARK
RICHMOND, VIRGINIA

ROOMS ARE AVAILABLE AT
THE MARRIOT HOTEL 1 (800) 228-9290

PLEASE ASK FOR THE RABIN/WILLIS WEDDING

www.TheKnot.com/OurWedding/MerylRabin&JohnathanWillis

INVITATION TO FOLLOW

Meryl's and John's pre-invitation wedding announcement.

* Woodland Heights is a retirement community extraordinaire. I reside in an apartment with a living and dining room combination, bedroom, library, kitchen and two baths, and a balcony that overlooks Little Rock. Woodland Heights has various amenities including a library, exercise room, billiards room, lounge, salon, heated pool and hot tub. Food is top quality.

One may believe Woodland Heights is a prescription for banality—a life vacation on Gilligan's Island. Albeit, a table guest at dinner shared a thought with me with which I concur, "I cannot believe I am as old as I am, but if you've got to be old, this is a great place to be."

Friends have come. Mike and Mildred McGinnis have come to visit in Woodland Heights. So have Dalene, church secretary, and Mary Ann (Willis) Copeland. They just dropped by. My Monticello friends Buddy, Monteene, Mary Ann Jones, and Kay Grant, whom I had as a student teacher, have joined me for scheduled monthly lunch and afternoons of canasta.

* The 2010 Christmas holidays were memorable. Both sons, both stepdaughters, and my six grand children visited me, though not all at the same time. The one missing among my progeny was great-grandson Jaeger. Bethany left him in Delaware with his wonderful daddy.

When Hayley and Hope came to visit, we had a great time, as we always do. On Tuesday, December 28, we ate lunch at Ya-Ya's Euro Bistro, went to two movies, *The King's Speech* and *True Grit,* and returned to Ya-Ya's for dinner. We had the same meal both times: Ya-Ya's delicious Diver Sea Scallops, with warm, freshly baked bread and baba ghanoush.

On Sunday, January 16, 2011, to celebrate Buddy's ninetieth birthday, I returned to Monticello for the first time since leaving. To know Buddy is to love him. His day was celebrated with a catered dinner at the Methodist church attended by 250 of his family and friends. To the extent anyone can, Buddy lives "in the love of the common people," as described by Paul Young in his song "Love of the Common People."

* I have experienced great joy and great sorrow. During these times, my full attention was given to the present moment. When I was captured within these extreme emotions, their singular moments consumed my attention until I could not escape them to contemplate other moments.

Author, children and grandchildren, except Jaeger at 2011 Willis Reunion.

Author with his children and grandchildren, except great grandchild Jaeger, and spouses at 2011 Willis Reunion.

Author and first wife Mary Ann with all their children, grandchildren and great grandchild Jaeger, 2011 Willis Reunion.

Today, I am enthusiastically, euphorically *content*, which I have found is not a feeling halfway between joy and sorrow. Contentment is a separate, third state of feeling, one of freedom, tranquility and leisure. It is a feeling that lingers, allowing me time to wallow in its care free pleasure.

I think, perhaps, my default mode is *alone*. Albeit, when that position came up, without thought, I searched for another one.

As said previously, I have given up hope for a better past. My contentment, my *now* time, holds *mundane* moments of fine dining, good shows, interesting books, witty conversation, and loving associations with family and friends. I am in awe of my progeny and stepdaughters. I am proud of them and I love them.

How will I move from the mundane to sublime? My death will be sublime.

Elie Wiesel survived the Holocaust at Austerlitz for 13 months, later a Nobel Laureate, was to say in 1983, "Between the dead and the rest of us there exists an abyss that no talent can comprehend"—*Grief Wept Without Tears*, p. vii.

When Lazarus was resurrected, no record exists of anyone asking him what death was like; where he had been, whom he had seen or what he had done. Their failure of curiosity allows us to imagine death with the truth we wish.

When Buddhism arrived in Japan in the Ninth Century, the Japanese adopted it to their more meditative culture. They call it Zen Buddhism. Zen became a path that uses contemplative questions on which to meditate, such as, "What did your face look like before you were born?"

While meditating on it, I began to realize afterlife is a word in a dictionary. Forelife is not a word. Albeit, next month, next year, many people on earth not yet born will be. Maybe death is like unborn. Time does not exist.

.

James Geary, a world-renowned expert of word and phrase origins and author of the *New York Times* bestseller *The World in a Phrase,* wrote in a subsequent book, *I is an Other*, "'Truth'—a term . . . distilled from Icelandic, Swedish, Anglo-Saxon, and other non-English words meaning 'believed' rather than 'certain'"

Each of us thinks we are rational; therefore, following rational precepts, we doubt any information that is not consistent with other ideas or conformable with facts and does not pass a practical test of experience and common sense. We, also, know we must be especially suspicious of believing true anything convenient for us to believe; what we very much want to believe or hope we can believe.

We follow these and other rational criteria to ascertain what is true, *except* when what we are asked to believe pertains to religion. Then, we disengage from rational constraints and believe anything we want to or hope for, no matter how far removed it is from logical thought or preposterous it is to a rational person.

David Eck is a New Mexico State University Archeologist. Part of his job is to assist groups who wish scientifically to confirm the authenticity of which among various competing archeological sites may prove who discovered America before Columbus—in other words, he helps them find truth. He offered his insight into the problem of this endeavor: "When people begin wanting to believe, they quit thinking"—*Who Really Discovered America*, History Channel (14 June 2011).

As mentioned previously, among psychologists is a popular theory that of all illusions, the most difficult one to give up is the belief that consciousness exists after death. The reason it is the most difficult illusion to give up is everyone wants to believe we can live forever among those we have known and loved.

Quest for a world beyond our senses is one of the oldest and deepest yearnings of mankind. Even the keenest minds are easily deceived. The temptation is too delicious, too intoxicating not to succumb.

On a Walmart parking lot in Paris, Tennessee, a bumper sticker on a pickup read, "Are you saved?" To emphasize the importance of this question, the sticker's author added in all caps, "THIS IS THE ONLY QUESTION."

This bumper sticker concept of Christianity is an insult to the life of Christ, which was love, and his message from the cross, which was forgiveness. Love and forgiveness: the bumper sticker message is so stupid it is an insult to stupid.

Hamlet tells us the question is "To be, or not to be?" We quickly, loudly, joyfully exclaim the obvious answer, "To be!"

Sam, the philosophical piano player in *Casablanca*, told the world, "The fundamental things apply as time goes by," and as time goes by, we learn that unless we change our perspective on death, we can make a calamity of so long a life. Not being able to die would be a terrible thing.

Youth believe their strength is immortality. Their power is not immortality; it is choice. As is the way of youth, when I was young, I thought I was immortal. Now, as is the way of age, I am daily aware of my mortality. Some people are of the opinion that when one dies, one will have all questions answered.

I believe when my last breath frees me from flesh, I will no longer have a question I need answered. To compensate me death will solve all my problems.

"Death is nothing to us, for that which is dissolved is without sensation; and that which lacks sensation is nothing to us"—Epicurus (341-270 B.C.)

William Shakespeare had long, long thoughts about death, which he artfully placed in the mind and voice of Julius Caesar.

The Roman calendar designated the day of a month the moon is full as the *ides* of that month. In 44 BC, the ides of March was the fifteenth day. A soothsayer had warned Caesar, "Beware the ides of March." On that date, family and friends begged him to remain home.

Instead, he went forth, explaining, "Of all the wonders that I yet have heard, the strangest is men's fear of death. Seeing death a necessary end will come when it comes"—*Julius Caesar, Act* I, scene ii.

Renowned British poet, orator and Anglican cleric, George Herbert, knew he was dying of consumption, today called tuberculosis Herbert struggled through the phases a person's does when facing his death, recognized by Elizabeth Kulber-Ross in her 1969 book *Death and Dying*: denial, anger, bargaining, depression, and acceptance the final phase. Shortly before

Hebert died in 1633, he reached the final stage. The poet explained his acceptance of his death in the last stanza of his final poem aptly named *The Forerunners*:

> Go birds of spring; let winter have its fee.
> *Let a bleak paleness chalk the door,*
> *So all within be livelier than before.*

Author's oldest son Wesley with Jaeger, his first grandchild, 2011 Willis Reunion.

Finis.